# Wildlife Conservation

## Edited by Hilary D. Claggett

The Reference Shelf
Volume 69 • Number 2

The H. W. Wilson Company
New York • Dublin
1997

# The
# Reference
# Shelf

# The Reference Shelf

The books in this series contain reprints of articles, excerpts from books, and addresses on current issues and social trends in the United States and other countries. There are six separately bound numbers in each volume, all of which are generally published in the same calendar year. Numbers one through five are each devoted to a single subject, providing background information and discussion from various points of view and concluding with a comprehensive bibliography that lists books, pamphlets and abstracts of additional articles on the subject. The final number of each volume is a collection of recent speeches. This number also contains a subject index to all the articles in an entire Reference Shelf volume. Books in the series may be purchased individually or on subscription.

Visit H.W. Wilson's web site: http://www.hwwilson.com

**Library of Congress Cataloging-in-Publication Data**

Wildlife Conservation / edited by Hilary D. Claggett.
    p.   cm. — (The reference shelf ; v. 69, no. 2)
    Includes bibliographical references (p.   ) and index.
    ISBN 0-8242-0915-X
    1. Wildlife conservation.  I. Claggett, Hilary D., 1964–
II. Series.
QL82.W55  1997
333.95' 16—dc21
                                                      97-14000
                                                         CIP

*Cover:* Three white Bengal tiger cubs. The endangered Bengal tiger, which is found in India, Nepal, and parts of Asia, is disappearing at a rate of 500 per year.

*Photo:* AP/Wide World Photos

Printed in the United States of America

# Contents

## IV. Managing Ecosystems

## V. New Directions in Wildlife Conservation

## Bibliography

# Preface

It is tempting to introduce the topic of wildlife conservation with a litany of previous rates of extinction in history, a listing of endangered species, or an enumeration of various efforts, in the United States and elsewhere, to conserve our biological heritage. But the selections reprinted here address all these topics and more, including some of the controversies spawned by attempts to deal with the imperatives of wildlife conservation in the public policy arena. Furthermore, the ever-evolving nature of the conservationist's unending task—to halt or reverse the decline in the Earth's biodiversity, which is short for biological diversity—makes it difficult to pin down the status of any given species or conservation project. Even those species that are listed as endangered are not all known to be still in existence; a few of them are suspected of having become extinct already but are nonetheless listed in the hope of discovering a new population. In any case, the goal of this book is not to provide a comprehensive history of preservation efforts but to introduce the most salient issues in wildlife conservation today. While the majority of the selections were chosen with the needs of the nonspecialist reader in mind, it is hoped that professionals—from the relatively new fields of conservation biology and ecotourism to the more traditional arenas of politics and academia—will learn something new about an aspect of this broad topic that may have until now seemed merely tangentially related.

Broadly conceived, wildlife conservation is all about scale. Whether considering what is being conserved, who is implementing conservation, and how and when it is accomplished, one is faced with vast extremes of time, space, and size. Conservation can benefit everything from the most obscure, little-known insects and weeds to large, far-ranging mammals as well as entire ecosystems (ecological communities and their environment) or biota (a region's flora and fauna). As many of the authors featured here explain, wildlife conservation can also benefit humanity itself. Conservationists, again broadly defined, can range from individuals who take steps to save members of a threatened species to wildlife biologists to the collective membership of nonprofit organizations. They can be amateurs or professionals, writers of natural history or philosophers, scientists or hunters, entrepreneurs or politicians. Local legislation, state and federal laws, national policy, and international treaties all must deal with the thorny questions of managing conservation programs, among the most contentious of which is who bears the costs.

Only by understanding the intricate web of ethical, scientific, political, economic, and managerial considerations that inform both conservation science and policy can one hope to begin to understand the myriad ways in which wildlife conservation touches our lives. The organization of this book reflects this broadbrush approach. Section I, "Why Conserve Wildlife?" deals with premises on which all the subsequent selections are based. The writers featured here, among them Aldo Leopold, the father of modern wildlife conservation, and Edward O. Wilson, the Harvard entomologist, discuss the need for the development of an "ecological conscience," the benefits to humanity of maintaining biodiversity, and the mythology surrounding our concept of wilderness. Section II, "Endangered Species and Their Enemies," deals with some of the threats to wildlife: cli-

1

matic change, disease, war, illegal trade in endangered animals, and tourism. Section III, "Legislation and Politics," contains a discussion of congressional efforts to undercut the Endangered Species Act (1973) and other environmental protection legislation. Another article in this section illuminates the alliance between hunters and environmentalists. Section IV, "Managing Ecosystems," comprises several examples of ecosystem management: our national parks, sustainable forests, and the "accidental" wildlife refuges provided by the vast land holdings of military bases and the absence of human habitation in the demilitarized zone dividing the two Koreas. Section V, "New Directions in Wildlife Conservation," focuses on the changing missions of zoos, the effects of ecotourism on wildlife, and the controversial role of hunting in conservation. This final section is followed by an extensive bibliography for further reading, abstracts of other recent articles on this topic, a list of organizations (including phone numbers and web sites), and the names of people involved in conservation whose lives you can read about in *Current Biography*, another Wilson reference book.

The editor wishes to thank the authors and publishers who kindly granted permission to reprint the material in this collection. Special thanks are due to Bob Little, a student of ethics and philosophy; Miriam Helbok, an associate editor of *Current Biography* who formerly worked at the the Wildlife Conservation Society (formerly the New York Zoological Society); and Peter Claggett and Susan Lamont, a geographer and an ethnobotanist, respectively. All of these individuals gave freely of their ideas while the editor was preparing this issue of the Reference Shelf.

**Hilary D. Claggett**
**February 1997**

# I. Why Conserve Wildlife?

## Editor's Introduction

The selections in this section concern the philosophical aspects of wildlife conservation, including the ethics of conservation, ecologically sound habits of thought and action, the meaning of biodiversity, and the nature of wilderness itself.

The author of the first essay is Aldo Leopold, a pioneer in forestry, game management, recreation planning, and soil erosion control. Born in Burlington, Iowa, in 1887, he eventually settled on a farm in Wisconsin, where he wrote his landmark collection of natural-history writings, *A Sand County Almanac*. Published in 1949, a year after his death, this volume enjoyed renewed popularity with the growth of the environmental movement in the 1960s and 1970s; it is now a classic, widely regarded as the conservationist's bible.

In the selection reprinted here, "The Ecological Conscience" (1947), parts of which were revised and incorporated in "The Land Ethic" in *A Sand County Almanac*, Leopold discusses several conservation issues that, as Section III of this book demonstrates, remain unresolved to this day. Foremost among them is the tension between the desire for economic reward and the moral imperative of conserving wildlife. He argues, in effect, that the moral benefits of conservation and proper land use, if understood properly, outweigh the short-term financial rewards that may in some cases accrue to those who mistreat the land and its endangered wildlife.

In the second selection, Mark Jerome Walters, a veterinarian, teacher, and writer, emphasizes the need for "a philosophy of caring" for entire species that can be learned from examples of extinctions. Noting that "no rituals mark the passing of a species," he reminds us that we can nonetheless learn lessons from such losses, which "teach us that to preserve animals we must first preserve the multitude of habitats in which they live."

Among the reasons for caring about biodiversity offered by Roger L. DiSilvestro, a professional conservationist and a former editor and writer for the National Audubon Society, is that "protection of biodiversity, of wildness, offers us a diversity of opportunities for experience." In other words, by conserving wildlife, we give ourselves the chance to abandon the familiar role of spectator and to choose, instead, to participate in the natural world and to make connections to the past. "As long as wild places exist, we can go home again," he writes in the third selection, because "ultimately we are one with wildness." Therefore, if we degrade the environment, we degrade ourselves. Asking whether economic and real estate development is worth the long-term consequences in lost species, he concludes that choosing short-term gain over the preservation of wild places "reveal[s] a horrifying depravity in the human spirit."

Tracing the origins of that depravity to the emotionalism that drives the engine of human progress regardless of the price, the respected Harvard entomologist Edward O. Wilson contends, in the fourth selection, that we need to give reason a chance to tame our irrational impulses. To do this, he argues, it is necessary to overcome our vast "ignorance of our origins" on this planet. "The more closely we identify ourselves with the rest of life," he writes, "the more quickly we will be able to discover the sources of human sensibility and acquire the knowledge on which an enduring ethic, a sense of preferred direction, can be built." He suggests that our evolutionary history is evident today in the strength of our attractions and aversions to natural phenomena. Among those to which we are attracted is wilderness itself, which, aside from all its practical benefits to humanity, enhances the spirit as well, according to Wilson. He prescribes the study, protection,

and restoration of biodiversity, adding that conservation appeals to a wide range of inidi-
viduals, whether religious believers or atheists, animal rights activists or human suprema-
cists. "An enduring environmental ethic will aim to preserve not only the health and freedom of our species," he concludes, "but access to the world in which the human spirit
was born."

In the fifth selection, William Cronon, the editor of *Uncommon Ground: Toward
Reinventing Nature*, from which this essay was adapted for publication in *Utne Reader*,
calls for a new conceptualization of wilderness that is less romantic than the conventional
view but that demands just as much protection of wild places. Surveying the history of
humanity's relationship to the wild, he demonstrates that far from being an untouched
sanctuary free from human influence, wilderness as we know it today is a creation of civilization, weighted with symbolism harking back to the myth of the frontier. "The removal
of Indians to create an 'uninhabited wilderness'—uninhabited as never before in the
human history of the place—reminds us just how invented, just how constructed, the
American wilderness really is," he writes. For conservationists, the problem with the pre-
vailing definition of wilderness as a place from which humans are absent, according to
Cronon, is that we distance ourselves from nature, thereby abdicating responsibility for its
preservation. Conversely, he also points out that responsible behavior is only possible
when we recognize that our interests are not always the same as those of wild plant and
animal species. The main portion of his essay addresses this paradox.

# The Ecological Conscience[1]

Everyone ought to be dissatisfied with the slow spread of conservation to the land. Our "progress" still consists largely of letterhead pieties and convention oratory. The only progress that counts is that on the actual landscape of the back forty, and here we are still slipping two steps backward for each forward stride.

The usual answer to this dilemma is "more conservation education." My answer is yes by all means, but are we sure that only the *volume* of educational effort needs stepping up? Is something lacking in its *content* as well? I think there is, and I here attempt to define it.

The basic defect is this: we have not asked the citizen to assume any real responsibility. We have told him that if he will vote right, obey the law, join some organizations, and practice what conservation is profitable on his own land, that everything will be lovely; the government will do the rest.

This formula is too easy to accomplish anything worthwhile. It calls for no effort or sacrifice; no change in our philosophy of values. It entails little that any decent and intelligent person would not have done, of his own accord, under the late but not lamented Babbitian code.

No important change in human conduct is ever accomplished without an internal change in our intellectual emphases, our loyalties, our affections, and our convictions. The proof that conservation has not yet touched these foundations of conduct lies in the fact that philosophy, ethics, and religion have not yet heard of it.

I need a short name for what is lacking; I call it the ecological conscience. Ecology is the science of communities, and the ecological conscience is therefore the ethics of community life. I will define it further in terms of four case histories, which I think show the futility of trying to improve the face of the land without improving ourselves. I select these cases from my own state, because I am there surer of my facts.

> *"Ecology is the science of communities, and the ecological conscience is therefore the ethics of community life."*

## Soil Conservation Districts

About 1930 it became clear to all except the ecologically blind that Wisconsin's topsoil was slipping seaward. The farmers were told in 1933 that if they would adopt certain remedial practices for five years, the public would donate CCC labor to install them, plus the necessary machinery and materials. The offer was widely accepted, but the practices were widely forgotten when the five-year contract period was up. The farmers continued only those practices that

[1]Speech delivered by Aldo Leopold on June 7, 1947, to the Conservation Committee of the Garden Club of America; published later that year in the club's *Bulletin*. Revised portions of this speech formed the basis for his essay "The Land Ethic," which appeared in his *A Sand County Almanac* (1949). Speech reprinted from *The River of the Mother of God and Other Essays by Aldo Leopold*, edited by Susan Flader and J. Baird Callicott. Copyright ©1991 The Aldo Leopold Shack Foundation. Reprinted with permission of the University of Wisconsin Press.

yielded an immediate and visible economic gain for themselves.

This partial failure of land-use rules written by the government led to the idea that maybe farmers would learn more quickly if they themselves wrote the rules. Hence, in 1937, the Wisconsin Legislature passed the Soil Conservation District Law. This said to the farmers, in effect: "We, the public, will furnish you free technical service and loan you specialized machinery, if you will write your own rules for land-use. Each county may write its own rules, and these will have the force of law." Nearly all the counties promptly organized to accept the proffered help, but after a decade of operation, *no county has yet written a single rule*. There has been visible progress in such practices as strip-cropping, pasture renovation, and soil liming, but none in fencing woodlots or excluding plow and cow from steep slopes. The farmers, in short, selected out those remedial practices which were profitable anyhow, and ignored those which were profitable to the community, but not clearly profitable to themselves. The net result is that the natural acceleration in rate of soil-loss has been somewhat retarded, but we nevertheless have less soil than we had in 1937.

I hasten to add that no one has ever told farmers that in land-use the good of the community may entail obligations over and above those dictated by self-interest. The existence of such obligations is accepted in bettering rural roads, schools, churches, and baseball teams, but not in bettering the behavior of the water that falls on the land, nor in the preserving of the beauty or diversity of the farm landscape. Land-use ethics are still governed wholly by economic self-interest, just as social ethics were a century ago.

To sum up: we have asked the farmer to do what he conveniently could to save his soil, and he has done just that, and only that. The exclusion of cows from woods and steep slopes is not convenient, and is not done. Moreover some things are being done that are at least dubious as conservation practices: for example marshy stream bottoms are being drained to relieve the pressure on worn-out uplands. The upshot is that woods, marshes, and natural streams, together with their respective faunas and floras, are headed toward ultimate elimination from southern Wisconsin.

All in all we have built a beautiful piece of social machinery—the Soil Conservation District—which is coughing along on two cylinders because we have been too timid, and too anxious for quick success, to tell the farmer the true magnitude of his obligations. Obligations have no meaning without conscience, and the problem we face is the extension of the social conscience from people to land.

## Paul Bunyan's Deer

The Wisconsin lumberjack came very near accomplishing, in reality, the prodigious feats of woods-destruction attributed to Paul Bunyan. Following Paul's departure for points west, there followed an event little heralded in song and story, but quite as dramatic as the original destruction of the pineries: there sprang up, almost over night, an empire of brushfields.

*"Land-use ethics are still governed wholly by economic self-interest, just as social ethics were a century ago."*

Paul Bunyan had tired easily of salt pork and corned beef, hence he had taken good care to see that the deer of the original pineries found their way regularly to the stewpot. Moreover there were wolves in Paul's day, and the wolves had performed any necessary pruning of the deer herd which Paul had overlooked. But by the time the brushfields sprang into being, the wolves had been wiped out and the state had passed a buck-law and established refuges. The stage was set for an irruption of deer.

The deer took to the brushfields like yeast tossed into the sourdough pot. By 1940 the woods were foaming with them, so to speak. We Conservation Commissioners took credit for this miracle of creation; actually we did little but officiate at the birth. Anyhow, it was a herd to make one's mouth water. A tourist from Chicago could drive out in the evening and see 50 deer, or even more.

This immense deer herd was eating brush, and eating well. What was this brush? It consisted of temporary short-lived sun-loving trees and bushes which act as a nurse crop for the future forest. The forest comes up under the brush, just as alfalfa or clover come up under oats or rye. In the normal succession, the brush is eventually overtopped by the forest tree seedlings, and we have the start of a new forest.

In anticipation of this well-known process, the state, the counties, the U.S. Forest Service, the pulp mills, and even some lumber mills staked out "forests" consisting, for the moment, of brush. Large investments of time, thought, cash, CCC labor, WPA labor, and legislation were made in the expectation that Nature would repeat her normal cycle. The state embarked on a tax subsidy, called the Forest Crop Law, to encourage landowners to hang onto their brushfields until they were replaced by forest.

But we failed to reckon with the deer, and with deer hunters and resort owners. In 1942 we had a hard winter and many deer starved. It then became evident that the original "nurse-trees" had grown out of reach of deer, and that the herd was eating the oncoming forest. The remedy seemed to be to reduce the herd by legalizing killing of does. It was evident that if we didn't reduce the herd, starvation would, and we would eventually lose both the deer and the forest. But for five consecutive years the deer hunters and resort owners, plus the politicians interested in their votes, have defeated all attempts at herd reduction.

I will not tire you with all the red herrings, subterfuges, evasions, and expedients which these people have used to befog this simple issue. There is even a newspaper dedicated solely to defaming the proponents of herd reduction. These people call themselves conservationists, and in one sense they are, for in the past we have pinned that label on anyone who loves wildlife, however blindly. These conservationists, for the sake of maintaining an abnormal and unnatural deer herd for a few more years, are willing to sacrifice the future forest, and also the ultimate welfare of the herd itself.

The motives behind this "conservation" are a wish to prolong easy deer hunting, and a wish to show numerous deer to tourists.

These perfectly understandable wishes are rationalized by protestations of chivalry to does and fawns. As an unexpected aftermath of this situation, there has been a large increase of illegal killing, and of abandonment of illegal carcasses in the woods. Thus herd control, of a sort, is taking place outside the law. But the food-producing capacity of the forest has been overstrained for a decade, and the next hard winter will bring catastrophic starvation. After that we shall have very few deer, and these will be runty from malnutrition. Our forest will be a moth-eaten remnant consisting largely of inferior species of trees.

The basic fallacy in this kind of "conservation" is that it seeks to conserve one resource by destroying another. These "conservationists" are unable to see the land as a whole. They are unable to think in terms of community rather than group welfare, and in terms of the long as well as the short view. They are conserving what is important to them in the immediate future, and they are angry when told that this conflicts with what is important to the state as a whole in the long run.

There is an important lesson here: the flat refusal of the average adult to learn anything new, i.e., to study. To understand the deer problem requires some knowledge of what deer eat, of what they do not eat, and of how a forest grows. The average deer hunter is sadly lacking in such knowledge, and when anyone tries to explain the matter, he is branded forthwith as a long-haired theorist. This anger-reaction against new and unpleasant facts is of course a standard psychiatric indicator of the closed mind.

We speak glibly of conservation education, but what do we mean by it? If we mean indoctrination, then let us be reminded that it is just as easy to indoctrinate with fallacies as with facts. If we mean to teach the capacity for independent judgment, then I am appalled by the magnitude of the task. The task is large mainly because of this refusal of adults to learn anything new.

The ecological conscience, then, is an affair of the mind as well as the heart. It implies a capacity to study and learn, as well as to emote about the problems of conservation.

## Jefferson Davis's Pines

I have a farm in one of the sand-counties of central Wisconsin. I bought it because I wanted a place to plant pines. One reason for selecting my particular farm was that it adjoined the only remaining stand of mature pines in the county.

This pine grove is a historical landmark. It is the spot (or very near the spot) where, in 1828, a young lieutenant named Jefferson Davis cut the pine logs to build Fort Winnebago. He floated them down the Wisconsin River to the fort. In the ensuing century a thousand other rafts of pine logs floated past this grove, to build that empire of red barns now called the Middle West.

This grove is also an ecological landmark. It is the nearest spot where a city-worn refugee from the south can hear the wind sing in tall timber. It harbors one of the best remnants of deer, ruffed grouse, and pileated woodpeckers in southern Wisconsin.

My neighbor, who owns the grove, has treated it rather decently through the years. When his son got married, the grove furnished lumber for the new house, and it could spare such light cuttings. But when war prices of lumber soared skyward, the temptation to slash became too strong. Today the grove lies prostrate, and its long logs are feeding a hungry saw.

By all the accepted rules of forestry, my neighbor was justified in slashing the grove. The stand was even-aged; mature, and invaded by heart-rot. Yet any schoolboy would know, in his heart, that there is something wrong about erasing the last remnant of pine timber from a county. When a farmer owns a rarity he should feel some obligation as its custodian, and a community should feel some obligation to help him carry the economic cost of custodianship. Yet our present land-use conscience is silent on such questions.

## The Flambeau Raid

The Flambeau was a river so lovely to look upon, and so richly endowed with forests and wildlife, that even the hard-bitten fur traders of the free-booting 1700s enthused about it as the choicest part of the great north woods.

The freebooting 1800s expressed the same admiration, but in somewhat different terms. By 1930 the Flambeau retained only one 50-mile stretch of river not yet harnessed for power, and only a few sections of original timber not yet cut for lumber or pulp.

During the 1930s the Wisconsin Conservation Department started to build a state forest on the Flambeau, using these remnants of wild woods and wild river as starting points. This was to be no ordinary state forest producing only logs and tourist camps; its primary object was to preserve and restore the remnant of canoe water. Year by year the Commission bought land, removed cottages, fended off unnecessary roads, and in general started the long slow job of re-creating a stretch of wild river for the use and enjoyment of young Wisconsin.

The good soil which enabled the Flambeau to grow the best cork pine for Paul Bunyan likewise enabled Rusk County, during recent decades, to sprout a dairy industry. These dairy farmers wanted cheaper electric power than that offered by local power companies. Hence they organized a cooperative REA and applied for a power dam which, when built, will clip off the lower reaches of canoe water which the Conservation Commission wanted to keep for recreational use.

There was a bitter political fight, in the course of which the Commission not only withdrew its opposition to the REA dam, but the legislature, by statute, repealed the authority of the Conservation Commission and made County Commissioners the ultimate arbiters of conflict between power values and recreational values. I think I need not dwell on the irony of this statute. It seals the fate of all wild rivers remaining in the state, including the Flambeau. It says, in effect, that in deciding the use of rivers, the local economic interest shall have blanket priority over state wide recreational interests, with County Commissioners as the umpire.

The Flambeau case illustrates the dangers that lurk in the semi-honest doctrine that conservation is only good economics. The defenders of the Flambeau tried to prove that the river in its wild state would produce more fish and tourists than the impounded river would produce butterfat, but this is not true. We should have claimed that a little gain in butterfat is less important to the state than a large loss in opportunity for a distinctive form of outdoor recreation.

We lost the Flambeau as a logical consequence of the fallacy that conservation can be achieved easily. It cannot. Parts of every well-rounded conservation program entail sacrifice, usually local, but none the less real. The farmers' raid on our last wild river is just like any other raid on any other public wealth; the only defense is a widespread public awareness of the values at stake. There was none.

*"The practice of conservation must spring from a conviction of what is ethically and esthetically right, as well as what is economically expedient."*

## The Upshot

I have described here a fraction of that huge aggregate of problems and opportunities which we call conservation. This aggregate of case histories show one common need: an ecological conscience.

The practice of conservation must spring from a conviction of what is ethically and esthetically right, as well as what is economically expedient. A thing is right only when it tends to preserve the integrity, stability, and beauty of the community, and the community includes the soil, waters, fauna, and flora, as well as people.

It cannot be right, in the ecological sense, for a farmer to drain the last marsh, graze the last woods, or slash the last grove in his community, because in doing so he evicts a fauna, a flora, and a landscape whose membership in the community is older than his own, and is equally entitled to respect.

It cannot be right, in the ecological sense, for a farmer to channelize his creek or pasture his steep slopes, because in doing so he passes flood trouble to his neighbors below, just as his neighbors above have passed it to him. In cities we do not get rid of nuisances by throwing them across the fence onto the neighbor's lawn, but in water management we still do just that.

It cannot be right, in the ecological sense, for the deer hunter to maintain his sport by browsing out the forest, or for the bird hunter to maintain his by decimating the hawks and owls, or for the fisherman to maintain his by decimating the herons, kingfishers, terns, and otters. Such tactics seek to achieve one kind of conservation by destroying another, and thus they subvert the integrity and stability of the community.

If we grant the premise that an ecological conscience is possible and needed, then its first tenet must be this: economic provocation is no longer a satisfactory excuse for unsocial land-use, (or, to use somewhat stronger words, for ecological atrocities). This, however, is a negative statement. I would rather assert positively that decent land-use should be accorded social rewards proportionate to its social importance.

I have no illusions about the speed or accuracy with which an ecological conscience can become functional. It has required 19 centuries to define decent man-to-man conduct and the process is only half done; it may take as long to evolve a code of decency for man-to-land conduct. In such matters we should not worry too much about anything except the direction in which we travel. The direction is clear, and the first step is to *throw your weight around* on matters of right and wrong in land-use. Cease being intimidated by the argument that a right action is impossible because it does not yield maximum profits, or that a wrong action is to be condoned because it pays. That philosophy is dead in human relations, and its funeral in land-relations is overdue.

# The Meaning of Extinction[2]

I recently visited the Smithsonian museum in Washington, D.C., where corridors are lined with dioramas and display cases of extinct species. In one display, nine stuffed passenger pigeons perch on a branch against a painted autumn backdrop of a beech-oak forest in the Appalachian Mountains. This pigeon, as you have heard, once may have been the most abundant bird in the world. A nearby case displays Martha, the last passenger pigeon, who died in captivity at the Cincinnati Zoological Gardens on September 1, 1914.

*"We now have an economic philosophy. We have a philosophy of government. But we have yet to develop a philosophy toward extinction. We barely have learned to grieve."*

Below Martha is a reconstructed skeleton of a stocky flightless bird known as the dodo from the island of Mauritius in the Indian Ocean. In 1681, within a century of its discovery, hunters wiped out the dodo. Also on display is the great auk, a species that once lived in the far north and wintered as far south as Florida; the last was killed in 1844. A few specimens over is a case displaying a pair of heath hens. A staple food of the early New England colonists, the birds were so common in the wooded areas of early Boston that they were often served for dinner several times a week. By 1927, disease, bad weather, poachers, and legions of feral cats had reduced the number to about a dozen. In 1932, the last heath hen was seen.

Many other species are in those cases at the Smithsonian. But, in fact, only a part of the museum's collection of extinct species is in public view.

Tucked away in drawers, among many others, are skins of the last dusky seaside sparrows, birds that once lived in the salt marshes along the Indian and Banana rivers of east central Florida. In the 1960s, the Kennedy Space Center was built in dusky habitat. For a time...the birds lived in the shadow of Launch Complex 39, the spot from which humans were first launched to the moon. But, because the salt marsh bred bothersome mosquitoes that hampered the space program, the land was diked and permanently flooded to destroy the insects' breeding areas. The sparrow's breeding areas were flooded as well. Housing developments, highways, and wildfires finally did in the rest. The last dusky seaside sparrow died in captivity, near Orlando, in 1987....

The Greek scholar Dionysius of Halicarnassus said that history is philosophy learned from examples. What does the passenger pigeon say to us? What does the great auk whisper? Can the dodo tell us anything we do not already know? The dusky? We will never know until we consider past extinctions with far greater deliberation than we have so far.

We now have an economic philosophy. We have a philosophy of government. But we have yet to develop a philosophy toward

---

[2]Article by Mark Jerome Walters, a veterinarian, teacher, and writer, from *Sanctuary* p16-17 N/D '93. Copyright © 1993 *Santuary* and the Massachusetts Audubon Society. Reprinted with permission.

extinction. We barely have learned to grieve. Indeed, as Aldo Leopold wrote, "For one species to mourn the death of another is a new thing under the sun." How do we begin to shape examples of extinction and our growing awareness of loss into a philosophy of caring for all life? How do we chart a positive course from a history of annihilation?

Rarely are the lessons of history explicit. But perhaps Martha tells us that numbers alone are no assurance against extinction. Abundance should not decrease an animal's value in our eyes. Ten million bison on a western plain are no less deserving of our protective care than the last twenty in a zoo.

Science can teach us cause and effect, but only philosophy can teach the meaning of kinship; that interconnectedness means more than mere mutual dependency. Dionysius might have told us that the extinction of the dusky seaside sparrow teaches us that outward journeys—even to the moon—can never take us as far as inward ones; that searching is different from seeking; and that facts about the universe are no substitute for a philosophy of caring for life on earth.

The litany of extinctions can teach us how to feel about the loss of species. We mourn the death of individuals, but no rituals mark the passing of a species. Death is the end of a life, but extinction is the end of birth. Holmes Rolston III, wrote, "Extinction kills essences beyond existences—the soul as well as the body. To superkill a species is to shut down a story of millennia and leave no future possibilities."

After spending the morning around the glass display cases at the Smithsonian, I rode the metro across town to the National Zoo. I saw the giant panda, palm cockatoos, tigers, cheetahs, mountain gorillas, and the endangered Guam rail. I stood before these endangered species as people must have once stood before the last living passenger pigeons.

I suddenly imagined the Smithsonian entry hall two centuries from now, a stuffed black-and-white bearish creature poses in a gallery of plastic bamboo. A sign reads: *Giant panda. Thousands once roamed the clouded highland forests in parts of China. Habitat transformed by farming. The last specimen died in captivity in Wolong, China, in 2115.* In the museum's corridors, the display cases have multiplied. They hold a Bachman's warbler, a Guam rail, a palm cockatoo, a hyacinth macaw, and hundreds of newcomers. In the Gallery of Extinct Mammals is a Bengal tiger, a cheetah, and numerous other animals.

But celebrities such as the giant panda do not necessarily teach the realities of extinction. It is the little things that run the world. For every endangered large mammal, tens of thousands of plants, invertebrates, and little-known birds languish in anonymity.

Not far from the panda yard—in a small feeder spring along Rock Creek, which defines a portion of the zoo's boundary—there is an endangered species known as the Hay's spring amphipod. Almost no one knows about this shrimplike crustacean. Hundreds could fit in the palm of your hand, and it is little noted in the drama of

*"Death is the end of a life, but extinction is the end of birth."*

endangered species conservation. If it became extinct tomorrow, who would know or care? Is there anything to learn from an animal we barely knew was here? If we are unaware of the examples that matter most, how are we to find a philosophy that matters at all?

If Dionysius is right, even as many species become extinct, a philosophy of caring learned from the examples of loss is still something we have every reason to hope for. What is philosophy but lessons learned the hard way?

# Biodiversity: Saving Wilderness[3]

The entire cause of the conservation movement has been, in recent years, boiled down to a single word. Unfortunately, that word is *biodiversity*, which does not have the ring of a clarion call to arms. Unlike such phrases as *endangered species* and *save the whale*, or the all-encompassing *save the Earth*, biodiversity smacks of the scientific and the esoteric. It is not a term with which to move the masses and win ardent public support. And yet it is, in fact, synonymous with saving the Earth, or at least with saving enough of it to ensure that our economic and social lives can continue without threat of catastrophic disruption.

Biodiversity is shorthand for biological diversity, which in turn describes a fairly complex set of conditions.

On one level, biodiversity refers to the variety of life forms found in a given area or ecosystem or on the planet as a whole. We can refer to the biodiversity of the rainforest or of the desert or of the entire globe.

No one knows exactly how diverse life is on the planet. Biologists have named about 1.5 million species (a species may be roughly defined as a group of genetically related organisms that can produce fertile offspring). This is only a fraction of the planet's total array of life forms, which has been estimated at anywhere from 5 million to 30 million species, estimates that show we lack the foggiest notion of how diverse life really is.

The concept of biodiversity incorporates more than mere numbers. It also alludes to the interrelationships of species. It is probably safe to say that all species interact with others on some level. This is certainly true of the species that we see all around us. Birds and insects interact with trees and shrubs. Squirrels interact with birds, cats, dogs, and people. Wolves interact with moose and caribou. Species interactions can be as simple as a grizzly preying upon a ground squirrel, but they can also be subtle and complex. They are often vital. Some plants can reproduce only if pollinated by a particular species of insect. For example, most tropical orchid species can be fertilized only by a single species of bee. Each orchid species has its own pollinating bee species. Should an insect species involved in such a relationship vanish, so will the associated plant. When the plant disappears, so do other species dependent on it. The importance of biodiversity is thus underscored by the vital interrelationships that exist among species.

On the second level, biodiversity refers to the genetic diversity each species represents. Consider the house mouse, as Harvard biologist E[dward] O. Wilson does in the opening chapter of *Biodiversity*. The cell nucleus of a house mouse contains about

*"...biodiversity refers to the variety of life forms found in a given area or ecosystem or on the planet as a whole."*

---

[3]Chapter by the conservationist Roger L. DiSilvestro, a former editor and writer for the National Audubon Society, from his book *Reclaiming the Last Wild Places: A New Agenda for Biodiversity*. Copyright ©1993 John Wiley & Sons, Inc. Reprinted with permission of John Wiley & Sons, Inc.

100,000 genes, each organized from four strings of genetically encoded chemicals called DNA. DNA molecules are microscopic, but if the cellular DNA were uncoiled it would measure more than three feet. Enlarged to the diameter of kite string, the DNA molecule would run about 650 miles long, with about 20 "letters" of genetic code per inch. If the letters of the molecule were enlarged to the size of the typeface on this page, they would fill nearly all 15 editions of the *Encyclopedia Britannica* published since 1768.

The vast amount of information contained within an individual mammal constitutes a small amount of the genetic diversity represented by an entire species. Each individual, except in species that reproduce without exchanging genetic information through crossbreeding, is genetically different from all other individuals. The more individuals a species contains, the greater the genetic diversity of that species. When something reduces a species' numbers, such as poaching or habitat destruction, vast amounts of genetic diversity are lost even if the species continues to survive.

Globally, we are losing biodiversity at a terrific rate. Wilson estimates that in tropical rainforests alone we are losing about 17,500 species yearly—roughly 1,000 to 10,000 times the rate at which marine species vanished at the end of the Paleozoic and Mesozoic eras, which until now marked the quickest rate of extinction in the past 65 million years. Present losses are caused primarily by human activities and are much more thorough than those brought on by nature. In the Paleozoic and Mesozoic eras, most plant species survived; today, both animals and plants are rapidly vanishing.

But what has this to do with us?

## Why Worry about Biodiversity?

"Why" is a question ever on the minds of conservationists, and the irreducible answer is *people*. The central concern of most conservationists is the physical, spiritual, and emotional well-being of humankind. All these things are subsumed in wildness, in nature, which is what we preserve when we protect biodiversity. "In wildness is the preservation of the world," wrote Henry David Thoreau—to which might be added Loren Eiseley's observation: "Nature is the receptacle which contains man and into which he finally sinks to rest. It implies all, absolutely all, that man knows or can know." When we chip away at the biodiversity of planet and homeland, we chip away at our potential for knowing more about, and surviving better in, the world.

The protection of biodiversity gives us our city parks, our zoos, our wildlife refuges. It gives us Yellowstone and Yosemite national parks. It gives us national seashore recreation areas where we can walk among sand dunes and listen to the rumble of the surf.

The protection of biodiversity lies at the heart of many emotional, intellectual, and spiritual pleasures. Protection of biodiversity, of wildness, offers us a diversity of opportunities for experience, which in turn offers a solution to at least one discouraging aspect of modern life: the extent to which we have all become spectators.

*"The central concern of most conservationists is the physical, spiritual, and emotional well-being of humankind."*

Most of us spend more time watching other people engaging in various activities than we do actively participating ourselves. Urban life especially is built around watching rather than doing. Urban dwellers pride themselves on the variety of things they can watch: theater, films, ballet, symphony orchestras, museums, zoos, sports, television, television, television. How often does conversation with friends, family, and associates gravitate toward events that one or all have merely witnessed?

If wild places offer us anything they offer us this: participation. Even a nature trail in a city park is participatory. Your body must work to get there and work to be there. If the place is big enough to get lost in and perhaps be attacked in—if only by ticks and black flies—so much the better. You have broken into the realm of participation, you have escaped a world in which there is a great deal of cause and no real effect. You are compelled to plan or contemplate or decide what you yourself must do, rather than merely watch others make decisions.

But wild places offer us more than participatory recreation. They offer us connections as well.

Among the crumbling arches of the Roman Colosseum, or the marbled ruins of the Forum, or the tawny stonework of the pyramids of Egypt, we can sense connections to an ancient past, to the shadows of vanished hopes and dreams. These monuments tie us to the lost societies from which we sprang, to the homelands of our individual ancestors—Italians to the Romans, British to the Celts, French to the Gauls, Germans to the Vikings, African Americans to the Ashanti, Chinese to the dynastic nobles, Japanese to the Samurai.

But wildness takes us to something far older and deeper, returns all of us, regardless of race or nationality, to one and the same place: the birthing ground of humanity, where all our ancestors, regardless of present race, color, or creed, spent much of their time chipping tools from stone, hunting animals, gathering plants, and huddling around open fires. Wildness brings us all back home and reveals the world that shaped, created, and nurtured us. As long as wild places exist, we can go home again. We can meet unvarnished the fears and trials faced by our earliest human ancestors and measure the broad limits of our species' ability to survive. We can learn how resilient and tough and independent we really are.

But in wildness we learn about more than ourselves. Said John Muir, one of the premier defenders of natural places at the turn of the century, "The clearest way to the Universe is through a forest wilderness." For those eternally locked in human society, whose primary concerns are money and status, this may not seem much of an offering. But to those blessed with a desire to understand life itself, it is invaluable. Social critic Christopher Lasch, in *The Culture of Narcissism*, pointed out that few people today, caught in the web of earnings and status, escape a feeling of meaninglessness, a malaise of life. They lack a *purpose* in life. As novelist Russell Hoban put it, the central question of life is not *what does it all mean*, but *who are we doing it for*?

The answer lies well outside ourselves, for life, that is to say, *Life*, is not synonymous with humanity. Our species is only a small part of life, a type of life. Trying to understand the purpose of our strivings and joys by studying humanity, by focusing on humanity, is like trying to define a giant sequoia by looking at a single plant cell. Humanity as we know it has tramped over the surface of the globe for about a million years. Life, however, has been here for 3.5 *billion* years. We have much to learn from examining life in all its variety and interaction, from looking outward rather than inward. We must plunge into the pool of life—into tropical rainforests, deserts, mountains, oceans, and streams. To live happily, we need to discover our links to the larger world, to wildness, and we need to escape the ego-focused doctrines that salve our desire for personal importance while undercutting the ecosystems that give us life.

*"When we seek to protect wildness, we seek to protect eternity..."*

When we seek to protect wildness, we seek to protect eternity, to protect that which came before us and produced us, that which nurtures and preserves us, that which will provide for all future generations. We may destroy the natural world, but we cannot escape it, for ultimately we are one with wildness. As Muir put it, spend time in the wild and eventually "you lose consciousness of your separate existence: you blend with the landscape, and become part and parcel of nature."

We cannot, in the end, be separated from the natural world. We absorb directly our physical environment. Our lungs take in air, and if that air is riddled with pollutants, then those pollutants are incorporated into our muscles, our blood, and our bones. Thousands of years from now, if scientists still exist, they will be able to distinguish our bones from those of 16th-century people by the amount of industrial pollutants incorporated into our bodies' most durable organs. We drink water, and our digestive tract absorbs whatever minerals and pollutants it contains. We eat animals, and our bodies absorb and hold the steroids we have pumped into livestock and the pollutants we have pumped into wild systems. Pesticides sprayed on southern cotton fields have migrated north on the wind to settle in rainfall upon the Great Lakes, where microscopic creatures have absorbed them, and the pesticides have worked their way up the food chain into lake trout that are also depositories for a variety of other Great Lakes pollutants, including cancer-causing toxins. From the trout the toxins have worked their way into eagles and otters and us.

When conservationists suggest that the planet's biodiversity is decreasing, they are talking about a potential catastrophe for humankind. At worst, rapid loss of species could undercut our own biological supports, stranding us in a denuded world for which we are not adapted and in which we cannot survive. At best, we will almost certainly lose species that could be of critical importance to our well-being and to the improvement of our daily lives.

And now we are down to the hardcore pragmatic reasons for protecting biodiversity. Even people who have little regard for the spiritual and emotional benefits of biodiversity protection will likely be interested in the fundamental things that wild species bring to our daily lives, such as food, medicine, and even jobs.

"Wild species are in fact both one of the Earth's most important resources and the least utilized," wrote Wilson. "We come to depend completely on less than 1 percent of living species for our existence, the remainder waiting untested and fallow. In the course of history...we have utilized about 7,000 kinds of plants for food; predominant among these are wheat, rye, maize, and about a dozen other highly domesticated species. Yet there are at least 75,000 edible plants in existence, and many of these are superior to the crop plants in widest use."

You need look no further than the pharmaceutical industry to see another way in which the survival of the natural environment is critical to human society. For the past quarter-century, 25 percent of the prescriptions sold in the United States have contained plant extractions as active ingredients. Some 119 medicinal chemicals used worldwide are extracted from plants. These plants number fewer than 90 species, but the planet produces about 250,000 species of plants. The bulk of these have never been tested for their potential value as medicinal substances, and some valuable plant species are disappearing. For example, in the Pacific Northwest, the yew tree was until recently cut down and burned as a trash species. In the 1980s scientists discovered that yew bark contains a chemical effective against some types of cancer. Unfortunately, large quantities of bark are needed to produce useful amounts of the chemical, and too few yew trees of adequate size remain to make the natural source promising. Similarly, in the heavily logged Philippine rain forest some 1,500 plant species are used in traditional medicine. Many of these may offer little more than a placebo effect, but if even a fraction of them are medically useful their extinction would be a major loss to human society.

Wild plants are also valuable because they can help ensure the health or enhance the utility of crop plants. Wild relatives of domestic crop plants sometimes contain genes that give them resistance to threatening diseases. An African species of wild coffee contains a gene that makes it resistant to rust, a disease that in recent years jeopardized the world's coffee crop. Crossbreeding domestic coffees with the wild variety halted the epidemic. A wild grass discovered about 10 years ago in Mexico proved to be a relative of domestic corn. Corn is an expensive crop because it must be grown from seed each year. The Mexican wild grass regrows without reseeding. If its genes for reproductive strategy can be bred into domestic corn, the once-obscure wild grass's potential value—translated into income and jobs—will top $7 billion yearly.

It is impossible to calculate the dollar value of every species because complex and indispensable relationships between species compound the value of any given type of plant or animal. A species that seems to have no intrinsic worth might be critical to the survival of another, more clearly valuable species. For example, the

Brazil nut is a valuable export crop, bringing in about $1 billion annually to Brazil. But it has never been successfully cultivated—it exists only in the wild. No one knows why it cannot be cultivated, but probably the Brazil nut is in some way dependent on the hidden activities of certain other species, such as insects or rodents. Thus the billion-dollar Brazil-nut industry might depend ultimately on the fate of some unknown moth.

Even a species of obvious value to humans may have greater value to its ecosystem. The African elephant, for example, is critically related to a wide number of other species. During droughts, elephants dig waterholes in river beds, providing moisture for uncounted other species. The seeds of some trees, such as the acacia, germinate best when they have passed through an elephant's digestive tract. Elephants knock down mature trees, helping to keep grasslands open—a critical factor for many grazing species, such as antelopes. The elephant's value is thus more than the price of its tusks or the money it brings from tourism. It is the value of nearly all the large animals that share the elephant's habitat.

*"Wild plants are also valuable because they can help ensure the health or enhance the utility of crop plants."*

The mutual dependence of species makes the protection of biodiversity critical. As we remove species from any ecosystem, we begin to upset the balance of all species. Remove enough species, or a keystone species such as the elephant, and the whole system veers toward collapse.

Underlying the survival of all species is habitat itself. Without proper habitat—whether it be virgin forest, open grassland, the bottom of the sea, or the human intestine—no species can survive. Habitat protection, which includes the protection of everything from wilderness areas to city parks, is the foundation of all efforts to protect species, to preserve biodiversity. This is why it is so vital to save such vanishing habitats as the temperate rainforests of the Pacific Northwest and the tall-grass prairies of the Midwest. They represent the last of a certain type of ecosystem. When they are gone, we risk losing all that these ecosystems offer us. This is equally true of wetlands and coastal zones. The loss of these habitats results in a net loss of species, a diminishing of biodiversity and all that it promises us in foods, medicines, and other products.

Many of those who stand to profit from environmental destruction would argue that biodiversity is of no consequence. Extinction, they say, is a natural process that began long before the arrival of humankind. Like glaciers and comets, humanity is merely another cause of extinction, neither more nor less natural as an agent of species loss.

This argument overlooks the scientific point that we are causing extinctions at thousands of times the rate of anything in the past and that we are destroying the entire spectrum of species—everything from plants to insects to mammals. When the ecological bottom drops out and ecosystems begin to collapse, a domino effect comes into play so that even species that are not directly touched by human activities could vanish. If we destroy enough species and disrupt enough ecosystems, we will almost certainly destroy the way of life to which we have become accustomed.

It will happen by slow degrees. We already find ourselves unable to eat fish from certain bodies of water, or to breathe comfortably the air in some urban communities, or to swim along some ocean beaches—and we adjust our lives accordingly. We will continue to adjust and adjust as more and more warning signs are erected along rivers, lakes, and seas—*do not fish here, do not swim here.* And though as a species we quite likely will survive, right down to the most extreme scenario short of global conflagration, nevertheless if we persist in our actions we will bring down the ecological super-structure on which is mounted our social, political, and economic life, and we will find ourselves living a less desirable, much degrad-ed existence.

Fortunately, we need not function with the mindless inexorability of a glacier. If we so choose, we can be barriers to death, destruc-tion, and extinction. We can empathize with wild places and crea-tures for their sake as well as our own. Australian geneticist O. H. Frankel, quoted in the Worldwatch Institute's booklet "On the Brink of Extinction: Conserving the Diversity of Life," observed, "We are *not* the equivalent of an ice age or a rise in sea level: we are capa-ble of prediction and control. We have acquired evolutionary responsibility."

Because we have a choice, we can pause in our actions and ask ourselves what we are sacrificing biodiversity for. William Faulkner, in *The Bear,* put it neatly when he had Ike McCaslin say over the dead body of a buck he has shot, "I slew you; my bearing must not shame your quitting life. My conduct forever onward must become your death."

Is our conduct worthy of the untolled species and vast ecosystems we have wiped out? We sacrificed the dusky seaside sparrow—a bird abundant along the eastern Florida coast a mere 20 years ago—to suburban houses and insect spray. A land developer in Oregon wants to sacrifice the Oregon silverspot butterfly for the construc-tion of a golf course. Southern California real-estate developers want to sacrifice the Stephen's kangaroo rat for housing tracts—the same sort of tracts that threaten California cougar populations. Loggers want to sacrifice the last expanses of ancient forests in the Pacific Northwest for perhaps five more years of work, after which they will be both treeless and jobless. These actions reveal a horri-fying depravity in the human spirit.

But that depravity did not arise wholecloth in our time. To find its origin, and the challenge that human society poses to biodiversity and to its own survival, we need to catapult back about 15,000 years and trace the roots of biodiversity protection. The world then was in many ways a much more complex place, biologically at any rate, because more species were thriving. Many large mammals now extinct were still living and breeding. Complex forests grew where now we see human-caused deserts, as in the Middle East and parts of India. Vast herds of bison, antelope, wisent, mammoths, and woolly rhinos roamed the land, and countless ducks, geese, wild pigeons, and other birds crowded the skies. No park boundaries had yet been drawn on the land, nor were they needed.

# The Environmental Ethic[4]

The sixth great extinction spasm of geological time is upon us, grace of mankind. Earth has at last acquired a force that can break the crucible of biodiversity....

The creation of that diversity came slow and hard: 3 billion years of evolution to start the profusion of animals that occupy the seas, another 350 million years to assemble the rain forests in which half or more of the species on Earth now live. There was a succession of dynasties. Some species split into two or several daughter species, and their daughters split yet again to create swarms of descendants that deployed as plant feeders, carnivores, free swimmers, gliders, sprinters, and burrowers, in countless motley combinations. These ensembles then gave way by partial or total extinction to newer dynasties, and so on to form a gentle upward swell that carried biodiversity to a peak—just before the arrival of humans. Life had stalled on plateaus along the way, and on five occasions it suffered extinction spasms that took 10 million years to repair. But the thrust was upward. Today the diversity of life is greater than it was a 100 million years ago—and far greater than 500 million years before that.

Most dynasties contained a few species that expanded disproportionately to create satrapies of lesser rank. Each species and its descendants, a sliver of the whole, lived an average of hundreds of thousands to millions of years. Longevity varied according to taxonomic group. Echinoderm lineages, for example, persisted longer than those of flowering plants, and both endured longer than those of mammals.

Ninety-nine percent of all the species that ever lived are now extinct. The modern fauna and flora are composed of survivors that somehow managed to dodge and weave through all the radiations and extinctions of geological history. Many contemporary world-dominant groups, such as rats, ranid frogs, nymphalid butterflies, and plants of the aster family Compositae, attained their status not long before the Age of Man. Young or old, all living species are direct descendants of the organisms that lived 3.8 billion years ago. They are living genetic libraries, composed of nucleotide sequences, the equivalent of words and sentences, which record evolutionary events all across that immense span of time. . . . Each species is the product of mutations and recombinations too complex to be grasped by unaided intuition. It was sculpted and burnished by an astronomical number of events in natural selection, which killed off or otherwise blocked from reproduction the vast majority of its member organisms before they completed their lifespans. Viewed from the perspective of evolutionary time, all other species are our

---

[4]Chapter by the Pulitzer Prize-winning author Edward O. Wilson, the Frank B. Baird Jr. Professor of Science and Curator in Entomology, Museum of Comparative Zoology, Harvard University, from his book *The Diversity of Life* Copyright © 1992 Edward O. Wilson. Reprinted with permission of Harvard University Press.

distant kin because we share a remote ancestry. We still use a common vocabulary, the nucleic-acid code, even though it has been sorted into radically different hereditary languages.

Such is the ultimate and cryptic truth of every kind of organism, large and small, every bug and weed. The flower in the crannied wall—it *is* a miracle. If not in the way Tennyson, the Victorian romantic, bespoke the portent of full knowledge (by which "I should know what God and man is"), then certainly a consequence of all we understand from modern biology. Every kind of organism has reached this moment in time by threading one needle after another, throwing up brilliant artifices to survive and reproduce against nearly impossible odds.

Organisms are all the more remarkable in combination. Pull out the flower from its crannied retreat, shake the soil from the roots into the cupped hand, magnify it for close examination. The black earth is alive with a riot of algae, fungi, nematodes, mites, springtails, enchytraeid worms, thousands of species of bacteria. The handful may be only a tiny fragment of one ecosystem, but because of the genetic codes of its residents it holds more order than can be found on the surfaces of all the planets combined. It is a sample of the living force that runs the Earth—and will continue to do so with or without us.

*"...a fifth or more of the species of plants and animals could vanish or be doomed to early extinction by the year 2020 unless better efforts are made to save them."*

We may think that the world has been completely explored. Almost all the mountains and rivers, it is true, have been named, the coast and geodetic surveys completed, the ocean floor mapped to the deepest trenches, the atmosphere transected and chemically analyzed. The planet is now continuously monitored from space by satellites; and, not least, Antarctica, the last virgin continent, has become a research station and expensive tourist stop. The biosphere, however, remains obscure. Even though some 1.4 million species of organisms have been discovered (in the minimal sense of having specimens collected and formal scientific names attached), the total number alive on earth is somewhere between 10 [million] and 100 million. No one can say with confidence which of these figures is the closer. Of the species given scientific names, fewer than 10 percent have been studied at a level deeper than gross anatomy. The revolution in molecular biology and medicine was achieved with a still smaller fraction, including colon bacteria, corn, fruit flies, Norway rats, rhesus monkeys, and human beings, altogether comprising no more than a hundred species.

Enchanted by the continuous emergence of new technologies and supported by generous funding for medical research, biologists have probed deeply along a narrow sector of the front. Now it is time to expand laterally, to get on with the great Linnean enterprise and finish mapping the biosphere. The most compelling reason for the broadening of goals is that, unlike the rest of science, the study of biodiversity has a time limit. Species are disappearing at an accelerating rate through human action, primarily habitat destruction but also pollution and the introduction of exotic species into residual natural environments. I have said that a fifth or more of the species of plants and animals could vanish or be doomed to early extinction by the year 2020 unless better efforts are made to save them. This estimate comes from the known quantitative relation between the area of habitats and the diversity that habitats can sustain. These area-biodiversity curves are supported by the general but not universal principle that when certain groups of organisms are studied closely, such as snails and fishes and flowering plants, extinction is determined to be widespread. And the corollary: among plant and animal remains in archaeological deposits, we usually find extinct species and races. As the last forests are felled in forest strongholds like the Philippines and Ecuador, the decline of species will accelerate even more. In the world as a whole, extinction rates are already hundreds or thousands of times higher than before the coming of man. They cannot be balanced by new evolution in any period of time that has meaning for the human race.

Why should we care? What difference does it make if some species are extinguished, if even half of all the species on Earth disappear? Let me count the ways. New sources of scientific information will be lost. Vast potential biological wealth will be destroyed. Still undeveloped medicines, crops, pharmaceuticals, timber, fibers, pulp, soil-restoring vegetation, petroleum substitutes, and other products and amenities will never come to light. It is fashionable in some quarters to wave aside the small and obscure, the bugs and weeds, forgetting that an obscure moth from Latin America saved Australia's pastureland from overgrowth by cactus, that the rosy periwinkle provided the cure for Hodgkin's disease and childhood lymphocytic leukemia, that the bark of the Pacific yew offers hope for victims of ovarian and breast cancer, that a chemical from the saliva of leeches dissolves blood clots during surgery, and so on down a roster already grown long and illustrious despite the limited research addressed to it.

In amnesiac revery it is also easy to overlook the services that ecosystems provide humanity. They enrich the soil and create the very air we breathe. Without these amenities, the remaining tenure of the human race would be nasty and brief. The life-sustaining matrix is built of green plants with legions of microorganisms and mostly small, obscure animals—in other words, weeds and bugs. Such organisms support the world with efficiency because they are so diverse, allowing them to divide labor and swarm over every square meter of the earth's surface. They run the world precisely as we would wish it to be run, because humanity evolved within living communities and our bodily functions are finely adjusted to the idiosyncratic environment already created. Mother Earth, lately called Gaia, is no more than the commonality of organisms and the physical environment they maintain with each passing moment, an environment that will destabilize and turn lethal if the organisms are disturbed too much. A near infinity of other mother planets can be envisioned, each with its own fauna and flora, all producing physical environments uncongenial to human life. To disregard the diversity of life is to risk catapulting ourselves into an alien environment. We will have become like the pilot whales that inexplicably beach themselves on New England shores.

Humanity coevolved with the rest of life on this particular planet; other worlds are not in our genes. Because scientists have yet to put names on most kinds of organisms, and because they entertain only a vague idea of how ecosystems work, it is reckless to suppose that biodiversity can be diminished indefinitely without threatening humanity itself. Field studies show that as biodiversity is reduced, so is the quality of the services provided by ecosystems. Records of stressed ecosystems also demonstrate that the descent can be unpredictably abrupt. As extinction spreads, some of the lost forms prove to be keystone species, whose disappearance brings down other species and triggers a ripple effect through the demographies of the survivors. The loss of a keystone species is like a drill accidentally striking a powerline. It causes lights to go out all over.

> *"The loss of a keystone species is like a drill accidentally striking a powerline. It causes lights to go out all over."*

These services are important to human welfare. But they cannot form the whole foundation of an enduring environmental ethic. If a price can be put on something, that something can be devalued, sold, and discarded. It is also possible for some to dream that people will go on living comfortably in a biologically impoverished world. They suppose that a prosthetic environment is within the power of technology, that human life can still flourish in a completely humanized world, where medicines would all be synthesized from chemicals off the shelf, food grown from a few dozen domestic crop species, the atmosphere and climate regulated by computer-driven fusion energy, and the earth made over until it becomes a literal spaceship rather than a metaphorical one, with people reading displays and touching buttons on the bridge. Such is the terminus of the philosophy of exemptionalism: do not weep for the past, humanity is a new order of life, let species die if they block progress, scientific and technological genius will find another way. Look up and see the stars awaiting us.

But consider: human advance is determined not by reason alone but by emotions peculiar to our species, aided and tempered by reason. What makes us people and not computers is emotion. We have little grasp of our true nature, of what it is to be human and therefore where our descendants might someday wish we had directed Spaceship Earth. Our troubles, as Vercors said in *You Shall Know Them*, arise from the fact that we do not know what we are and cannot agree on what we want to be. The primary cause of this intellectual failure is ignorance of our origins. We did not arrive on this planet as aliens. Humanity is part of nature, a species that evolved among other species. The more closely we identify ourselves with the rest of life, the more quickly we will be able to discover the sources of human sensibility and acquire the knowledge on which an enduring ethic, a sense of preferred direction, can be built.

The human heritage does not go back only for the conventionally recognized 8,000 years or so of recorded history, but for at least 2 million years, to the appearance of the first "true" human beings, the earliest species composing the genus *Homo*. Across thousands of generations, the emergence of culture must have been profoundly influenced by simultaneous events in genetic evolution, especially those occurring in the anatomy and physiology of the brain. Conversely, genetic evolution must have been guided forcefully by the kinds of selection rising within culture.

Only in the last moment of human history has the delusion arisen that people can flourish apart from the rest of the living world. Preliterate societies were in intimate contact with a bewildering array of life forms. Their minds could only partly adapt to that challenge. But they struggled to understand the most relevant parts, aware that the right responses gave life and fulfillment, the wrong ones sickness, hunger, and death. The imprint of that effort cannot have been erased in a few generations of urban existence. I suggest that it is to be found among the particularities of human nature, among which are these:

• People acquire phobias, abrupt and intractable aversions, to the objects and circumstances that threaten humanity in natural environments: heights, closed spaces, open spaces, running water, wolves, spiders, snakes. They rarely form phobias to the recently invented contrivances that are far more dangerous, such as guns, knives, automobiles, and electric sockets.

• People are both repelled and fascinated by snakes, even when they have never seen one in nature. In most cultures the serpent is the dominant wild animal of mythical and religious symbolism. Manhattanites dream of them with the same frequency as Zulus. This response appears to be Darwinian in origin. Poisonous snakes have been an important cause of mortality almost everywhere, from Finland to Tasmania, Canada to Patagonia; an untutored alertness in their presence saves lives. We note a kindred response in many primates, including Old World monkeys and chimpanzees: the animals pull back, alert others, watch closely, and follow each potentially dangerous snake until it moves away. For human beings, in a larger metaphorical sense, the mythic, transformed serpent has come to possess both constructive and destructive powers: Ashtoreth of the Canaanites, the demons Fu-Hsi and Nu-kua of the Han Chinese, Mudamma and Manasa of Hindu India, the triple-headed giant Nehebkau of the ancient Egyptians, the serpent of Genesis conferring knowledge and death, and, among the Aztecs, Cihuacoatl, goddess of childbirth and mother of the human race, the rain god Tlaloc, and Quetzalcoatl, the plumed serpent with a human head who reigned as lord of the morning and evening star. Ophidian power spills over into modern life: two serpents entwine the caduceus, first the winged staff of Mercury as messenger of the gods, then the safe-conduct pass of ambassadors and heralds, and today the universal emblem of the medical profession.

• The favored living place of most peoples is a prominence near water from which parkland can be viewed. On such heights are found the abodes of the powerful and rich, tombs of the great, temples, parliaments, and monuments commemorating tribal glory. The location is today an aesthetic choice and, by the implied freedom to settle there, a symbol of status. In ancient, more practical times the topography provided a place to retreat and a sweeping prospect from which to spot the distant approach of storms and enemy forces. Every animal species selects a habitat in which its members gain a favorable mix of security and food. For most of deep history, human beings lived in tropical and subtropical savanna in East Africa, open country sprinkled with streams and lakes, trees and copses. In similar topography modern peoples choose their residences and design their parks and gardens, if given a free choice. They simulate neither dense jungles, toward which gibbons are drawn, nor dry grasslands, preferred by hamadryas baboons. In their gardens they plant trees that resemble the acacias, sterculias, and other native trees of the African savannas. The ideal tree crown sought is consistently wider than tall, with spreading lowermost branches close enough to the ground to touch and climb, clothed with compound or needle-shaped leaves.

*"In the United States and Canada more people visit zoos and aquariums than attend all professional athletic events combined."*

• Given the means and sufficient leisure, a large portion of the populace backpacks, hunts, fishes, birdwatches, and gardens. In the United States and Canada more people visit zoos and aquariums than attend all professional athletic events combined. They crowd the national parks to view natural landscapes, looking from the tops of prominences out across rugged terrain for a glimpse of tumbling water and animals living free. They travel long distances to stroll along the seashore, for reasons they can't put into words.

These are examples of what I have called *biophilia*, the connections that human beings subconsciously seek with the rest of life. To biophilia can be added the idea of wilderness, all the land and communities of plants and animals still unsullied by human occupation. Into wilderness people travel in search of new life and wonder, and from wilderness they return to the parts of the Earth that have been humanized and made physically secure. Wilderness settles peace on the soul because it needs no help; it is beyond human contrivance. Wilderness is a metaphor of unlimited opportunity, rising from the tribal memory of a time when humanity spread across the world, valley to valley, island to island, godstruck, firm in the belief that virgin land went on forever past the horizon.

I cite these common preferences of mind not as proof of an innate human nature but rather to suggest that we think more carefully and turn philosophy to the central questions of human origins in the wild environment. We do not understand ourselves yet and descend farther from heaven's air if we forget how much the natural world means to us. Signals abound that the loss of life's diversity endangers not just the body but the spirit. If that much is true, the changes occurring now will visit harm on all generations to come.

The ethical imperative should therefore be, first of all, prudence. We should judge every scrap of biodiversity as priceless while we learn to use it and come to understand what it means to humanity. We should not knowingly allow any species or race to go extinct. And let us go beyond mere salvage to begin the restoration of natural environments, in order to enlarge wild populations and stanch the hemorrhaging of biological wealth. There can be no purpose more enspiriting than to begin the age of restoration, reweaving the wondrous diversity of life that still surrounds us.

The evidence of swift environmental change calls for an ethic uncoupled from other systems of belief. Those committed by religion to believe that life was put on earth in one divine stroke will recognize that we are destroying the Creation, and those who perceive biodiversity to be the product of blind evolution will agree. Across the other great philosophical divide, it does not matter whether species have independent rights or, conversely, that moral reasoning is uniquely a human concern. Defenders of both premises seem destined to gravitate toward the same position on conservation.

The stewardship of environment is a domain on the near side of metaphysics where all reflective persons can surely find common ground. For what, in the final analysis, is morality but the command of conscience seasoned by a rational examination of consequences? And what is a fundamental precept but one that serves all generations? An enduring environmental ethic will aim to preserve not only the health and freedom of our species, but access to the world in which the human spirit was born.

# The Trouble with Wilderness; or, Getting Back to the Wrong Nature[5]

The time has come to rethink wilderness. This will seem a heretical claim to many environmentalists, since the idea of wilderness has for decades been a fundamental tenet—indeed, a passion—of the environmental movement, especially in the United States. For many Americans wilderness stands as the last remaining place where civilization, that all too human disease, has not fully infected the Earth. It is an island in the polluted sea of urban-industrial modernity, the one place we can turn for escape from our own too-muchness. Seen in this way, wilderness presents itself as the best antidote to our human selves, a refuge we must somehow recover if we hope to save the planet. As Henry David Thoreau once famously declared, "In Wildness is the preservation of the World."

But is it? The more one knows of its peculiar history, the more one realizes that wilderness is not quite what it seems. Far from being the one place on Earth that stands apart from humanity, it is quite profoundly a human creation—indeed, the creation of very particular human cultures at very particular moments in human history. It is not a pristine sanctuary where we can encounter the last remnant of an untouched, endangered, but still transcendent nature without the contaminating taint of civilization. Instead, it is a product of that civilization, and it could hardly be contaminated by the very stuff of which it is made. Wilderness hides its unnaturalness behind a mask that is all the more beguiling because it seems so natural. As we gaze into the mirror it holds up for us, we too easily imagine that what we behold is Nature when in fact we see the reflection of our own unexamined longings and desires. For this reason, we are mistaken when we suppose that wilderness can be the solution to our culture's problematic relationships with the nonhuman world, for wilderness is itself no small part of the problem.

Go back 250 years in American and European history, and you do not find nearly so many people wandering around remote corners of the planet looking for what today we would call "the wilderness experience." Wilderness in the 18th century bore biblical connotations: it was "deserted," "savage," "desolate," "barren"—in short, a "waste," the word's nearest synonym. The emotion one was most likely to feel in its presence was "bewilderment"—or terror. Whatever value wilderness might have had arose solely from the possibility that it might be "reclaimed" and turned toward human ends—planted as a garden, say, or turned into a city on a hill. In its raw state, it had little or nothing to offer civilized men and women.

But by the end of the 19th century, the wastelands that had once

[5]Essay by William Cronon, editor of *Uncommon Ground: Toward Reinventing Nature.* Adapted version published in *Utne Reader* p76-79 My/Je '96. Copyright © 1995 William Cronon. Reprinted with permission of W. W. Norton & Company, Inc.

seemed worthless had for some people come to seem almost beyond price. When John Muir arrived in the Sierra Nevada in 1869, he would declare, "No description of Heaven that I have ever heard or read of seems half so fine." One by one, various corners of the American map came to be designated as sites whose wild beauty was so spectacular that a growing number of citizens had to visit and see them for themselves. Niagara Falls was the first to undergo this transformation, and it was soon followed by the Catskills, the Adirondacks, Yosemite, and Yellowstone. (Yosemite was deeded by the U.S. government to the state of California in 1864 as the nation's first wildland park, and Yellowstone became the first true national park in 1872.) The sources of this rather astonishing transformation were many, but they can be gathered under two broad headings: the sublime and the frontier.

In the wilderness the boundaries between human and nonhuman, between natural and supernatural, have always seemed less certain than elsewhere. By the 18th century this sense of the wilderness as a landscape where the supernatural lay just beneath the surface was expressed in the doctrine of the sublime, a word whose modern usage has been so watered down by commercial hype and tourist advertising that it retains only a dim echo of its former power. Sublime landscapes were those rare places where one had a better chance than elsewhere on Earth to glimpse the face of God. God was on the mountaintop, in the chasm, in the waterfall, in the thundercloud, in the rainbow, in the sunset. One has only to think of the sites that Americans chose for their first national parks—Yellowstone, Yosemite, Grand Canyon, Mount Rainier, Zion—to realize that virtually all of them fit one or more of these categories. Not until the 1940s would the first swamp be honored, in Everglades National Park, and to this day there is no national park in the grasslands.

No less important than the sublime was the powerful national myth of the frontier. In the writing of historian Frederick Jackson Turner, for instance, wild country became a place not just of religious redemption but also of national renewal, the quintessential location for experiencing what it meant to be an American. It is no accident that the movement to set aside national parks and wilderness areas began to gain real momentum at precisely the time that laments about the vanishing frontier reached their peak. To protect wilderness was in a very real sense to protect the nation's most sacred myth of origin.

The idea of the sublime and the frontier myth converged to remake wilderness in their own image, freighting it with moral values and cultural symbols that it still carries. In the decades following the Civil War, more and more of the nation's wealthiest citizens sought out wilderness for themselves in enormous estates (disingenuously called "camps") in the Adirondacks and elsewhere: cattle ranches for would-be rough riders on the Great Plains, guided big-game hunting trips in the Rockies, and luxurious resort hotels wherever railroads pushed their way into sublime landscapes. The

*"In the wilderness the boundaries between human and nonhuman, between natural and supernatural, have always seemed less certain than elsewhere."*

irony, of course, is that wilderness came to reflect the very civilization its devotees sought to escape. There are other ironies as well:
The movement to set aside national parks and wilderness areas followed hard on the heels of the final Indian wars; after the prior
human inhabitants were rounded up and moved onto reservations,
tourists could safely enjoy the illusion that they were seeing their
nation in its pristine, original state. (Today, the Blackfeet continue
to be accused of "poaching" on the lands of Glacier National Park
that originally belonged to them.) The removal of Indians to create
an "uninhabited wilderness"—uninhabited as never before in the
human history of the place—reminds us just how invented, just
how constructed, the American wilderness really is.

I hope it is clear that my criticism is not directed at wild nature
per se, or even at efforts to set aside large tracts of wild land—for
nonhuman nature and large tracts of the natural world do deserve
protection—but rather at the specific habits of thinking that flow
from this complex cultural construction called wilderness. If by definition wilderness leaves no place for human beings, save perhaps
as contemplative sojourners enjoying their leisurely reverie in God's
natural cathedral, then also by definition it can offer no solution to
the environmental and other problems that confront us.

Defenders of "biological diversity" (a seemingly more "scientific"
concept than "wilderness" that is employed by organizations like
the Nature Conservancy), for instance, often point to "untouched"
ecosystems as the best and richest repositories of the undiscovered
species we must certainly try to protect. There is a paradox here, of
course. To the extent that biological diversity (indeed, even wilderness itself) is likely to survive in the future only by the most vigi-
lant and self-conscious management of the ecosystems that sustain
it, the ideology of wilderness is potentially in direct conflict with the
very thing it encourages us to protect.

Another example of the problematic use of "wilderness" is in
Earth First! founder Dave Foreman's description of the ideal "Big
Outside" in his promotion of the "wilderness experience," which
bears an uncanny resemblance to that of the frontier myth: wide
open spaces and virgin land with no trails, no signs, no facilities, no
maps, no guides, no rescues, no modern equipment, a land where
hardy travelers can support themselves by hunting with "primitive
weapons (bow and arrow, atlatl, knife, sharp rock)." When radical
environmentalists express the popular notion that our environmental problems began with the invention of our agriculture (as
Foreman does in 1991's *Confessions of an Eco-Warrior*), they push
the human fall from natural grace so far back into the past that all
of civilized history becomes a tale of ecological declension. From
such a starting place, it is hard not to reach the conclusion that the
only way human beings can hope to live naturally on the Earth is
to follow the hunter-gatherers back into a wilderness Eden and
abandon virtually everything that civilization has given us.

But if nature dies because we enter it, then the only way to save
nature is to kill ourselves. It is not a proposition that seems likely

*"The removal of Indians to create an 'uninhabited wilderness'... reminds us just how invented, just how constructed, the American wilderness really is."*

to produce positive or practical results, yet radical environmental-ists and deep ecologists all too frequently come close to accepting it as a first principle. It may indeed turn out that civilization will end in ecological collapse or nuclear disaster, whereupon one might expect to find any human survivors returning to a way of life clos-er to that celebrated by Foreman and his followers. For most of us, though, the debacle would be cause for regret, a sign that humani-ty had failed to fulfill its own promise and failed to honor its own highest values—including those of the deep ecologists. Viewing nature and ourselves in such stark, absolute terms leaves us little hope of discovering what an ethical, sustainable, honorable human place in nature might actually look like.

In critiquing wilderness, I'm forced to confront my own deep ambivalence about its meaning for modern environmentalism. On the one hand, any way of looking at nature that encourages us to believe we are separate from nature—as wilderness tends to do—is likely to reinforce environmentally irresponsible behavior. On the other hand, it is no less crucial for us to recognize and honor non-human nature as a world we did not create, a world with its own independent, nonhuman reasons for being as it is. Any way of look-ing at nature that helps us remember—as wilderness also tends to do—that the interests of people are not necessarily identical to those of every other creature or of the Earth itself is likely to foster *responsible* behavior.

If the core problem of wilderness is that it distances us too much from the very things it teaches us to value, then the question we must ask is what it can tell us about home, the place where we actually live. To the extent that we live in an urban-industrial civi-lization but at the same time pretend to ourselves that our real home is in the wilderness, we give ourselves permission to evade responsibility for the lives we actually lead. We inhabit civilization while holding some part of ourselves—what we imagine to be the most precious part—aloof from its entanglements. We work our nine-to-five jobs in its institutions, we eat its food, we drive its cars (not least to reach the wilderness), we benefit from the intricate and all too invisible networks with which it shelters us all the while pre-tending that these things are not essential part of who we are. So how can we take the positive values we associate with wilderness and bring them closer to home?

Our challenge is to stop thinking of things according to a set of bipolar moral scales in which the human and the nonhuman, the unnatural and the natural, serve as our conceptual map for under-standing and valuing the world. Instead, we need to embrace the full continuum of a natural landscape that is also cultural, in which the city, the suburb, the pastoral, and the wild each has its proper place, which we permit ourselves to celebrate without needlessly denigrating the others. We need to discover a common middle ground in which all of these things, from the city to the wilderness, can somehow be encompassed in the word *home*. Home, after all, is the place for which we take responsibility, the place we try to sustain so we can pass on what is best in it (and in ourselves) to our children. And calling a place home inevitably means that we will use the nature we find in it, for there can be no escape from manipulating and working and even killing some parts of nature to make our home.

Wilderness is more a state of mind than a fact of nature, and the state of mind that today most defines wilderness is *wonder*. When we visit a wilderness area, we find ourselves surrounded by plants and animals and physical landscapes whose otherness compels our attention. In forcing us to acknowledge that they are not of our making, that they have little or no need of our continued existence, they recall for us a creation far greater than our own. Wilderness gets us into trouble only if we imagine that this experience of wonder and otherness is limited to the remote corners of the planet, or that it somehow depends on pristine landscapes we ourselves do not inhabit. In the wilderness, we need no reminder that a tree has its own reasons for being, quite apart from us; the same is less true in the gardens we plant and tend ourselves: There it is far easier to forget the otherness of the tree.

> *"Wilderness is more a state of mind than a fact of nature..."*

The tree in the garden is in reality no less other, no less worthy of our wonder and respect, than the tree in an ancient forest that has never known an ax or a saw. The tree in the garden could easily have sprung from the same seed as the tree in the forest, and we can claim only its location and perhaps its form as our own. Both trees stand apart from us; both share our common world. The special power of the tree in the wilderness is that it can teach us to recognize the wildness we did not see in the tree we planted in our own backyard. By seeing the otherness in what is most unfamiliar, we can learn to see it too in what at first seemed merely ordinary. If wilderness can do this—if it can help us perceive and respect a nature we had forgotten to recognize as natural—then it will become a part of the solution to our environmental dilemmas rather than part of the problem.

We can thus still join Thoreau in declaring that "in Wildness is the preservation of the World," for *wildness* (as opposed to wilderness) can be found anywhere: in the seemingly tame fields and woodlots of Massachusetts, in the cracks of a Manhattan sidewalk, even in the cells of our own bodies. As Gary Snyder wisely said, "A person with a clear heart and open mind can experience the wilderness anywhere on Earth. It is a quality of one's own consciousness. The planet is a wild place and always will be."

Learning to honor the wild—learning to remember and acknowledge the autonomy of the other—means striving for critical self-consciousness in all of our actions. It means that deep reflection and respect must accompany each act of use, and means too that we must always consider the possibility of non-use. It means looking at the part of nature we intend to turn toward our own ends and asking whether we can use it again and again and again—sustainably—without its being diminished in the process. Most of all, it means practicing remembrance and gratitude, for thanksgiving is the simplest and most basic of ways for us to recollect the nature, the culture, and the history that have come together to make the world as we know it.

If wildness can stop being (just) out there and start being (also) in here, if it can start being as humane as it is natural, then perhaps we can get on with the unending task of struggling to live rightly in the world—not just in the garden, not just in the wilderness, but in the home that encompasses them both.

# II. Endangered Species and Their Enemies

## Editor's Introduction

The threats to many endangered species are both clearly identifiable and potentially amenable to alleviation. In the first selection reprinted here, Jon R. Luoma discusses the possible effects of global warming—the gradual rise in the Earth's temperature as a result of the accumulation in the atmosphere of carbon dioxide and other gases—on wildlife habitats. The impact of human-influenced diseases on animal populations is discussed in the second selection, Traci Watson's "Outbreak Meets Bambi." In the third selection, Paul F. Salopek reports on the miraculous survival of the mountain gorillas that live on the slopes of the Virunga volcanoes. During the civil war in Rwanda, which had killed at least half a million people by October 1995, when his article was originally published in *National Geographic*, only one of an estimated 300 Virunga gorillas had been confirmed a casualty of the war.

In the fourth selection, Donovan Webster reports on his investigation for the *New York Times Magazine* of the international black market in endangered plants and animals, which brings in an estimated $10 billion to $20 billion annually. The focus of his article is the island of Madagascar, off the southeast African coast, whose wildlife evolved undisturbed by human influence until only 2,000 years ago. As a result, Madagascar possesses many unique animals, including all 32 species of lemur and a host of exotic snakes and tortoises. Prized for their parts and as pets, many of these already threatened creatures are becoming increasingly endangered by the fast-growing illegal smuggling trade, which, Webster reports, is second only to the drug trade in terms of its cash value and is approximately equal to the illegal weapons trade, according to a spokeswoman for the U.S. Fish and Wildlife Service quoted by Webster.

The emerging field of ecotourism has been broadly defined to include any tourism activity that has an environmental component. More narrowly delimited, the term signifies tourism that somehow contributes to wildlife conservation, environmental protection, and/or the welfare of indigenous peoples. In the fifth selection, "The Perils of Success," Perri Knize reports on the potentially negative environmental impact of tourism, especially in places whose natural environments are the main tourist attraction. In western Montana, Knize shows, some wildlife habitat has been lost to the development boomlet created by increasing numbers of tourists' desire to see Montana's pristine environment. As tourists become residents in ever-increasing numbers, many Montanans—longtime residents and newcomers alike—worry about the diminishment of their quality of life. Protecting it, many have come to realize, means protecting wildlife and its habitat from overdevelopment.

# Warming the Wild[1]

Just beneath the surface of recent headlines lies troubling news for polar bears and arctic caribou, for coastal mangroves and rare alpine flowers, for ancient cedars and subterranean truffles, and for a host of other species, from elephants to tree frogs.

In a series of reports issued this spring, the United Nations Environment Programme, the most comprehensive scientific panel ever assembled to study the world's climate, has concluded that global warming is probably already upon us and, will accelerate in the next century.

Indeed, a handful of experimental studies is offering strong initial confirmation that even moderate warming could cause dramatic disruption of existing wild habitats.

If you happen, for instance, to be wandering the grounds of Colorado's Rocky Mountain Biological Laboratory, you might come upon a curious assemblage of infrared heaters suspended over an alpine meadow. Since 1991 the heaters have been bathing five experimental plots of mountain landscape—totaling about 180 square yards—with heat radiation.

Day and night, the heaters provide enough warmth to raise soil temperatures by one to two degrees centigrade—the same amount that a predicted doubling of carbon dioxide in the atmosphere could cause in this region.

The results of the study have been dramatic. "We're already see-ing major changes in vegetation and nutrients and soil critters," says one of the project's founders, ecologist John Harte of the University of California, Berkeley. Notably, he says, "we're seeing a shift from a grass- and forb-dominated meadow to a meadow dom-inated by brush."

How big a deal is that? Not much if it were only Harte's little bit of meadow that was at stake. But, says the scientist, "there are vast areas of high montane grassland on the planet, including areas like the Tibetan Plateau. It's obvious that if you change the dominant vegetation pattern, you're going to restrict the availability of food for mammals. For instance, here in the Rockies, elk much prefer a diet of grasses and forbs to brush."

As limited as the Colorado experiment is, it amounts to one of the first pieces of proof that for many habitats, even a modest amount of warming will cause changes that will cascade through food chains and ecosystems, putting a host of species at risk.

Some threats are obvious. A warming earth would mean warmer and expanding oceans and higher sea levels, which could flood coastal marshes, destroying or damaging habitat for species ranging from mammals such as the salt-marsh harvest mouse of the coastal

*"...a handful of experimental studies is offering strong initial confirmation that even moderate warming could cause dramatic disruption of existing wild habitats."*

---

[1]Article by Jon R. Luoma from *Audubon* 98:102 + Jl/Ag '96. Copyright © 1996 Jon R. Luoma. Reprinted with permission.

United States to shorebirds, especially those like the California clapper rail, which has been pushed to the brink of extinction.

For example, thanks to vigorous protection under the Endangered Species Act, Hawaii's Laysan teal has rebounded from a population of only 7 individuals to about 500. But the bird is restricted to a single low-lying island whose highest point is less than 40 feet above the current sea level. With higher sea levels, much of the island might be inundated and the bird's habitat lost. Coral reefs—among the most biologically rich ecosystems on Earth—are also likely to be affected as seas rise and tropical storms become more frequent and fierce.

Even as the oceans rise, climate models predict warmer, drier summers in many midcontinent regions. One grim consequence: the drying of prairie wetlands of the northern Great Plains, where as many as 80 percent of North America's ducks are hatched. This could cause populations to decline by more than 20 percent.

*"Projections from Glacier National Park suggest that its very name could become an irony."*

Other potential problems are less obvious, and would often be the result of a complex chain of sometimes surprisingly related events. A sample:

• Projections from Glacier National Park suggest that its very name could become an irony. According to an analysis by National Biological Service scientists and collaborators, even if warming simply continues to increase as it has in recent decades, the park may lose its glaciers, and surprisingly soon. Daniel Fagre, a research ecologist with the service, relies on a sort of ecosystem in a computer—a program that, he says, can "grow the ecosystem, tree by tree," allowing park managers to assess what could happen under various warming scenarios. Although Fagre emphasizes that such models are limited, the picture isn't a pretty one. In one scenario, he says, "the glaciers would be gone by perhaps the year 2030, and certainly no later than 2050. A number of our seasonal streams would dry up, meaning the loss of macroinvertebrates—bugs—which in turn are important for species like our bull trout."

A warmer, drier climate would also lead to increased forest fires and what Fagre calls a "nixing out" of such rare alpine plants as the park's northern eyebright and the whitlowwort. The model shows that although already abundant trees like lodgepole pine and mammals like white-tailed deer might extend their range, overall species diversity could collapse. If, for instance, a 500-year-old cedar forest in the Lake McDonald valley were wiped out by fire, the trees would be unable to reestablish themselves in a hotter and drier climate. That would mean the demise here of such rare species as the red-backed vole, which thrives on the subterranean fungal truffles of old woods like this one.

• To the north, Canadian wildlife biologists worry that changes in the extent of ice floes could have a dramacic effect on the polar bear, which does most of its feeding—as much as 90 percent—during the cold months, when it preys heavily on seals. During the summer the bear lives almost entirely on fat reserves. According to at least one study, the bears could become extinct if the Arctic

Ocean were to become completely ice free during the summer.

More snow would also fall in a warmer Arctic, and with warmer temperatures the snowpack would become deeper and crustier. The combination of more and harder snow would make tundra vegetation more difficult for caribou and musk oxen to reach, and vanished ice bridges would make migration to new feeding areas difficult or impossible.

At the same time, studies suggest that the mosquitoes and biting flies that swarm in the Arctic in the warmest summer years already reduce the mammals' feeding time—and that an insect boom brought on by a warming in the range of two to four degrees centigrade could decrease feeding time by about 7 percent, leading to fewer surviving newborns from poorly nourished mothers.

• Predicted warming will be most severe near the poles and in some midcontinent regions, probably least severe in the tropics. But Maureen Donnelly, a herpetologist at Florida International University, says that based on preliminary "armchair biology," she's become convinced that even in warm regions, some reptiles and amphibians will lose.

In general, she says, "species that already tolerate a broad range of conditions might come out winners, but those that are more specialized lose. The bottom line is a potentially less diverse tropics." Likely losers: species like the crowned tree frog, which breeds only in moist tree holes and lives most of its life cycle in bromeliads in a belt of tropical forest from southern Mexico to Panama. On the other hand, species like the cane toad might do well. These creatures are so amenable to human disturbance that they will happily steal dog food.

• Donnelly and other researchers point to another surprising threat: Among some lizards, crocodiles, and turtles, an embryo's sex is determined by the incubation temperature of the egg, which can be influenced by factors such as the depth the egg is buried in sand. But an overall warming of, for instance, sands on the Mexican breeding beaches of a species like the endangered Kemp's ridley turtle could skew the proportions of males and females. The effect would be to lower the effective breeding size of an already tiny and troubled population.

• Some scientists suggest that warming could cause disruptions in animal behavior and, ultimately, reproduction. Insects, for instance, secrete minuscule amounts of pheromones for sexual communication, a process that Princeton University biologist Daniel Rubenstein says is finely tuned to each insect's environment. Even a subtle change in pheromone-evaporation rates could disrupt that process.

At the other end of the animal size scale, says Rubenstein, changes in rainfall patterns could disrupt elephant breeding. In eastern Africa, breeding cycles are timed so that dominant bull elephants become reproductively active just as females cluster in groups on the savanna, during the wet season. But should global warming dry the climate, females could remain dispersed in fragmented groups around patches of swamp.

*"In eastern Africa, breeding cycles are timed so that dominant bull elephants become reproductively active just as females cluster in groups on the savanna, during the wet season."*

The Earth's climate has fluctuated before. But Adam Markham, director of the World Wildlife Fund's climate-change campaign, says the speed of the new, human-initiated warming of the earth could simply overwhelm the ability of ecosystems and species to adapt. For instance, forests can move over time. Scientists believe that the average migration rate amounts to about 12 to 15 miles per century. But under the presently predicted global-warming scenario, tree species would have to move about 180 miles northward per century to keep up.

Ultimately, says Markham, if we fail to control global warming by limiting emissions of greenhouse gases, the changes it wreaks on ecosystems could be the final push for species that we've already reduced in numbers and habitats that we've isolated into pockets of remaining wild.

"People ask me, 'Haven't species adapted to major changes before?' My answer is 'Yes, but we weren't here then,'" says Markham. "We hadn't fragmented and taken over their habitats. Without the alterations humans have made to the Earth, climate change might not be a disaster for animals. *With* those alterations, it could be a catastrophe."

# Outbreak Meets Bambi[2]

No hospitals, no antibiotics, no 24-hour pharmacies—and predators always ready to pounce on those weakened by illness. That's the fate of sick animals living in the great outdoors. But wildlife faces another enemy in its struggle to stay healthy: people.

Across the United States and around the world, wild animals are dying of infectious diseases worsened by human influence, which alone can be enough to start an epidemic. In Tanzania's Serengeti National Park, for example, a thousand lions died in a recent distemper outbreak spread by unvaccinated pet dogs. Disease outbreaks are also more troubling when they hit species humans have already decimated: The mass deaths of endangered manatees in Florida—250 have perished this year compared with 201 in all of 1995—have biologists investigating the possibility of viral disease. Whatever the cause, the impact of the die-off is severe because there are so few manatees left.

Wildlife diseases pose risks beyond the loss of Bambi and Flipper. Illnesses spawned in the wild can infect domestic animals, destroying whole flocks or forcing farmers to kill their livestock. And microbes—microscopic organisms—occasionally jump species barriers; the AIDS virus is believed to have hopped from monkeys to humans. Experts say other disease-causing microbes will almost certainly take the same path. By goading on animal disease, humans help create their own future afflictions.

Skeptics say there is no hard evidence the incidence of wildlife disease is rising. And plenty of animal sickness emerges and spreads without human help. Some experts blamed pollution when hundreds of dead bottlenose dolphins washed onto American beaches a few years ago. But later research showed the dolphins were felled by a virus.

**Unsporting legacy**. In other cases, however, the role of human beings is all too clear. One example: the recent events in Montana's Madison River. Rainbow trout and anglers both love the river's riffle-dotted west fork. But a few years ago, scientists say, someone decided to enrich the Madison, illegally spiking the river with fish. The trout turned out to carry an often-lethal cartilage disorder known as whirling disease, which primarily kills young fish. Infected rainbows chase their tails obsessively, then eventually weaken into good targets for parasites. In recent surveys of the Madison, several generations of young rainbows were nowhere to be found.

Nor are small swimming creatures the only animals that have suffered from sportsmen's enthusiasm. Game farms, which raise deer, elk and other animals for hunting or meat, have grown more

*"By goading on animal disease, humans help create their own future afflictions."*

---

popular. But the loosely regulated ranches also offer a breeding ground for hard-to-detect disease organisms. And when game-farm animals are shipped around the country, diseases hitch along. Over the past few years, several mule deer and coyotes have tested positive for bovine tuberculosis in southeastern Montana. Bovine TB kills wild animals and also can jump to dairy herds. The Montana outbreak may have begun, state officials say, with animals at a local game farm.

Even animal lovers can inadvertently help spread disease by feeding wildlife. White-tailed deer in Michigan's Upper Peninsula have become solidly infected with bovine tuberculosis. Well-meaning souls who fed the deer helped the outbreak along: Nose-to-nose with other deer over hay and apples, the animals made a ripe target for TB germs that would have a harder time spreading in the wild. Now 4 percent to 5 percent of the deer in a 13-square-mile area are infected. "If you treat animals like cattle, they get cattle diseases," says Margo Pybus, a wildlife-disease specialist with Alberta Fish and Wildlife in Canada.

*"Some suburbanites persist in feeding deer despite warnings from state wildlife agencies about the risk of spreading illness."*

Some suburbanites persist in feeding deer despite warnings from state wildlife agencies about the risk of spreading illness. White-tailed and mule deer in parts of Colorado and Wyoming are dying from chronic wasting disease, caused by a mysterious bug that seems to be transmitted at backyard hay stations. "In all honesty, some people are too selfish to stop doing what makes them happy," says Michael Miller, a wildlife veterinarian with the Colorado Division of Wildlife. "If it makes them happy to have deer eating out of a trough in their back yard, that's what they're going to do."

**Boundary jumpers**. The growth of suburbs can also be deadly to animals. Until 50 years ago, avian cholera existed only on poultry farms. But as minimalls and housing tracts replaced wetlands, huge numbers of migrating birds were forced to crowd onto small scraps of marsh, creating a teeming hunting ground for the cholera germ. Today, the disease—so virulent that it causes die-offs of thousands of ducks, geese and other waterfowl—has spread across the nation.

In other countries, too, humans jump-start wildlife illness. In the Serengeti case, the distemper virus spread by unvaccinated dogs killed a third of the park's lions in 1994, and scientists worry it will now strike the endangered cheetah. In South Africa, rhinos and elephants may be the next targets for bovine TB—already rife in African buffalo, which probably contracted it from cattle.

Perhaps the most disturbing result of humans' contribution to animal disease is the risk to humans themselves. Many disease-causing microbes can survive only in a narrow range of animals. But others can and will jump boundaries between species. Animals also serve as holding pens for germs known to infect humans. Rabies provides a chilling example: For decades, raccoons in the northeastern United States were rabies free. But in 1977, some unknown shipper brought rabies-infected raccoons to West Virginia to stock hunting clubs. That began an epidemic of raccoon rabies that has spread to Maine, raising the risk of human infection. Says Lt. Col. Tom Lipscomb, a veterinary pathologist at the Armed Forces Institute of Pathology: "When you study these things, you realize there are no real separations between animal disease and human disease. We share the same environment and many of the same infectious diseases. We're all basically in the same boat."

Humans already have done their share of damage, but experts say further harm can be prevented. By vaccinating pet dogs in Africa, for example, scientists hope to forestall further distemper outbreaks in wildlife. Better controls on game farms would go a long way toward stopping the spread of TB. Most important, experts say, people shouldn't act as if wild animals are their play-things. Feeding deer might be fun, but the cost can be much higher than the price of hay.

# Gorillas and Humans: An Uneasy Truce[3]

In the dry season the Virunga volcanoes are the palest shade of blue, translucent as old glass, a hue almost too delicate to hold the eye. Barely 40 miles long, the chain of peaks rises above the borders of Rwanda, Zaire, and Uganda like jagged shards of sky. On the upper slopes of the volcanoes, primeval forests of bamboo and hagenia trees shelter half the world's remaining population of mountain gorillas. Higher still, a soft wind blows over subalpine meadows from the south, from Rwanda. This wind carries the silence of the dead.

At least 500,000 people died in Rwanda's four-year civil war. Entire families, most of them from the minority Tutsi tribe, were massacred last year in an orgy of violence that culminated in the overthrow of the Hutu-led government. Yet even while this human tragedy dominated the world stage, environmentalists warned of another potential disaster.

The Virungas were a battle zone. The Rwandan side of the volcanoes had been seeded with land mines. And thousands of soldiers and refugees had trampled through the forests, exposing the gorillas to both gunfire and lethal human diseases. The world's most endangered great apes, it seemed, would only slip closer to extinction.

For several weeks last spring, often on foot, I roamed the gorilla parks that encompass the Virungas, expecting the worst. But instead of casualties, I found gorillas in robust shape, going about their unhurried lives without disruption on the watercolor slopes of the volcanoes.

Only one out of an estimated 300 Virunga gorillas has been confirmed killed in the fighting. A silverback, Mrithi, was shot in 1992 by frightened soldiers who mistook him for the enemy. The world's only other mountain gorillas, some 300 animals out of the line of fire in the Impenetrable Forest of Uganda, have actually fared worse. Four adults were speared to death by poachers this year.

How did the Virunga gorillas survive? By virtue of rugged topography and the lobbying efforts of conservation groups. By the price tag that gorillas have come to represent in tourist dollars. And, more profoundly, by the grace of the Africans themselves: the peasant farmers, the unpaid park wardens, the gorilla trackers who faced bullets to protect them.

That quiet heroism—or, in the least case, tolerance—was a source of wonder as I set out in the aftermath of war to visit places whose names ring like a machete cutting bamboo—Karisoke, Kinigi, Bukima, Nyagakenke.

---

[3]Article by Paul F. Salopek, from *National Geographic* 188:72-83 O '95. Copyright © 1995 Paul Salopek/National Geographic Society. Reprinted with permission.

## KARISOKE RESEARCH CENTER, RWANDA

"Teenagers," Craig Sholley grumps. "Same the world over."

Sholley—an American gorilla expert and former director of Rwanda's Mountain Gorilla Project—is crouched with photographer Michael "Nick" Nichols, an unflappable Rwandan tracker named Alphonse Nemeye, and me in a prickly nettle patch near the looted ruins of Karisoke, the research post founded by the late primatologist Dian Fossey. Above us the equatorial sun beats down like a hammer. Fifteen feet ahead swaggers our problem.

The ape is perhaps seven years old and weighs close to a hundred pounds. She has separated from a group of 18 gorillas to challenge us, shambling forward on her knuckles, half aggressive, half curious, coughing a warning. Sholley, head bent in submission, grunts back. Pursing her lips nervously, the shaggy adolescent bats a wrist-thick stalk of senecio shrub down onto our heads. Sholley shakes a fern frond in retaliation. The gorilla sits, pretends to feed on wild celery—a nervous tic, like biting fingernails, that experts call displacement behavior. Sholley peels his own celery stalk, smacking his lips loudly. "She's showing off," he whispers over his shoulder.

As if on cue, the gorilla cartwheels backward into a wall of leaves, rump over teakettle, leathery black heels flying. Her companions hoot and grunt like a ragged cheering section.

"This," Sholley says, trying to stifle a laugh, "is what keeps me coming back." Gorilla charm. Superficially, at least, there isn't much about mountain gorillas to find endearing. Unlike the clownish and hyperactive chimpanzee, the gorilla is sleepily low-key—a hulking introvert. Gorillas do play, of course. But even their humor seems tentative, embarrassed. For the most part, they live out their 30 to 40 years lounging in high-altitude shrubbery, pensively munching on thistles and bamboo shoots. About the only thing that sparks real aggression is sex. Males will go to almost any extreme—fights to the death, infanticide, incest—to jockey for breeding rights over the females in his group.

Still, it is their monkish calm that has recently captured the Western imagination and earned gorillas a cult following in the conservation movement.

"Why do people love gorillas?" Sholley asked me when I first arrived in Africa. "Because we project our desires onto them." Later he refined this idea. "If people tend to think of gorillas as a blank slate, it's because when we look at them we see a lot of what we'd like to be. The gentleness. The tolerance."

The day after Sholley's grunting match, I raise this point with Fidele Nshogoza, a taciturn man who has been monitoring gorillas at Karisoke for 18 of his 44 years. Nshogoza, who got his start at Karisoke by washing dishes for Fossey, can recite gorilla genealogies back three generations. We are tagging after a group led by a silverback named Titus. From a distance comes the hollow *thup-thup-thup* of gorilla chest slapping.

"When I was a boy, I heard that gorillas were men who were very bad and who went to live in the forest," Nshogoza tells me during a break on a hill above Fossey's old research station. "But the gorillas are better than us."

Better?

Nshogoza nods gravely. "They are peaceful. They have no tribes. When they fight, it is for a good reason. We cut one another with machetes for zero."

He points his own machete to the smoke-blue passes that lead toward Zaire. An ethnic Hutu, he fled over the volcanoes after the 1994 Tutsi victory. Two of his children almost died of cholera in a Zairean refugee camp. His house in the village of Kanyamiheto was ransacked by soldiers. And his elderly father was an early casualty of war—enfeebled, he starved to death in his home when Tutsi forces overran the area. Nshogoza's story is typical of those I heard in Karisoke, where 25 men—Hutu and Tutsi—have trickled back from Zaire to monitor the gorillas. The taproot of ethnic strife in Rwanda runs deep. The majority Hutu are farmers, a stocky people who have tilled the valleys surrounding the volcanoes for generations. The Tutsi, by contrast, descend from tall warrior-herdsmen who brought cattle and conquest to the region centuries ago. Their kings ruled over the Hutu virtually until independence in 1962, and last year's massacre was only the latest—and most brutal—of Hutu score-settling.

"I am happy to be back watching gorillas," Nshogoza says, his voice thickening as the noose of his memories tightens. "I don't want to think about the war. I only wish the scientists would come back too."

Embarrassed by tears, he stares down at his gum boots, then averts his face, staring over his shoulder. At two mountain gorillas.

They have crept up behind us, perhaps drawn in by our voices. Nshogoza identifies them as members of Titus's group, descendants of Fossey's celebrated patriarch Uncle Bert, killed in 1978 by poachers. The gorillas and Nshogoza gaze at each other with easy familiarity, even tenderness. And for the first time in our two-day acquaintance I hear his grudging laughter.

*"By the start of the civil war in 1990 the gorillas had become both a national totem and a national meal ticket for Rwanda—bald eagle and cash cow rolled into one."*

## KINIGI, RWANDA

The fierce loyalty of Rwanda's wildlife guards and trackers has been a key to the apes' survival. But shrewd packaging hasn't hurt either.

By the start of the civil war in 1990 the gorillas had become both a national totem and a national meal ticket for Rwanda—bald eagle and cash cow rolled into one.

Gorilla-watching provided the third largest source of foreign exchange, after coffee and tea, as much as ten million dollars each year. Dian Fossey was convinced that Rwandans were interested only in poaching gorillas, but soon after her death in 1985 the animals were being displayed on postage stamps and idolized in pop radio tunes. In Kigali, the capital, I saw silverbacks staring somberly from photographs in bullet-scarred hotels.

"Gorillas are our only renewable resource," says Nsengiyumva

Barakabuye, the new tourism officer at Volcanoes National Park, headquartered in the village of Kinigi. "Some have said, 'Give the park to returning refugees!' But we will never do that. The gorillas are too valuable."

Barakabuye is an intense, bamboo-thin Tutsi, one of 700,000 exiles who have poured back into Rwanda since the war. In Zaire, where he was born, he grew up playing in the western jungles of the Virungas, longing to become a forest ranger. Barred from a park service job by his Rwandan nationality, he spread the gospel of rain forest conservation to Zairean villages for the World Wide Fund for Nature. Then came the war and its bittersweet consequences: seven dead relatives and the chance to help rebuild the shattered park service of his homeland.

One afternoon I travel with Barakabuye to visit Kinigi—the destination, in better days, of thousands of foreign tourists eager to plunk down nearly $200 to spend an hour with habituated gorillas.

We jounce up lava-rock roads in a rented pickup steered by its owner, a hulking man named Didi. Sullen-faced farmers watch us pass. The dark corduroy mounds of potato fields loom above, nudging against the park's forest boundary at 8,500 feet. After clearing two roadblocks manned by the Rwanda Patriotic Army, we roll into the park compound with the truck's radiator steaming.

Barakabuye comes here daily, but his jaw muscles still clench at the sight of the ruined facility. We poke about collapsing tourist bungalows and a roofless restaurant. Puddles of rainwater reflect skeletal beams against a gray sky. Human excrement fouls the concrete floors. There is broken glass. On the walls, charcoal graffiti denounces the new Tutsi regime as "cockroaches." Barakabuye shows me the office of his Hutu predecessor, a small cubicle ankle deep in ashes: Looters had burned flyers about gorilla biology, photographs of the gorillas, and all but a few copies of a poem by Fabien Iyamuremye, a seventh grader, titled *La Beauté du Parc des Volcans*.

"We must rebuild fast, fast, fast," Barakabuye declares, sifting through the damp scab of burned papers. "We must give the gorillas back to the world. We must give them back to the Rwandans. We want to make Rwandans proud again."

*"Before the war Rwanda was one of the brightest conservation stars in Africa."*

Before the war Rwanda was one of the brightest conservation stars in Africa. The 48 square miles of Volcanoes National Park were protected by a crack antipoaching corps. World renowned through its association with Dian Fossey, the Karboke Research Center had become an autonomous, scientific mini-state within Rwandan borders. And an association of conservation groups was spending an average of $1,250 a year on the health and safety of each ape—four times the Rwandan per capita income.

Today organizations like the International Gorilla Conservation Program and the Dian Fossey Gorilla Fund are trying to pick up the pieces of that model program. Two-thirds of the Rwandan park service staff is dead or in exile. Only two national park vehicles out of 50 made it through the war. And just about the only gorilla tourists these days are United Nations peacekeepers.

"We need outside help," Barakabuye acknowledges. But he gives me a hard look to make sure there is no misunderstanding. "The park, including Karisoke, is Rwandan. We want more Rwandans to see the gorillas. We want more Rwandan control." Leaving the rubble of Kinigi behind, we rattle to the base of the volcanoes in Didi's ancient truck. The fuel needle is on empty, so we coast the whole way down.

## BUKIMA RANGER STATION, ZAIRE

The gorilla is a young male—only three or four years old—and a broken snare set for bush-buck is gouging into his left foot. Crushed together for weeks, his toes have lost their hair. The naked flesh is the color of a bruised peach. Dribbling spittle onto his black index finger, the gorilla rubs saliva into the wire cut.

"It can die from infection," whispers Augustin Kambale, a guard at Virunga National Park in Zaire, a fearless man with a shaved head, an M14 rifle, and degrees in biology and chemistry. "We must save it." Peering over his shoulder, I can't see how. Kambale huddles with two trackers. After a brisk exchange in French, he decides to rescue the gorilla on the spot, before septicemia sets in: "We will circle him, throw our bush jackets over him, and pull the snare off."

The injured gorilla eyes us warily and limps off, trailing the frayed, snapped end of the wire behind. We follow. As the trackers begin circling, holding their old army coats out like matadors, I notice a shadow, very big and very still, in a nearby bamboo thicket.

"Silverback," I hiss to Kambale, who pauses, his own coat already shrugged half off. "*Le grand chef,*" he mutters, squinting through the feathery bamboo.

It's the big chief all right, an ape named Ndungutse—or "benefits," as in ecotourism dollars—that dominates this local band of 30 gorillas. At about 400 pounds, Ndungutse has a head as big as a bull's and a back the size of a door. The stricken youngster had been keeping close to the burly patriarch the whole time.

In the end—to my enormous relief and the trackers' clear disappointment—Kambale calls off the rescue. We slip and skid down the mountain to Bukima village, where Kambale radios for help at the ranger station.

Weeks later I hear that a veterinarian based in Rwanda has darted the youngster, saved his foot, and christened him Bahati—Swahili for "luck."

Luck, however, is a dwindling commodity in Zaire. Attempts to oust President-for-life Mobutu Sese Seko from power have plunged the country into near anarchy, derailing, among other things, a promising gorilla conservation program. The Zairean park service has habituated six gorilla groups for tourism. But with government soldiers machine-gunning hippos for meat within sight of the Virungas, visitors are understandably scarce. Park rangers like Kambale haven't been paid in months; they have been kept working only by handouts from conservation groups and the World

Food Program.

This chaos is compounded by Zaire's refugee crisis. At the time of my visit seven huge camps sprawled on the Zairean side of the Virungas, mini-cities of fluttering blue and green plastic tarps. Together they sheltered some 746,000 ethnic Hutu—one-tenth of Rwanda's total prewar population. Most of the exiles had spilled over the Zaire border days before the Tutsi rebel victory in July 1994. Fearing reprisals, many have refused to go home. Meanwhile they have hacked down, for firewood, several square miles of Virunga National Park—a world heritage site that encompasses one of the oldest rain forests in Africa.

"Even though the deforestation hasn't hit gorilla habitat yet, the sheer scale of the problem puts them at risk," a UN environmental expert tells me. Whipping out a pocket calculator, he tallies the damage. "Very, very roughly? Two hundred thirty truckloads of trees are coming down per day."

Kibumba camp, the largest tent-city with 200,000 people, sends out 16,000 wood gatherers every morning. They have stripped the nearby foothills of almost every tree. Mountain gorillas live in forests only a four-hour walk away.

"We know the cutting is very bad," says Elie Sebigoli, a Rwandan park warden languishing in Kibumba. " But we have to cook to eat."

Sebigoli is a big Hutu man with a friendly round face, who, in a world of barrel latrines, scabies, and rationed corn, talks ebulliently about gorillas. He knows the haunts of gorilla bands in the Virungas. He says he used to travel from village to village in Rwanda, showing conservation films on a portable screen.

Will he ever go back?

"They will kill me," he says of the Tutsi, as if by rote. "There will be no coexistence. No reconciliation. Never."

Sebigoli has built his family's green plastic shack to face the cone of Mount Karisimbi. The volcano rises, ethereal, above the camp's hovels, a majestic reminder of home.

Sebigoli assures me that he hurt no one in the war. He blinks slowly, staring at the peak, when I tell him that his old office at Volcanoes National Park headquarters is in ruins, scattered with the charred poems of schoolchildren.

## NYAGAKENKE, UGANDA

"A stool," Ezekiel Nsanzumuhile says tonelessly, standing before his cracked mud hut. "Two plastic water jugs. A cook pan." He holds each item up as if it were an exhibit in a trial. "A bamboo basket. A pot. That's all."

Nsanzumuhile lists his worldly possessions for me and jabs a spidery finger to the soaring slopes of Mgahinga Gorilla National Park, Uganda's small slice of the Virungas. He tells me that his four-acre farm and the house his family lived in for 20 years were seized to make way for new parkland in 1992.

"I have two wives and eight children," he says. " The gorillas get saved, and we starve."

Mgahinga's expansion—actually the reclamation of former park-land that's been encroached on since the 1950s—is an unprecedented sign of gorilla clout in East Africa. Over the past seven decades, as the regional population exploded, half the Virunga ecosystem in Rwanda was converted to agriculture. But to save habitat for gorillas here in Uganda, almost 2,000 farmers have been ejected from 3,500 acres of prime land.

From the doorway of his new homestead, Nsanzumuhile can see his former fields on the green slopes of the volcanoes. It's a beautiful view—luminous, quivering sheets of grasses—that only reminds him of what he's lost. Like his 25 goats, which he sold to pay for the food he can no longer grow.

"When I was young, we used to see gorillas eating in the trees, it was nothing," Nsanzumuhile remembers. "Now the white people come and see them, and the government says they will help us. We will be porters. But I have seen no benefits from tourists."

Ugandan officials insist that Mgahinga's expansion is more than an attempt to grab gorilla business from Rwanda and Zaire. "We want to do things right," said Alfred Labongo, a national park service planner I met in Kampala, Uganda's capital. "We want to bring the local people into the park system. We want them to feel the parks are theirs, for Africans."

Mgahinga (and the nearby Impenetrable Forest) will offer neighboring villagers 10 percent of the revenue from gorilla tourism. This money will pay for schools and water projects. Labongo is also issuing local villagers licenses to collect medicinal plants, keep bees, and harvest edible bamboo inside national parks. In the new Uganda, even forest-dwelling Pygmies must carry user permits.

Whether or not this economic approach to conservation will succeed remains to be seen. But if it fails, it is hard to imagine how the gorillas in Uganda or anywhere else can hold out. The humanity surrounding their remnant forests is swelling fast: Rwanda's prewar population of seven million represented a sevenfold increase in this century. The number is predicted to double again in just 25 years.

"Think too far ahead about gorilla conservation and you get depressed," admits Craig Sholley. "But just remember that for the first time ever, gorillas and people depend on each other for survival. Now you can't separate the fate of the two."

Remarkably, even those who suffered the most in Rwanda's years of violence—a Kigali taxi driver whose entire family was killed, a Ugandan park ranger who lost a leg to a land mine—cheer on this economic alliance.

Yet for me, it will always be the gorilla's capacity to bridge the gulf between humans and animals that argues most strongly for their preservation. This thought strikes home on a steamy afternoon when Sholley and I join a group of tourists slogging through the mud of the Impenetrable Forest.

Soft cathedral light filters down through the rain forest canopy. Copper-winged butterflies float by, snatching stray sunbeams. Suddenly, up ahead, the Ugandan guides freeze. Twenty feet away,

*"...to save habitat for gorillas here in Uganda, almost 2,000 farmers have been ejected from 3,500 acres of prime land."*

wreathed by a thicket of wild celery, a female gorilla cradles an infant on her lap. The baby, dependent on its mother for its first three or four years, is the size of a human toddler. Both pause, and regard us with shining, umber eyes that seem ageless, depthless.

I'm not sure what people see in those liquid irises—recognition? lost innocence?—but the young German woman next to me giggles with delight. A travel-jaded Australian on safari through Africa stands speechless, her mouth agape. I realize I have stopped taking notes, and that I am grinning. And that Craig Sholley is grinning back at me.

# The Looting and Smuggling and Fencing and Hoarding of Impossibly Precious, Feathered, and Scaly Wild Things[4]

As the world's largest exotic reptile show—the National Reptile Breeders Expo—was about to get under way last August in Orlando, Fla., special agents from the United States Fish and Wildlife Service's division of law enforcement were ready to move in. For more than three years, they had been tracking a fast-moving smuggling ring out of Germany and Canada, and two members of the ring had just arrived to sell more than $100,000 worth of rare and protected snakes and tortoises from Madagascar.

They spotted Simon David Harris at the Orlando airport. Harris, 25, was a British citizen living in South Africa. He was carrying in his suitcases 61 Madagascan tree boas and 4 spider tortoises, both of which are protected species. Customs officials arrested him. He would be the bait.

Two days later in a restaurant outside Orlando, Harris's partner, a 33-year-old German named Wolfgang Michael Kloe, was eating breakfast with his wife and two children, waiting for the remainder of his shipment to arrive. Harris showed up, but unbeknown to Kloe, he had agreed to cooperate with federal officials. The two men left the restaurant to add Harris's cache to Kloe's, which was in a parked van nearby. Kloe had a haul of Madagascan boas; over the years, his ring had smuggled in more than 100 boas and 51 radiated tortoises, which since 1975 have been protected by the Convention on International Trade in Endangered Species (Cites), signed by 130 nations. The radiated tortoise, indigenous only to southwestern Madagascar, has a yellow head and a domed shell with brilliant yellow-and-black star bursts, making it one of the most coveted tortoise species on earth.

As Kloe climbed into his van, two Fish and Wildlife officers confronted him. He went quietly—until he got in the car.

"I handcuffed him with his hands in front instead of behind his back," one of the officers recalls. "I thought it would be more comfortable during our ride." The officer drove Kloe toward Orlando for his arraignment. He slowed the car as they approached a tollbooth on the East-West Expressway, and then: "*Boom*—Kloe was out of the car and running."

Kloe shot out across the 10-lane highway, dodging speeding cars and trucks. He jumped the railing of a bridge and scampered down an embankment before disappearing inside a plumbing-supply

---

[4]Article by Donovan Webster, from the *New York Times Magazine* 6:26+ F 16 '97. Copyright © 1997 The New York Times Company. Reprinted with permission.

warehouse. With the sirens of backup police units blaring in the distance, Kloe slipped out a rear door, where a pair of warehouse workers grabbed him. They mistook him for a petty thief.

Kloe eventually pleaded guilty and was fined $10,000 and sentenced to 46 months in prison for conspiracy, smuggling, money laundering, attempted escape and violating the Lacey Act, which bans interstate and international transport of endangered or protected species that have been illegally captured. For Fish and Wildlife, breaking up Kloe's ring was a result of thousands of agent-hours, including international detective work and audio- and video-taped stings. Why all this time, money and effort to stop the smuggling of...a few dozen snakes and turtles from Madagascar?

Wildlife for sale. The trade in exotic animals—especially protected, threatened and endangered species—is not usually thought to occupy a huge share in the global market of illegal goods smuggled across borders. But in recent years, only illegal drugs have outstripped the cash value of the living and dead wildlife that sluices through a black market toward trophy hunters, pet enthusiasts and devotees of traditional medicines. "The business is roughly equal to that of smuggled weapons," says Anne-Berry Wade, a Fish and Wildlife spokeswoman. "And very few nations do anything about it."

Between $10 billion and $20 billion in plants and animals were traded illegally around the world last year, with the United States leading the list of buyers—spending about $3 billion (compared with $30 billion for contraband drugs). The cargo comes in many forms. Like the snakes and tortoises shipped to Orlando, they may be live "pets," pulled from the wild to be sold for thousands of dollars to collectors. They might be dead animals or animal parts whose use and value spans every interest: rare butterflies and beetles caught and killed for collectors; potions made from the horns of endangered black rhinos or the bones of tigers, both of which are said in some cultures to increase male sexual potency, or exotic skins used in designer clothing.

In the end, however, animal smuggling is essentially an environmental problem. According to Fish and Wildlife authorities and a chorus of independent biologists and ecologists, life on Earth may be nearing a doorway it does not want to enter. They suggest that if the decimation of animal populations and their habitats continues, the tapestry of life across whole blotches of the map may start to unravel. Though few scientists agree on the timing or severity of this scenario, they have given it a name: ecosystem collapse.

Perhaps nowhere on Earth have exotic animal species come under more pressure than on Madagascar, a 1,000-mile-long island off the southeast coast of Africa with the planet's most distinctive skein of life. Given that the high-profile arrests in Orlando last summer concerned some of Madagascar's most coveted tortoises and snakes, I decided to see firsthand what the animal trade looks like from the supply end, and what it does to an environment under attack. I

*"Between $10 billion and $20 billion in plants and animals were traded illegally around the world last year..."*

boarded a jet for the 30-hour flight.

Antananarivo—or Tana, as the locals call it—is the island's capital, a city of 1.5 million souls clinging to the sides of 12 red-dirt hills. Studded with apartment houses that are either porch-fronted French colonials or third-world brick cubes, Tana is a city of poverty and dusty beauty. The roads are edged with carts drawn by zebu, a curving-horned mix of cow and ox; farther on lie pastel-green rice paddies. Pedestrians carry live chickens slung across their backs for the evening's meal.

Closer to Antananarivo's downtown, an almost medieval flavor overtakes the city. Many of the houses have interior courtyards and darkly lighted passageways leading to backyards. There are broad stairways rising over the city's hills and roadway tunnels beneath them. Merchants sell litchi nuts, while open-air barbers proffer empty chairs. And all across Antananarivo, on days when the wind blows hard, the sky is thick with smoke from the burning forests and grasslands.

*"As the world's appetite for exotic pets grows, Madagascar has found that its hoard of snakes and tortoises and lemurs, displaced by deforestation, are a very convenient export product."*

A geologic orphan, neither part of Africa nor Asia—the island occupies its own tectonic plate, which has slid southeast over the ages—Madagascar was unpopulated until roughly 2,000 years ago, when Malay-Polynesian mariners called the Malagasy arrived. On Madagascar, the wide, slow arc of biological evolution had been allowed to continue its curve for at least 80 million years, unkinked by human intervention.

Consequently, many of the island's animals and plants are unique. All 32 species of lemur (prehensile-tailed mammals that seem equal parts fox, cat, raccoon and monkey) live only in Madagascar. As does the Parson's chameleon, a three-foot-long arboreal lizard whose limbs move ponderously and whose bulging eyes rotate independently. As did, until a few hundred years ago, the comically gigantic Aepyornis, a 10-foot-tall bird, now extinct, whose shattered eggs—each larger than a rugby ball—are still glued together and sold as $500 souvenirs by Malagasy locals. Then there are the various tortoises and snakes, many of which rank among the planet's most threatened species.

In 1960, when Madagascar gained full independence from France, its population was six million. Today, 12 million people live there (they speak both French and Malagasy), and the population is expected to at least double again by 2015. To feed all these people, jungles are being replaced by rice paddies and grazing land; every year, nearly a third of the island's former scrub forest and desert is set afire to keep it arable. With widespread unemployment and a government still adapting to free-market democracy after shifting in 1993 from a Communist dictatorship, Madagascar is being squeezed by economic and environmental forces on all fronts.

As the world's appetite for exotic pets grows, Madagascar has found that its hoard of snakes and tortoises and lemurs, displaced by deforestation, are a very convenient export product. And for smugglers, with a large pool of collectors willing to pay top dollar for the privilege of owning a fast-evaporating piece of life on earth, Madagascar is a pirate's paradise—especially given that local enforcement isn't very tight.

Of course, Madagascar isn't the only place where smugglers thrive: huge profits are being made from Brazilian monkeys, Indonesian reptiles, Australian birds. "Animal smugglers do it because enforcement and prosecution aren't priorities compared to other crimes," says Tom Striegler, Fish and Wildlife's chief of law enforcement. According to Striegler, a padded vest studded with 40 eggs from Australia's endangered black palm cockatoo, each worth at least $10,000, is far easier to smuggle than an equal-valued cache of cocaine, simply because customs officials aren't looking for cockatoo eggs. "And there's not a stigma attached to being an animal smuggler," Striegler says. "If you get caught illegally transporting animals on a first offense, it's possible you won't even do jail time. You can't say the same for running drugs." (All told, Kloe's gang smuggled in animals worth more than $250,000, which earned him 46 months' jail time and a $10,000 fine; a similarly priced haul of cocaine sold by the kilogram would net a smuggler 121 to 151 months in jail, with potential fines of $175,000 or more.)

Snakes are among the most common live contraband because of their availability and because they, like tortoises, can survive a long trip without food or water. Larger and more fragile live animals, especially monkeys and birds, are more difficult to smuggle (the survival rate for smuggled birds is only 10 percent) and are, therefore, often more expensive.

Madagascar is hardly the only country where habitat destruction and illegal animal collection are endangering the environment. A 1996 study by the World Conservation Union called the loss of biodiversity one of the world's most pressing environmental problems, noting a sharp increase in the pace of extinction of birds and mammals. And with exploding human populations, especially in the third world, the trend is expected only to grow.

"You go into these jungles where there once were abundant birds and parrots, and now they're empty," says the eminent biologist George Schaller, director of science at the Wildlife Conservation Society, about South America's equatorial rain forests. "Collectors removed immature birds before they had time to breed. Demand from the pet trade stripped those jungles like a disease. Who knows how many ways the loss of the birds will upset the balance of life in those jungles? But it will."

In Antananarivo, the place where smuggling-minded individuals can gain reliable information is a hotel and bar called Le Glacier— "the Ice Cream Maker." Ice cream may have been concocted here at one time, but the milk and flavorings have long been discarded to history, leaving only the ice. Which is used to cool Scotch whisky.

Le Glacier is Antananarivo's cultural crossroads. From inside, you look out onto Zoma, which the locals say is the world's second-largest outdoor market after Bangkok's: bananas and knockoff

Nikes, live ducks and musical instruments, butchered zebu and automobile radiators. Around you, Le Glacier's barroom is a dingy, tall-ceilinged place dotted with tables and trolled by bored hookers.

It takes a few minutes to navigate Le Glacier's social shoals, but soon I am talking with a well-dressed, gravel-voiced gentleman who seems to be a regular. When I ask about smuggled snakes and tortoises, he takes a puff of his Gauloise and grins. "That man, over there, he knows the smuggling," he says, pointing toward the bar. "Monsieur!" he shouts. "Come over to our table and join us."

The man does. His name is Patrice Grondin, and though only in his 50s, he is thin and battered. With a receding hairline and mahogany parchment skin, he is a caricature of the pirate outlaw. His eyes are rheumy, his teeth capped with silver. It's five in the afternoon, and he has been in the bar since before lunch.

After lighting a cigarette and ordering a white rum, Grondin settles in. "Since we all know the man who introduced us, I know we can speak freely," he says. "The smuggling is going on. Right now! Especially the radiated tortoise. It is in great demand by pet owners. Each tortoise's shell is unique. I've heard a story that once the Queen of England offered a lot of money—hundreds of thousands of dollars—to find two that are exactly alike. And still, with all that money at stake, it never happened."

Some of the tortoises, he says, are even shipped out of the country with the government's help. "It's amazing how it is all intertwined," he says, smoothing his hands over each other. Grondin then mentions the platter-size plowshare tortoise, one of the world's most endangered reptiles. It is estimated that only 400 to 1,000 plowshares still exist in Madagascar's wilds. On the night of May 6, 1996, 76 plowshares were stolen from a captive-breeding reserve along the country's northwest coast, destroying 10 years of work with the slow-to-breed animals. The theft and export of the plowshares was so solidly planned that they were advertised for sale in Europe days before they were stolen.

These days, Grondin tells us, animals are increasingly smuggled off Madagascar by fast trimarans or speedboats, bound for South Africa or the island of Reunion. "The airports are too controlled," he says, "so unless prior arrangements have been made, you can be caught. But there is no coast guard in Madagascar."

Once the Madagascan tortoises and snakes arrive in Reunion or South Africa, Grondin says, they are mixed with captive-bred exotics. Because these rare species don't exist naturally outside Madagascar, the newly smuggled animals are also assumed to have been bred in captivity. Eventually, false documents are generated for the illegal animals, since it's not against the law to transport a protected animal if its paperwork confirms that it never lived in the wild.

The conversation ebbs and flows. There are stories about would-be smugglers getting caught. One radiated-tortoise courier tried to board an outbound jet in Antananarivo wearing heavy winter clothes whose insulation was stuffed with tortoises. Another carried them aboard as cabin luggage—in a burlap sack marked

"Coconuts." Grondin laughs. "The bag looked good," he says. "It was about the right weight, and the round shape of the shells looked like coconuts under the fabric. Then the coconuts started to crawl and scratch inside the bag!"

Finally Grondin offers some specific directions: to trace the path of the radiated tortoise, he says, we must go to Tuléar, a seaport city in southwestern Madagascar. But first he issues an invitation: "Come with me, and we will leave one morning and come back with a few boas in the afternoon. It will take only four hours." I will definitely be heading to Tuléar. But, sure, I'd also like to see how boas, which are also protected by the Cites agreement, begin their trip from the Madagascan jungle to Orlando.

A few days later, I find myself bearing a letter from Grondin—he couldn't accompany me the day I wanted to go—and heading across the scarred and mountainous jungles of east-central Madagascar toward the town of Andasibe.

During the past few years, snakes have come to dominate the fast-growing animal smuggling trade. They are sought as pets (Michael Jackson and the rock guitarist Slash, both famous for their snakes, may have spurred the craze) and for their skins and body fluids. In Vietnam, I was once offered the blood and gall of a live grass snake. Before my eyes, the delicate green animal—narrow as a string—would be slit from tail to head, with the gall and blood squeezed into a glass of rice brandy. The elixir, I was told, would give me the strength of 10 men.

Snakes move through the black market in ways limited only by human imagination. One of the most creative ruses was undertaken by a Taiwanese man named Chine-Kuo Liu, who in July 1993 was arrested leaving Los Angeles International Airport with 52 North American snakes on his body. To carry the snakes, he would drop one into the toe of a nylon stocking, let the snake ball itself tight, then twist the stocking shut above the snake and drop in another, repeating the process until the stocking resembled a large string of pearls. Then he wrapped the stocking around his body and wore loose clothes for the airplane trip.

At Andasibe, home to the 2,000-acre Périnet nature reserve, I enter the railway hotel and give Grondin's letter to the maitre d'hotel. He reads it and smiles. "Yes," he says, "I will send for someone who can help."

I sit for lunch, and within five minutes two young farmers—Buddy, 24, and Julien, 29—approach the table. They're filthy, and they look hungry and a little nervous. "We have no boas today," Buddy says. "It is Friday, coming into the weekend. There are many tourists inside the reserve. So we don't hunt. We don't keep any in our possession on weekends, in case someone were to see. But we can get some. It will take only a few hours."

Julien, who is smaller and darker than Buddy, raises a hand to quiet him. "Will you be exporting these?" he asks. "If so, we can get smaller specimens. They're easier to hide. Or, we can get a large

*"During the past few years, snakes have come to dominate the fast-growing animal smuggling trade."*

one. We can get anything you'd like."

I say it doesn't matter. I'm only interested in seeing one.

The next morning at nine Buddy arrives at the hotel. "We have a ground boa," he says. "A beautiful one. But only one. The tourists were too many last night. We could not hunt. We have to walk the forest paths and roads using flashlights. It would have given us away."

We drive about two miles from the rail station, through a village of wood huts with dirt floors and backyard gardens and a circular rice paddy at its center. We turn up a side road that leads to the town's former schoolhouse, a three-room building whose windows, doors and roof have been destroyed. "A cyclone did that," Buddy says. Julien materializes from the jungle. He lifts a dirty white bag into the air and walks toward us. We step inside the wrecked schoolhouse, and Julien opens the bag. "It's a very nice specimen," he says. "We got another one like it recently. For a German. He bought it for $300. He paid in real U.S. currency."

*"I can do one of three things with these boas. I can leave them alone, and not have enough to eat. I can eat them. Or I can sell them to people.'"*

Slowly, the snake begins a long, easy-bodied slide out of the bag. Its head is triangular, its body a putty like brown blotched with dark diamond shapes along its back. The shapes grow larger as the snake's body increases in diameter. "This is a young one," Julien says. "It is only three or four feet long. They can be six feet long." He lifts the snake by its midsection. "It's also a female," he says. "And it is pregnant. I can feel the eggs. Soon there will be little snakes."

So if I were to take this one snake from the jungle, I would effectively be taking many more. "Is $300 a lot for a boa?" I ask Julien.

He bobs his head. "Yes," he says, "though they can be more expensive."

"In the United States," I tell him, "people would pay $2,000."

He looks shocked, as if I'd just slugged him. "Well," he says, "you have to pay for transportation—and sometimes for bribes. I am not an exporter. I am a cultivator. I farm rice. These days, I don't make enough money from that."

The Madagascan ground boa, Julien goes on, is indigenous only to the Andasibe area, but there are a lot of them. "So, to me," he says, "I can do one of three things with these boas. I can leave them alone, and not have enough to eat. I can eat them. Or I can sell them to people. I make enough from selling one snake to eat for a month—or more. What would you choose? Of course, I would rather make $2,000 than $300 from this snake. But the danger comes in the exporting."

Does he know how the snakes are exported?

"Not really," he says. "By boat, I think. Many of them."

Fortunately, the United States Attorney's indictment from the Orlando case fills in some gaps, at least in the case of Wolfgang Kloe's operation. Kloe and another defendant, Frank H. Lehmeyer, would travel from Germany to Madagascar, where they collected the snakes and tortoises and had them flown back to Germany, often by bribing airport officials. In Germany, the animals would be sold to a Canadian, Enrico Joseph Truant, who hired couriers to transport the animals back to Canada in what Kloe called a "special suitcase." From Canada, the snakes and tortoises would be driven into the United States and shipped by commercial airlines from Detroit. By this time, Lehmeyer would have sent a forged Cites permit for the animals to Truant, with instructions to show the permit only if necessary. If the permit went unused, Truant was to return it to Lehmeyer.

Back in the destroyed schoolhouse, Buddy and Julien still think I want to buy their snake for export. "She is very healthy," Buddy says. "So, are we ready for a sale?"

"No," I tell them, "I only wanted to see it. I don't want to buy it."

The two snake catchers are confused. They look at each other, their faces screwing tight. They each smoke a cigarette, watching me for a few minutes, asking for a second and third time if I don't want to buy the snake. After a moment of negotiation between themselves, they turn the snake loose on the schoolhouse floor. No use keeping evidence around.

*"The harvesting of wild animals wouldn't be nearly so profitable if there weren't such ardent collectors around the world..."*

Buddy tells me that because of their size and ability to adapt to different-shaped containers, snakes are far easier to export than radiated tortoises, which are generally heavy, bulky and more difficult to find. Also, when in distress, the tortoises urinate—sometimes a noxious, crimson liquid that can tip off a wildlife inspector. The urine's smell, Buddy says, can linger for hours or days after a tortoise has been taken. That is why most smugglers drop newly collected tortoises into mesh bags and swing them in circles above their heads, inciting the animals to spend their scent before export begins.

We talk for a few more minutes. I give Buddy and Julien about $15 each for their work. The snake, which isn't accustomed to sunlight, slithers tentatively across the wooden floor. A moment later, what must have seemed a windfall $300 to Buddy and Julien slides through a hole in the fractured floorboards, dropping onto the red soil of Madagascar.

The harvesting of wild animals wouldn't be nearly so profitable if there weren't such ardent collectors around the world, especially in America, Germany and Japan (where an estimated 1 in 10 males is a serious butterfly collector). And their demands have turned animal smuggling into something of a science.

When Fish and Wildlife officers raided a house in Redwood City, Calif., five years ago, they found an extensive collection of butterflies, including dozens of living specimens shrouded in glassine envelopes and chilled inside a dark refrigerator.

"It's done that way so the butterflies metabolize stored fat before they're killed," says Chris Nagano, an entomologist with Fish and Wildlife's Carlsbad, Calif., office who participated in the Redwood City case. "It creates the best specimens for sale to collectors, because then the fat can't melt out and spoil their wings once they die."

The keeper of these butterflies, as it turns out, was a pest exterminator and butterfly authority named Richard J. Skalski, known locally as "Bugman." In the end, investigators found that Skalski and his colleagues were in possession of 2,375 rare and protected butterflies from Mexico, Germany and the United States, a cache that Fish and Wildlife estimated to have a black-market value of more than $300,000. On the ceiling beams above his bed, Skalski had meticulously taped sections of paper toweling on which were mounted maturing chrysalides, so that he could monitor their development.

"He knew precisely what he was doing," Nagano says. "It was a system that left him pristine specimens.

By Nagano's reckoning, such behavior isn't that uncommon. The most obsessive collectors, he says, often become experts on their preferred species. "Pretty soon, they think, Hey, it's my animal," Nagano says. "Which results in the smuggling and, I think, a real lack of respect for the species."

Nagano remembers interviewing one rare-animal dealer who had seen so many zoologic obsessions that he coined a name for it: the Sickness. "He told me he could see it in their eyes," Nagano says. "The animal takes them over. He told stories of guys whose wives left them because of the Sickness. Guys who were ruined financially. It's ironic—they gain all this knowledge of a rare species, and rather than use it to help the animal, they internalize it. They have to possess it."

Of course, not all collectors are pathological. Richard D. Bartlett, 58, white-haired and thickbearded, has written 13 books and more than 400 articles about reptile behavior and collecting. He and his wife (and sometime collaborator), Patti, live near Gainesville, Fla., on a few acres draped with Spanish moss. They maintain a menagerie of about 100 animals—including 40 species of exotic snakes, birds, turtles, mudskippers and tortoises, among them a pair of radiated tortoises from Madagascar—collected over the years and kept in conditions that would put most public zoos to shame.

Bartlett has a particular soft spot for reptiles and amphibians. "I've been interested in them since I was old enough to understand there was life beyond me in this world," he says. "And I can't tell you why, exactly. I just find the roles that they play in life fascinating. They occupy an ecosystem niche that's not being used. They're so versatile.

"I can say, I think, that we don't have too many wild-collected animals in our collection. Oops, I'm lying—I have some temple vipers, from Sulawesi and Sumatra. I believe they are wild-collected. And I have the radiated tortoises, of course, which I got 45 years ago from a French dealer who couldn't give them away. But I got those before any protections existed. I wouldn't do it today."

These days, Bartlett says with conviction, he has joined with the scientists who believe that biodiversity is indeed being threatened and that animal smuggling is a significant part of the problem. "I'm here, in my backyard in Florida, with my snakes from around the world and my pet tortoises from Madagascar, and one of the messages I get is that the world has gotten really small," Bartlett says.

"You can get anything you want—anything you can imagine having—provided you're willing to pay for it. No matter how rare an animal is, you can get it. Think about the implications—there's something deeply frightening about it. That's why we have to change the way things are being done now. The time has come for that."

The harbor town of Tuléar in southwest Madagascar has a Caribbean-blue sea, deep coral lagoons and constant cool breezes, which make it feel like a tropical seaport. Yet a few hundred yards inland dust devils swirl inside walled courtyards, wild dogs crowd the patchy concrete streets and everywhere people are asking for money—begging and selling in equal proportion. Away from the beach the ground is a spiny desert, though one whose mosaic of plants, birds and animals appears healthy.

Everywhere beneath the placid surface of Tuléar's dusty streets a sort of Wild West desperation dwells, and it occasionally bursts into view. One afternoon, for example, I buy a few seashells from a woman who is subsequently beaten by a man nearby, though it's not clear for what. He shatters a large conch shell across her face, leaving her bleeding, crying and, it seems, perplexed. In another minute, the man is surrounded by a mob and beaten senseless. All this happens beneath an enormous, swaying palm tree, less than 200 yards away from my luxury beach hotel.

This is where I have come to look for illegally transported radiated tortoises, which can sell in the States for as much as $10,000 each. The most valuable specimen is an adult female that can reproduce; also, the more distinctive and brilliant the sunburst shell, the more valuable the tortoise. After a few hours of asking around, I drive away from town with a local gentleman who says he can guide me to where the tortoises are kept and sold.

"Some Malagasy think the tortoises are good luck to have around your house," he says. "Other people think they are a delicacy. They eat them—especially around Christmas. Still others export them. They put them in pirogues—you know, dugout canoes—at night, and take them to boats offshore, for export. Everyone knows that in other countries the tortoises are extremely valuable as pets. The adults live to be more than 100 years old. They can be very beautiful. This is why collectors like them so much."

Within 10 minutes we are snaking through a ghetto at the edge of town. Tall fences, made of woven sticks, line the dirt road and obscure our view. Ragged children run alongside our car. Finally, where the street ends, we get out and walk the village's maze. At one house, my guide tells me to wait, then steps inside a fence. He returns a minute later with a tall, 30-ish-looking woman in a print dress. "She has some tortoises she will show you," he says. "Come."

I step into her small house, built with scrap wood and a tin roof. In one corner, hemmed by plywood boards leaning against two beds, is a pen filled with radiated tortoises stacked two and three deep. The woman—"I don't want my name used," she says—pulls back a shade-giving sheet hanging on a string above the pen, and the afternoon's blistering daylight falls across the contraband. The tortoises jump and tumble. Each one is the size of a halved basketball. Their black-and-yellow star-burst designs are intricately beautiful, if somewhat dusty. The animals grunt and make hissing sounds, their little yellow heads craning from beneath the high domes of their shells, their tiny clawed feet scratching and scrabbling against the other tortoises' shells and the wooden walls of the pen. I count 24 of them. The room smells dirty. The tortoises do not appear to be in peak health.

Outside, our arrival has attracted a small crowd, and a few men poke their heads inside, menace in their demeanors. Everyone, apparently, knows this is where radiated tortoises are sold, and the men seem to be making sure that no trouble comes to our hostess.

I ask her if she knows that these tortoises are endangered.

"Yes," she says. "I sell them to local people for food, starting at 5,000 Malagasy francs"—about $1.35. "For people who aren't local, I sell them beginning at about 15,000 francs. Sometimes I sell them for much more than that. That depends on how many tortoises I have at the time, also who is buying them."Does she know what the nonlocal people who buy tortoises do with them? The woman looks at me, then glances at the shanty's dirt floor. "I don't want to talk about that," she says. "I don't know who those people are. All I know is that about once a week, usually late at night, a pirogue lands on the darkest part of the beach and someone comes and gets me, and we go and unload tortoises. The pirogue always lands on the beach. Never in the port."

She won't talk about where the tortoises go from there, or who does the exporting. There are intimations, however, that this is how smuggling systems are usually set up: no one knows too much about anyone else's part in the network. This way, even if someone gets caught, the pipeline can't be pieced together. In the pen, the tortoises are still grunting and hissing, trying to escape. The woman grabs a few, rearranging them, the thumping of their shells initiates even more bedlam.

As the woman lifts one of the larger tortoises from the pen, another woman steps inside the shanty. She is carrying an infant. The baby, it happens, belongs to the tortoise merchant. It is perhaps three months old. The woman sets the baby on a bed next to the tortoise pen, and the tortoise merchant lays the tortoise on its back near the infant. The baby lies helplessly on its back, too. Both are thrusting and kicking their hands and feet into the air.

The tortoise merchant lifts her baby, cradling it in one arm. With her free hand, she grabs the tortoise's carapace and flips it, with an unceremonious bunk, back into the pen, sending the animals into yet another round of grunting and hissing. The interview, she says, is over. It is time to nurse the baby.

Just one more question, I say: "Where do these tortoises come from?"

"From the south, a place many miles down the beach," she says. "From a place somewhere near the town of Betioky."

Betioky is a village of sand-floored wooden huts at the edge of the Mozambique Channel. The air is hot and dry, and a nonstop gale howls across the sand and sea. At the far edge of the lagoon, a half-mile off the shore, the deep azure ocean hammers the reef, waves frothing white against the palette of blues on a sea-and-sky horizon.

It took an entire day to drive from Tuléar, less than 100 miles, passing through rock-escarpment valleys, cactus-and-baobab savanna, spiny chaparral and, finally, the low pine and scrub of this sandy dune beach.

Along the route, a traveler can readily see what an ecosystem devoured to nothing looks like. For stretches that seem endless, the earth has been burned and seared to broken and charred stone. The area was originally logged and set aflame to create grazing areas, but a few years of low rainfall—a climatic change perhaps partly hastened by the biological one—have left it barren. No people. No lizards skittering up the roadbed ahead of the car as they do across the rest of Madagascar. It is a land consumed down to lifelessness.

Then, at the far end of this blotchy desert, the deep blue of the sea rises above the low dunes, and a narrow rind of life clings tight. In Betioky, the children are often naked, the adults barely dressed in rags. Electricity is still many miles away. The village's fishermen, who have seen their fortunes dwindle after overfishing much of the reef, use patchy sails made from burlap sacks to propel their dugouts. The sand is a pale white, so clean it nearly fluoresces. Beneath a Crayola-yellow sun and deep blue sky, small octopuses hang drying from racks in the afternoon heat, shifting in the wind.

I drop my baggage in Betioky and, after asking some questions in town, head off-road along the coast. After winding through the scrub and pine for five or six miles, I arrive at the place where, I was told, radiated tortoises are caught by an outlaw band. Their patron—father to most, clan leader to others—is a skinny, ebony-skinned man named Benjamin. He's 53 and lives in a prehistoric structure: a tiny, three-foot-tall mound of loose-woven pine boughs with an open cooking fire on its sand floor. The hut is set in a ravine, one dune off the beach. The afternoon's idiot wind continues to howl over our heads, occasionally whipping at the boughs of Benjamin's house, making it hard for us to speak at a polite distance.

Benjamin is wearing only a thin wrap of sarong, a rag with brightly printed colors. He is understandably suspicious—he knows that collecting tortoises is illegal. But soon, after I promise "No police, no police," he calms down.

"Yes, we get them most every day," he says. He reaches into his shelter and extracts a sack with five radiated tortoises, from a near-adult 20-pounder to a youthful specimen of perhaps two. I'm surprised by the vibrancy of their colors—their shells are like inlaid wood, their amber yellows and dark browns and midnight blacks practically giving off their own light. The difference between these healthy, newly collected specimens and the ones I saw in Tuléar, further up the pipeline, is astounding. In fact, until seeing these, I hadn't understood why these tortoises are so prized.

*"I'm surprised by the vibrancy of their colors—their shells are like inlaid wood, their amber yellows and dark browns and midnight blacks practically giving off their own light."*

Benjamin tells me that I am a day late. Today is Wednesday, and just yesterday he sent an outrigger full of tortoises to Tuléar—it probably arrived late last night. "It was beautiful," he says. "A boatful of them. Eighty tortoises in bags. They were not the largest ones, but we got 1,000 Malagasy francs"—about 30 cents—"for each of them."

There are not as many of these tortoises as there used to be, Benjamin says. "It's like the fishing. For 51 of my 53 years I have been a fisherman here. Now the fishing has gotten too hard, and I am growing too old. It is far harder work than collecting tortoises. But collecting tortoises is far more risky. Still, I have to. I have to eat. I have to feed myself and my family, and the fishing has been nearly used up."

I ask if he understands the restrictions, if protections on the tortoise make sense.

"The tortoises are here, and I have to eat," he says again. "That is all I need to know. My people have always done this. They have collected what is nearby for food and money. Why should that change?"

He smiles, confounded, as I mention—somewhat absurdly, I'm aware—the opinions of biologists and global eco-congresses. "We do this to eat," he keeps saying. "We are human. We need to eat." He smiles again and puts the tortoises back inside their sack.

I ask Benjamin if he is going tortoise hunting tomorrow, and if I can go along.

"Yes," he says. "Tomorrow we will go to the best collecting place. It is a distance away. There are many tortoises there. We can collect many in an hour. Ones much bigger than we get here, along the beach. Along the beach now, the tortoises are becoming hard to find. They are being depleted, like the fishing."

We make arrangements to meet at 5 A.M.

*"It strikes me that telling Benjamin not to hunt tortoises is a bit like telling an Iowa farmer: 'Sorry, you can't grow corn anymore, even if that's your livelihood. The inhabitants of Mars think it's a bad idea.'"*

That night, although I'm offered a shack in Tuléar, I opt to sleep on the beach. The wind is fresh, almost overpowering the din of waves breaking across the reef. The air is so clear that every star of the Southern Hemisphere seems visible. All night long, as I wrestle with the twisty economics of the radiated tortoise and the ground boa and the danger of collapsing ecosystems in the face of people trying to feed themselves, the constellations march steadily overhead.

If fishing has become too difficult, why shouldn't Benjamin turn to collecting tortoises for profit? People worldwide have always eaten and sold what's available—why should Benjamin starve because far-off biologists and statesmen decide the radiated tortoise is now off-limits?

"When the gendarmes catch me with tortoises," Benjamin told me earlier, "I can give them money and they forget about it. The police understand. But when the World Wildlife Fund comes out twice a year, I make sure not to have any tortoises in my possession. If they catch you, you are going to court and to prison. To me, they have the problem backward—let the tortoise live, so I can starve."

It strikes me that telling Benjamin not to hunt tortoises is a bit like telling an Iowa farmer: "Sorry, you can't grow corn anymore, even if that's your livelihood. The inhabitants of Mars think it's a bad idea."

And then I think of something I heard months earlier from Robert S. Anderson, senior trial counsel for the wildlife and marine resources section at the Department of Justice and the enforcement officer for Cites in Geneva. "The people who smuggle these animals into the U.S. usually aren't hobbyists gone astray," he said. "They're not doing this to eat. They're not trying to save the species. They're out to make a buck."

And I know that he's right, too.

So where does the shift happen? At what point does a radiated tortoise go from a piece of nature's bounty to contraband? Is it when they're dumped into the outrigger on Benjamin's beach, or into the darkened pens of Tuléar? Or as they exit the pipeline in Orlando—now worth hundreds or thousands of times more than they were in Madagascar?

On my way back along this beach, looking at the stars, I think of all the animals. Snakes in Asia and the United States. Birds from Guyana and Central America. Tigers in India and Siberia. Black rhinos. Red-kneed tarantulas. Black bears. According to the planet's most eminent biologists, the pace of biodiversity's decay is speeding up. And there is too much demand to discourage Benjamin and his colleagues around the world from supplying.

It's 4:28 A.M. In the east, the first slice of sunrise climbs into the sky. Off the beach, fishermen are already steering their square-rigged boats across the lagoon toward the reef. Soon the light of the sun blots out the stars, and in the village behind me roosters start crowing.

Forty-five minutes later, I arrive at Benjamin's camp, ready for a morning of tortoise hunting. We begin hiking to the collecting area, and in the cool of the morning the six men in Benjamin's hunting group say little. To me, they're a slightly threatening bunch. Wearing ragged clothes and broken shoes, each man carries a sharpened machete, and I can't help but think that I may have asked Benjamin too many questions the night before. Maybe he and his men think I'm a policeman. Might they set their machetes on me out in the bush?

An hour later, after hopscotching through burned-over savanna and intact chaparral, Benjamin points into the forest. "This is it," he says. We head away from the road, and within minutes we are walking through groves of low eucalyptus trees. The men spread out, and all across the area I can hear them hollering their good fortune.

"Got a large one," somebody yells.

"Another here," someone else shouts.

Benjamin has yet to find a tortoise. He searches beneath the eucalyptus shrubs, pressing back their branches to look around the roots. "The tortoises like it deep beneath the bushes," he says. "They eat the leaves and use the brush for shade."

Ahead, he points. "Ah," he says. "There."

Just beneath the edge of a shrub, a mature radiated tortoise—large as a boulder—rests in the shadows. As Benjamin approaches, the tortoise hisses and tries to escape deeper beneath the eucalyptus, but it is too late. Benjamin flips the tortoise onto its back, grasping its carapace at a natural handle where its left rear leg protrudes. The tortoise stares at Benjamin with its black, almond-shaped eyes. As Benjamin stands, holding the tortoise against his thigh, the tortoise urinates—a thin, red liquid that reeks of ammonia. "There it is," Benjamin says, laughing. "He thinks it will save him now."

Within an hour, Benjamin has caught nine tortoises. At one point, he finds two adults with a baby, the size of a small stone, wedged beneath them. He collects them all and, stripping a swath of bark from a tree with his machete, pulls the bark apart into several long strips. He then loops and ties the strips at the natural seam where the tortoises' bottom and top shells connect. It's a quick, neat trick. Soon, all the tortoises have a small handle, and Benjamin finds a long windfallen branch, smooths it with his machete and lashes each tortoise to the pole. He is working quickly, humming a little song to himself. "A very good day," he says.

*"...Benjamin tells me that the radiated tortoises now live in a very limited area, which is shrinking all the time."*

By the time we return to the road, the other men are there as well. An hour and a half has passed since we went into the forest. They have taken 54 mature radiated tortoises from the wild, plus a number of young ones—which I can't accurately count—which they either tied beneath the larger tortoises or stuffed into their pockets. It has been a banner day. If not sold as a Christmas meal to someone in Tuléar, each tortoise will be worth at least $2,000 once smuggled out of Madagascar, with the most exquisite of them commanding prices as high as $10,000. When this haul is transferred into pirogues on the beach near Betioky, Benjamin and his clan will take in roughly $16.

It is hard to imagine that two hours ago I was afraid of these guys. Now they are slapping my back and dancing, ecstatic at their harvest.

As we begin home, Benjamin tells me that the radiated tortoises now live in a very limited area, which is shrinking all the time. He tells me, too, that he knows each of the adult tortoises he collected today is older than he is. He knows, he says, that the tortoises will soon be gone.

"What will you do for food," I ask him, "when the tortoises disappear?"

Benjamin looks at me, my question flapping nervous as a bird behind his dark eyes. He stares down for a long moment, scanning the red soil. He shakes his head. He smiles. "I don't know," he says.

# The Perils of Success[5]

In northeastern Montana the roads undulate gently, rippling like ribbon candy; yet they are a straight shot to anywhere, so empty that it doesn't matter which side of the road you drive on. They are roads requiring a tall stack of tapes, preferably country-western or cowboy tunes, for those times when the radio's search function just goes round and round without a signal to rest on. They are roads to fear in the sudden summer rains, when their silica clay beds become gumbo and seize car tires and won't let go.

This is the region known in Montana travel literature as Missouri River Country, and the state's tourism promoters see it as the next hot destination. I see only one lonesome cottonwood tree isolated in the far distance, looking strange and lost, as if it had happened into the wrong landscape. At the dirt crossroad in Cleveland, Montana (pop. 3), in the yard of the one-room schoolhouse, stands a basketball hoop on a pole, surrounded by an endless sea of grass, looking as mournful and friendless out on the prairie as the cottonwood tree. These back roads of the Great Plains host nary a motel, nor espresso bar, nor art gallery, nor even any fly-fishing.

Hour after hour, with whole afternoons passing in the vastness between small towns, ring-necked pheasants fly into my windshield, flushed from the wheat fields. Wild lupine grows everywhere, and I gather some from the roadside to fill my car with fragrance. Driving under the open sky with wind in the wheat and rich purple flowers scenting the breeze, I think am in heaven.

In Zortman, a log-cabined, dirt-pathed community holed up in the Little Rocky Mountains, Leann M. nurses a cup of coffee at the Formica counter of the Miner's Club Cafe. She ranches just outside town and works as a security guard at the Pegasus gold mine. Leann is lanky, tough, in her 30s, has kids, and used to live in Hungry Horse, a community in western Montana's Flathead County, near Glacier National Park.

"I went back to Hungry Horse a couple of years ago and couldn't believe it," she says, tamping out a cigarette. "Everything I loved was paved over. I used to live out in the sticks there. Now it's all subdivided, people all right next to each other enjoying it!" She snorts. "If that's what tourism comes to, I'm against it. It's easier to raise cattle than to shoot tourists."

The ascendancy of tourism in western Montana has done more, however, than make residents grumble. Increasing numbers of visitors and paradise seekers—and the development to accommodate them—has meant the loss of wildlife habitat and agricultural lands, an increase in traffic and smog, an increase in noxious weeds; stress

---

5 Article by Perri Knize, from *Condé Nast Traveler* 30:158+ N '95. Copyright © 1995 Perri Knize. Reprinted with permission.

on already inadequate community infrastructure, resources, and services; and, in some cases, severe culture shock and cultural clashes. "[Newcomers] are used to the smog and traffic, and they don't notice it; we do," says Jay Printz, the Ravalli County sheriff who recently spearheaded a campaign to overturn the Brady Bill in Ravalli County. "To them, this is paradise. To us it was paradise."

The state has been goosed, in a matter of only a couple of years, from an agrarian culture, dreaming along sleepily in the 19th century, to the faster-paced, more urban culture of the late 20th century, complete with its crime, alienation, and other social ills. The mythology of the Old West, where rugged individualists freely do as they please, is dying as the frontier vanishes. The shift has been so sudden and dramatic that for many who feel their way of life is threatened, it is like undergoing the bends.

In western Montana, locals now say they are bracing themselves for the sequel to *A River Runs Through It*, Robert Redford's 1992 film about a Missoula, Montana, family obsessed with fly-fishing. It's called *A Realtor Runs Through It*. That's the acrid joke making the rounds of Missoula and Bozeman watering holes these days. And, in fact, 1,000 prospective real estate agents took Montana's licensing exam in 1993, a jump of 11.2 percent; some agents even specialize in fly-fishing properties.

At least one Montana angler, John Wilson, the managing director of the Montana Land Reliance, a conservation group in Helena, is worried about the pace of development. Wilson greets me in his dark warren of an office with a direct blue gaze that lends an air of integrity to a mien that is otherwise reminiscent of a used-car salesman—he's balding, fleshy, in his 40s, and he wears an inexpensive, badly fitting sport coat and no tie. At the bar of a popular coffee house a short walk from his office, Wilson tells of seeing *A River Runs Through It* on a theater marquee in Palo Alto, California. "After that movie, even people who don't fish will have a dream of coming to Montana," he says over an espresso and the roar of a coffee roaster in the corner. "Will they find what they saw in the movie? That depends. We're losing open space, beauty, lack of crime, friendly culture. We're getting more crowded. The handwriting is on the wall."

Yet it was Wilson, as the director of Travel Montana, the state's tourism promotion bureau, who led the team that sold the state to the American public. And he was phenomenally successful.

When John Wilson took the helm of Travel Montana in 1980, a market research firm told him that Montana had no national image except, perhaps, that it was cold and up north. Back then, the travel division had a budget of $600,000 a year, making it 49th in spending for promotion among the 50 states. Fifteen years and roughly $55 million later, Montana is one of the hottest destinations in the country and the envy of its neighbor states. And it is Wilson, with his vision, political savvy, and sheer salesmanship, who deserves much of the credit.

A transplanted native of Oswego, New York, and a dedicated environmentalist who fought in the trenches for the Montana Council of Trout Unlimited and the Montana Environmental Information Center, John Wilson saw tourism as the last best hope for Montana. The Treasure State is a poor one, ravaged by out-of-state moneyed interests who mine and log and then leave, taking their profits and abandoning Montana workers. This dependence on the boom-and-bust economy of extractive resources has led the state, like a third world country, to sacrifice its environment—the only left in the Lower 48 with its entire range of native species intact—for a paycheck.

One of the biggest Superfund sites in the nation is in Montana, and the soil and water surrounding Butte and Anaconda is so poisoned that the EPA doesn't know what to do about it. The Clark Fork River is full of toxins nobody can figure out how to remove. The rich forests of the northwest corner have been so severely logged on private lands that some national forests have cut their planned timber sales in half to protect the little that remains. Pulp mills and lead smelters smear the skies with a toxic haze. Most recently, to accommodate resource industries, the 1995 legislature gutted the state's water-quality regulations. The incessant cry for jobs in Montana has hamstrung environmentalists' best efforts for years.

Tourism, thought Wilson, is a renewable resource, light on the land. And tourism would give economic clout to the preservationists: Who could get away with despoiling a trout stream worth millions in tourism dollars? This vision of tourism as a tool of conservation and economic development ultimately gave Wilson the leverage he needed to persuade the legislature, the innkeepers, and the environmental community to support a four-percent tax on motel and hotel accommodations—called the bed tax—to fund the state's promotion efforts.

Wilson's first task was to get Travel Montana, languishing in a back office at the Department of Highways, moved to the Department of Commerce, where it could expand the agenda of economic development. With a minimum of support from the state legislature, he says, "what we were doing was like trying to start a car on only one cold cylinder."

Then in 1987, the legislature passed the bed tax bill. With Wilson's budget now enhanced a whopping 650 percent to $4.5 million, Travel Montana revved into high gear. The division's publicity team produced its first major television commercial, a foggy-lensed idyll of children romping in wildflower meadows in the mountains, called "When Montana Sings." It hosted familiarization tours for scores of writers and editors. Soon Montana was on the cover of a dozen national magazines. One Kalispell tour operator was shocked by the response: "Here I was, saying, 'Please, God, give me some tourists,' and then...wham!"

Wilson says he first knew the campaign had worked in the summer of 1989, when he and his publications director, Norma Tirrell, went on a drive together through the Flathead Valley. "There were Winnebagos and traffic everywhere, and it sunk in that now all the

*"This dependence on the boom-and-bust economy of extractive resources has led the state, like a third world country, to sacrifice its environment—the only left in the Lower 48 with its entire range of native species intact—for a paycheck."*

cylinders were running and we'd played a significant part. What we did was strike the match that lit the fire."

Now tourism in Montana is a conflagration the likes of which hasn't been seen here since the 1988 Yellowstone fires. Almost 8 million visitors came to this state of 840,000 residents last year. Revenues from the bed tax have soared an average of 10 percent each year, now bringing in nearly $8.1 million. Nonresident spending is soaring as well, to more than $1.2 billion in 1994, an increase of 8 percent over the previous year. Travel Montana and the state's six tourism regions now spend more than $7 million a year on promotion alone.

On a hot Sunday in July, the trailer homes and station wagons are creeping and stopping along Going-to-the-Sun Road in Glacier National Park. The long conga line of Winnebagos, Jeeps, pickup trucks, BMWs, and Airstreams stops as a body every few yards so someone can get out and take a family snapshot before a heart-stopping mountain vista, or watch white mountain goats lick antifreeze drips, or gaze into dank, ancient cedar groves. At Logan Pass, drivers circle the parking lot for an hour in an effort to view the granite majesty of America's most spectacular scenery from someplace other than the front seat of their car.

Both Glacier and Yellowstone national parks have set all-time records of two million and more than three million visitors, respectively. Yellowstone and Glacier's superintendents say that the national parks are at or nearing their carrying capacity and their budgets are stuck in 1980. "It's so full, it diminishes the experience the visitor should be having," says former Glacier superintendent Gil Lusk.

State and national forests are also hard-pressed. Facilities that haven't been maintained in a decade are crumbling under the bruising weight of traffic they weren't designed for. State park officials say their offices are understaffed and they are virtually helpless in the face of the onslaught. "Nobody asked us how to protect the resource and promote it at the same time," says Jim Domino, the former outdoor-recreation planner for Montana's Department of Fish, Wildlife, and Parks. "It all comes down to how much money we have." Now 6.5 percent of bed tax revenues goes to the 40 state parks for operations and maintenance, but in 1995 this amount came to only $530,000.

Although the goals of economic development have been fulfilled by the bed tax in a few regions of western Montana—for example, labor income has improved since the early 1990s in Flathead and Gallatin counties, almost entirely as a result of nonresident travel— not everyone who fought to pass the bed tax is happy. "The environmentalists thought tourism would be the salvation of Montana," recalls Sanna Kiesling, a former lobbyist for the Montana Environmental Information Center. "Now they're saying, 'Just give me a good, clean mine.'"

It isn't just the traffic congestion and smog filling western Montana's once-pristine valleys that have the environmentalists upset. The larger problem is that once people arrive, many—a great many—want to stay. In once-serene valleys where isolated lights glimmered faintly at night from a few ranch houses, there is now enough wattage to shout down the stars. Until the 1993 Montana legislature reformed the state's Subdivision and Platting Act, vast open spaces were carved into unregulated 20-acre parcels—called ranchettes—in country where 40 acres may be needed to support just one cow. Too small to ranch and too big to mow, these properties have become noxious weed beds spreading an insidious plague of knap-weed and leafy spurge throughout the region, destroying rangeland and forage for wildlife. The new subdivisions' wells and septic systems tax and degrade the state's extremely vulnerable and limited aquifers, and new houses and roads are playing a decisive role in the destruction of elk and bear habitat.

Wildlife biologists say that real estate development is a far greater threat to grizzly bears than logging or mining, fragmenting their range until the animals become isolated from one another and die out. Since 1980, the number of grizzlies in the Mission Mountains south of Glacier National Park, a tourism and real estate development hotbed, has dropped from 25 to between 10 and 15.

The construction industry is predicting that the Flathead Valley will have 200,000 residents in the next 10 to 20 years; it now has 60,000. The population of the Bitterroot Valley, some predict, will double by the year 2000. Populations in some regions of Gallatin County have already jumped 45 percent since the last census. "I think it will be worse than Aspen or Jackson Hole," says Wilson. "There is no ability to control development."

To Montana's promotional slogan, UNSPOILED, UNFORGETTABLE, one could easily add AND UNPREPARED. The state's tiny communities are overwhelmed trying to cope with this unforeseen and unplanned-for massive influx of out-of-staters. County sheriffs say they can no longer guarantee law-enforcement protection, pressed as they are by escalating violent crime and drug trafficking spread over immense distances, and by budgets and staff sizes that haven't changed in a decade. County governments warn home builders that they may not be able to find adequate water, get licensed for a septic system, have their mail delivered, or get their roads plowed or maintained. The tax base is too small, they say, to provide adequate infrastructure and services, and each new home puts the counties a little more in the hole, costing more in services than it pays in taxes.

Only a few years ago, one county planner was threatened with hanging for daring even to whisper the "z" word—zoning. In 1993, a building code department was created to allow the county to enforce the statewide uniform building code for the first time. But the department was quickly dissolved by a voter referendum with a majority of 70 percent. Residential developers still don't even need a building permit. Now Montanans are thronging to community planning meetings and organizing to raise money to hire planning

*"It isn't just the traffic congestion and smog filling western Montana's once-pristine valleys that have the environmentalists upset."*

consultants. Last year, a new Flathead County master plan that would have regulated and controlled growth was approved by the county commissioners as a result of such grassroots efforts. But then another group, Montanans for Property Rights, filed a lawsuit in district court to block the plan.

"We are still a conservative group of people up here," says Tom Esch, Flathead County Attorney. "We don't want the government telling us what to do. Even if the new master plan survives the lawsuit, implementing the regulations will be much harder; people won't go along."

To help the counties, some are calling for a repeal of the bed tax, or at the very least, a redirecting of some of its revenue to communities feeling the impact of tourism and development. In wet and foggy Kalispell, Brace Hayden, who works for Glacier National Park to shape development around the park, says he has found the community to be very concerned about its future. "The people I know say, 'Wait a minute, we're losing this place,'" he says. "I don't think the state has thought this through."

Annual surveys by the University of Montana's Institute for Tourism and Recreation Research, conducted at the discretion of the tourism industry, show that since 1991 Montanans have felt increasingly crowded by visitors. Although 72 percent of residents in little-visited Glendive, on the North Dakota border, view tourism favorably, the reaction in the heavily visited communities of western Montana is less enthusiastic: Only 43 percent of Whitefish residents and 49 percent of Bitterroot Valley residents believe that the benefits of tourism outweigh the costs.

According to political insiders, the tourism lobby, powered by bed tax revenues, has become invincible in Helena, the state capital, able to protect its vested interest. During the 1995 legislative session—the legislature meets for three months every two years—none of the many initiatives to reduce or redirect revenues from the bed tax went anywhere; they all died in committee. The state is now implementing a program to inform tourists about attractions in eastern Montana, far from the national parks, in an attempt to disperse the traffic.

Republican governor Marc Racicot says he is concerned about protecting Montana's quality of life, but he doesn't think the density of traffic has yet reached a level that demands control. "Any change will be discomfiting," Racicot says, "but all of us came from someplace else; we are all immigrants. Tourism poses its own special challenges. It is the consumption of something intangible. But it's given us a chance for economic development, and we think it's an important part of our future. We want to keep it strong and viable without threatening our culture."

On the road to Bozeman on a scorching Wednesday morning, the air is so parched that I've taken to spraying my throat with a saline-filled atomizer to keep bronchitis at bay, and I'm so dehydrated my lips have split open. A week before this trip, 14 wildland firefighters died on Storm King Mountain in Colorado, and this arid air has set the stage for the blow-torch that is to follow in Montana.

I enter Bozeman via North Seventh Avenue, a mile-and-a-half-long strip of national restaurant and motel chains and auto-parts centers. Downtown there is no place to park, but there are no parking meters, either. Fashionable clothing and shoes rivet my eyes to the store windows. Main Street, Bozeman, has gone from being the haunt of rodeo cowboys to being the Rodeo Drive of Montana. There is Italian on the menu of the newest restaurant, though that doesn't stop it from following the dictates of Montana gourmet cuisine: Put cream sauce on everything.

Bill Bryan, the owner of Off the Beaten Path, a company specializing in "Personal Itinerary Planning for the Rocky Mountain West," and I are having lunch, and we speculate about the effects on tourism of publishing an article entitled "Food of Montana."

Like John Wilson, Bryan spent many years as a professional environmentalist; in 1987 he started his own travel business. "When I got involved, I had romantic and naive ideas about responsible tourism. Now that I'm into it, I'm almost cynical as to whether there is anything responsible about tourism and whether tourism per se can be done in an appropriate manner for the economy and the community."

Bryan feels strongly that the state should stop promoting travel in Montana. "Instead, they should be wrestling with the long-term impact on the state as it grows," he says. "But the tourism industry isn't ready to think about responsible tourism—we're just thinking about making money."

Bryan suggests that those who do visit Montana can be responsible by hiring local naturalists, fishermen, hunters, and outfitters to guide them, so that the money they spend stays in the state instead of going to some national chain or outfitting company based elsewhere. These types of services, he feels, also encourage cultural exchange; visitors get to know people who are active in their communities and from whom they can learn what life in Montana is really like.

I spent such a day on the wild, snow-melt-swollen Big Blackfoot River—a trout fishery in recovery from decades of abusive mining and logging practices—with Bob Page, a Missoula-based itinerant logger who is looking for new economic opportunity as a fishing guide now that the timber supply in the Northwest is drying up. My father is in town from New Jersey for just a few days, and I want him to have a great time fishing a local river and meeting some terrific people. Page, with his affable personality, intimate knowledge of the Blackfoot, and deluxe pontoon boat, is just the person we are looking for.

We meet in the alley behind Bob's house in town, and the three of us pile into the cab of his pickup to brave a rainy June day on the river. (In western Montana, days in June are usually rainy.) The mountains surrounding the Potomac Valley are black with water-soaked pines, and the dark sky hangs low. While Bob mans the oars and hands out fishing tips with genial diplomacy—"downstream, now, to the shore, there's a good spot," he coaches—we thrash the wild water, casting our lines into the wind until our arms ache, our fingers numb in the cold. The day yields no trout, but there are other trophies: the music of water slapping the pontoons, the sight of bald eagles circling over us, the dark, arrowy pines gracing the shore, and plenty of goofy humor and bad puns expressed between slugs of beer.

While Page is doing his best to survive in Montana by switching from tree-felling to angling, others are hanging on to their way of life by sharing it with visitors. One program the state is developing along these lines is ranch recreation. Ranchers, who have always been hard-pressed to make their marginal livings from cattle and hay, are now taking guests into their homes and letting them help out with the chores for a fee, usually about $100 a night. Unlike dude ranches, these are not resorts, but real working cattle ranches.

One such ranch family is the Zimdarses, of the tiny hamlet of Polaris in southwest Montana. Lorie Zimdars, who grew up on a farm in northeastern Montana, and her husband, Calvin, bought their 2,800-acre dream ranch after a two-year search all over Montana and northern Wyoming, but they soon found they needed a way to subsidize their cattle and quarter horse operation. They built a two-bedroom log cabin about a quarter-mile down the lane from their historic two-story log home in the dry foothills of the East Pioneers and sent out the word that they and their three children—Charlie, 14, Clarissa, 10, and Jay, 5—would welcome families interested in experiencing ranch life.

"We've been in agriculture all our lives," says Lorie, a blond, round, sweet-natured woman who applies herself to ranching, wifing, mothering, and quarter horse breeding with verve and pride. She's wearing a sweatshirt that says CHILDREN FIRST. At the breakfast table she and her husband have a certain ease and comfort between them that feels good to be around; they tease each other affectionately. We're in the log-beamed great room of their beautifully crafted pioneer-era home. A big fan is blowing over Lorie's latest project—grass seed soaked overnight in a galvanized steel tub and now drying so it can be sown on her new lawn. In this arid region, it's been one of Lorie's dreams to have a lawn.

Calvin is scooping up a plateful of home fries. He's dressed for a cold morning on the range: a beat-up felt-brim hat decorated with feathers and dust, blue satin athletic jacket over a gray quilted vest, jeans, and mud-caked cowboy boots. He sports a handlebar mustache and the ubiquitous snoose in his teeth. In the dusty yard, he points out the shed where he reloads his own cartridges for his hunting rifles, a great passion of his.

The sun climbs through the fog as the Zimdarses' Suburban climbs onto the back of their federal grazing allotment, crushing the sagebrush so it sweetens the air as we go. Soon the view opens up. Mount Baldy rises over meadows and rolling, sage-dotted hills, and dark timber runs down to Farlin Creek, where pussy toes and lupine

*"Ranchers, who have always been hard-pressed to make their marginal livings from cattle and hay, are now taking guests into their homes and letting them help out with the chores for a fee, usually about $100 a night."*

grow among the quaking asps. Calvin and Lorie promise they'll let me come back and ride with them in the fall, when it's time to bring the cattle down.

John Wilson and I are walking the streets of Helena, talking about what the pressures of development could mean to operators like Page and the Zimdarses. "Tourism in Montana depends on open space and the agricultural/cowboy culture, fishing with scenery, grizzly bears, elk," he says. "What we need to do now is realize that these elements are the basis for our economic development and protect them—and we have failed miserably. We're killing the goose that laid the golden egg."

The state's new plan to disperse travel by extolling the virtues of Missouri River Country, the vast arid, windy plains of eastern Montana, to potential visitors is a strategy that is experimental at best; no one knows if it will help western Montana or what the impact on eastern Montana will be. But John Wilson says he sees potential. "We still have the opportunity to do things differently," he says. "There are no models for Montana. We are 20 years behind the rest of the nation in development. We're even more valuable now."

# III. Legislation and Politics

## Editor's Introduction

In the United States, persuading Congress to enact legislation that protects the environment is among the strategies most often employed to conserve wildlife. Because habitat protection is critical to a species' survival, laws that are good for the environment—for example, those promoting clean air and clean water—also preserve wildlife. Although studies have shown that a majority of the American public supports environmental-protection legislation, coalitions representing industry and development interests oppose federal rules and restrictions on their activities on the grounds that regulations are expensive and/or ineffective. The 104th Congress, which was elected in 1994 and served in 1995 and 1996, tried to enact a slew of measures under the banner of deregulation that would have undercut environmental-protection laws. As Vicki Monks explains in "Capitol Games," the first selection reprinted in this section, much of this activity took place with little or no public awareness. In many cases, riders were attached to appropriations bills; these amendments excluded certain areas or industries from complying with the very regulations specified in the legislation. The piecemeal, complicated procedures by which bills and riders can become law ensured that the battle would continue in the 105th Congress.

The second selection in "Legislation and Politics," a commentary reprinted from *Field & Stream*, exhorts sportsmen to take note of the threat posed to hunting and fishing resources by "takings" legislation, which the author, John McCoy, defines as "laws requiring government to pay compensation for any regulation limiting what property owners can do with their land." Whereas until recently property-rights law, rooted in the Fifth Amendment's declaration that "no property shall be taken for public use without just compensation," was interpreted narrowly, to mean that the government will pay landowners whose property or mineral rights it literally "takes," federal and state laws based on this principle are now being stretched by lobbyists for the so-called wise-use movement to encompass any infringement of landowners' rights. Many conservationists and sportsmen's groups are opposed to this concept of "takings" legislation. The alliance between hunters and environmentalists is addressed in the third selection, an article reprinted from *Sierra* by Ted Williams, who identifies himself as a hunter, fisherman, and environmentalist.

# Capitol Games[1]

During the late 1980s, when a series of unexplained illnesses felled livestock on Sue Pope's ranch in Midlothian, Texas, no one made a connection to the cement kiln down the road. Residents had heard that a nearby kiln was burning waste oil as fuel in the production of cement, but, Pope says, nobody thought much of it then. "For the longest time, we just thought that Lady Luck had stopped smiling on us," she says.

Cattle collapsed with mysterious neurological ailments and had to be destroyed. Calves were born with grotesque deformities, and several of Pope's prized Arabian horses could no longer produce foals. Then, Pope and many of her neighbors began to develop health problems of their own, including cancer, endometriosis, respiratory disease and heart trouble. "In 1991, someone handed me a pamphlet saying that these kilns were burning toxic waste," Pope says. "That's when everything clicked."

The kiln in this small town about 30 miles south of Dallas began supplementing its fuel with toxic waste in 1987. Last year alone it burned 130,000 tons of hazardous waste, mostly paint thinners, solvents and oil-refinery residues. Although Texas environmental officials so far have not connected kiln emissions directly to local health problems, cement kilns that burn toxic waste can release dioxins, heavy metals and other pollutants linked with cancer and other health problems. Consequently, the Environmental Protection Agency (EPA) has begun a study in Midlothian of the birth defects among local farm animals, and the Texas Health Department is investigating an unusual number of Down's syndrome children born to families living within 10 miles of the kiln.

Cement kilns for years have been burning thousands of tons of toxic waste annually in the United States. Because they burn toxics as fuel rather than as waste, the kilns have been regulated by interim federal rules that are not as strict as those for commercial hazardous-waste incinerators. However, a task force appointed by the chairman of the Texas Air Control Board recently concluded that regulations on the kilns should be tightened to bring them in line with regulations for toxic-waste incinerators, which burn many of the same materials.

The EPA agreed, and in 1995 was ready to set such standards. The proposed rules, the culmination of a decade-long examination, would require kilns to use the best technology available to reduce emissions. But just as those standards were about to become final, along came the 104th Congress, with a new majority elected in 1994.

The 104th Congress set out to undercut a broad range of environmental regulations. One rider on the EPA funding bill aimed to soft-

*"The 104th Congress set out to undercut a broad range of environmental regulations."*

---

[1]Article by Vicki Monks, from *National Wildlife* 34:22-28 Ap/My '96. Copyright ©1996 National Wildlife Federation. Reprinted with permission.

en the new cement-kiln rules and could have exempted some kilns from implementing the new technology-based air-emission controls.

That rider did not sit well with residents living near Midlothian's cement kiln. "If there had been hearings, if there had been any input from the public, it would be different," says Jim Schermbeck of Downwinders at Risk, a Midlothian citizens group. "But there was no opportunity for the public to participate. It's a backdoor way of getting these kilns off the hook."

The kiln rider illustrates how the [104th] Congress is bending 30 years of environmental laws to serve the needs of industry rather than the needs of the public at large. When the 104th Congress was called to order in January 1995, the new congressional majority set to work implementing House Speaker Newt Gingrich's (R-Georgia) Contract with America. One of the charges abundantly set forth in that document was the deregulating of America—cutting back on the rules and regulations that safeguard the health and safety of Americans at home, outdoors and in the workplace. The main argument advanced for these cutbacks: The regulations were too expensive for industry.

Though the Contract with America never explicitly mentioned the environment, the 104th Congress pursued an anti-environmental agenda astonishing in its scope. It included proposals to exempt oil refineries from the regulatory power of the Clean Air Act, speed up logging of dwindling remnants of old-growth forest, eliminate protection for at least 60 percent of remaining wetlands, and prohibit regulations that would limit arsenic, radon and microorganisms in drinking water.

In many cases, Congress never debated these proposals on their merits. Legislators slipped them stealthily into funding bills during committee sessions. These riders—like hitchhikers on a freight train—frequently bore little relationship to the legislative vehicles that carried them along. But using the appropriations process in this way helped to avoid messy showdowns over individual proposals and improved chances that otherwise unpopular measures might speed to passage.

The technique also gave Congress some leverage over White House objections. If both houses of Congress load critical funding bills with add-ons, the president must either accept amendments he finds distasteful or veto the entire package and face a shut-down of government services.

A major congressional push on deregulation last year shows how the rider ploy works. The story begins even before the 1994 elections, when Project Relief, an alliance of 350 powerful corporations, organized a campaign reportedly to roll back regulations that its members thought onerous. The group set the stage for its legislation by directing more than $19 million in contributions to congressional campaigns during one election cycle (two years for House members, six for senators). According to a 1995 study by the Environmental Working Group, a nonprofit research organization based in Washington, D.C., political action committees funded by

Project Relief contributed $87,126 to House Speaker Gingrich and more than $330,000 each to Senate Regulatory Task Force members Kay Bailey Hutchison (R-Texas) and Larry Craig (R-Idaho), all leaders in the regulation-reform movement.

The Project Relief effort seemed to pay off for industry when, in early 1995, the House approved regulatory reform as part of a bill euphemistically titled the Job Creation and Wage Enhancement Act. The bill would have set up a risk-assessment process requiring agencies to prove that benefits of government regulations outweigh potential costs. For instance, EPA would not be allowed to regulate carcinogenic benzene emissions from oil refineries unless the agency could prove that the dollar value of lives saved or health problems avoided is greater than the costs to the oil industry of installing pollution controls. Industry would be allowed to mount legal challenges at any step of the complicated process. Analysts on all sides of the issue acknowledged that this provision could make the initiation of important new public-health protections impossible—which was the ultimate goal, of course.

Reform advocates found smooth sailing in the new House of Representatives but hit stormy weather in the Senate, which was considering its own regulatory-reform legislation. Sponsored by Senate majority leader Bob Dole (R-Kansas), the bill included language to repeal the Delaney Clause, a law that since 1958 has prohibited cancer-causing pesticide residues in processed food. The White House Office of Management and Budget estimated that if the Senate version were enacted, the government would have to hire an additional 14,500 employees and spend an additional $3.5 billion yearly to perform the risk-assessment analyses the law required. In the end, opponents launched a filibuster to keep Dole from bringing the bill to a vote. After trying three times unsuccessfully to end the filibuster, Dole finally dropped the bill.

At this point, House Republicans sensed that reforms of the sort they wanted would not make it through the Senate if submitted as direct legislation. So early last November, House members tried an indirect approach, attaching to a critical spending bill a 112-page amendment that was virtually the same regulatory-reform wish list that Project Relief had been pushing. The vehicle for this rider—the debt-ceiling bill—was an essential piece of legislation needed to raise federal debt limits so the government would not default on loans. The Senate passed it, but President Clinton promptly vetoed it because of the House rider.

Congress repeated this pattern again and again, adding policy changes to omnibus budget legislation and to appropriations bills for nearly all government agencies. "Plenty of the attacks on environmental laws took place out in the open, but some of the more extreme measures were never publicly discussed," says Mary Marra, a National Wildlife Federation vice president and national staff director for conservation programs. "There's something wrong when so many important decisions are made behind closed doors. It's an affront to the democratic process."

*"'There's something wrong when so many important decisions are made behind closed doors. It's an affront to the democratic process.'"*

An embarrassing memo leaked last May revealed that an Endangered Species Act reauthorization bill introduced by Senator Slade Gorton (R-Washington) and designed to undermine the law's authority had been drafted by a coalition representing timber, mining, ranching, oil-and-gas and other businesses. Likewise, Representative Mike Oxley's (R-Ohio) bill revising Superfund contained language nearly identical to sections of a "working document" being promoted by major oil companies.

The *New York Times* reported last year that Republican leaders were "unapologetic about the access they are affording industry lobbyists," insisting that their alignment with business is little different from Democratic alliances with labor unions and environmental groups. But Marra demurs. "There's a tremendous difference between groups that are working to protect the health and safety of all Americans and industry associations seeking to improve their own profits at the public's expense," she says. "The failure to recognize that distinction is part of what's wrong in this Congress."

The 104th Congress has pursued its agenda even in the face of voter opposition. A wide range of opinion polls shows that a substantial majority of voters—both Republican and Democrat— oppose rolling back environmental protections. In an October TIME/CNN poll, two-thirds of the Republicans surveyed opposed reducing protection for endangered species, and an equal number objected to opening Alaska's Arctic National Wildlife Refuge to oil drilling. A majority of Republicans also expressed opposition to expanded logging, mining and ranching on public lands. The poll found comparable opinions among Democrats.

Similarly, an August Times-Mirror poll reported that 70 percent of Americans believe that pollution laws have not gone far enough, and 61 percent believe air-pollution controls are too weak. Even in the conservative state of Arizona, a majority said they would be willing to pay higher taxes if it meant greater protection for the environment, according to a Northern Arizona University survey.

The reason that many elected officials chose to ignore public opinion: money. According to the Environmental Information Center, a public-interest group, during a single five-year period, Oxley, who attempted to shrink the power of the Superfund law, accepted $321,310 in campaign funds from oil, insurance, waste-management and other companies seeking to reduce their liability for toxic-waste cleanups under Superfund. Another study found that during another five-year period, 54 political action committees (PACs) representing oil-and-gas interests contributed an average of $77,929 to each senator who later voted to open the Arctic National Wildlife Refuge to drilling.

According to an analysis of Federal Election Commission records conducted by the Washington, D.C.-based Public Interest Research Group (PIRG), industries lobbying to weaken the Clean Water Act made campaign contributions in excess of $57 million between 1989 and the 1994 election. The donations came from political action committees organized by chemical, pesticide, oil-and-gas, real-estate and agricultural interests. A similar link between donations and votes can be found on measures to relax pesticide restrictions, revoke endangered species protections and reduce wetlands protection.

In late November, the Federal Election Commission filed suit against the Republican political action committee GOPAC, charging that the organization illegally provided support for Gingrich's 1990 reelection campaign. Gingrich, who headed GOPAC until last May, denies any wrongdoing. Indeed, at a hearing held last fall to explore campaign-finance reform, Speaker Gingrich argued that PAC contribution limits should be increased to allow more money to flow into the political process.

This was the sort of political environment in which, last June, Republican budget writers released a list of 62 federal programs they wanted to stop funding. Included were the Endangered Species Act, water- and air-pollution standards and wetlands protection. Although these laws would not be repealed, GOP leaders sought to ensure that no money would be available to carry on the work. While the final budgets sent to President Clinton were not quite so extreme, deep cuts remained in most environmental programs. For example, the House proposed a 34 percent reduction in EPA funds that included a $560 million cut to the Superfund budget—translating into delays or suspension of toxic-waste cleanups at more than 250 communities in 44 states.

A selection of some of the other critical measures with which Congress worked last year shows how some legislators are trying to reconfigure American environmental protection:

• **The Clean Water Act:** On May 16, 1995, the House approved legislation that would have allowed greater discharges of industrial pollutants into U.S. waters; waived certain pollution limits for oil-and-gas, pulp-and-paper, mining and other industries; let cities dump more sewage into offshore coastal waters; rolled back controls on polluted runoff; reduced wetland protection; and required taxpayers to compensate landowners blocked from filling or draining wetlands on their property—even if the filling or draining would cause flooding on a neighbor's land.

A U.S. Army Corps of Engineers analysis concluded last year that under this legislation, more than 90 percent of the wetlands in South Carolina, Georgia and Alabama would lose protection. South Dakota, Nebraska, Wyoming and Florida could lose considerably more than half their wetlands. Even so, the revisions to the 1972 Clean Water Act easily passed the House.

The measure stalled in the Senate, however, when moderate Republican senator John Chafee [of] (R-Rhode Island)—who heads the Environment and Public Works Committee, which had jurisdiction over the bill—prevented the revised act from moving forward. To circumvent the Senate's delay, House members simply attached key Clean Water Act revisions as riders on the EPA appropriations bill. Representatives Sherwood Boehlert (R-New York), Louis Stokes

(D-Ohio) and other moderates sought to kill the amendments through the ensuing months. Nevertheless, in December an EPA spending bill with a few riders still firmly attached won approval in the House and Senate. President Clinton subsequently vetoed it.

• **Arctic National Wildlife Refuge**: Congress sought to open the last pristine stretch of Alaskan Arctic coastline—the 100 miles of shore in the Arctic National Wildlife Refuge—to oil-and-gas development by inserting an amendment into the omnibus budget reconciliation bill. Supporters claimed that the oil was needed for national security, but two facts fly in the face of this assertion: Last year, the House voted to lift a 22-year-old ban on the export of oil from Alaska's North Slope, and the Senate inserted a mandate into the energy-appropriations bill to sell 7 million barrels of oil from the nation's Strategic Petroleum Reserve.

Opening the refuge to drilling has long been opposed by environmentalists because development could jeopardize the area's wildlife species and the Native cultures dependent on them. Moreover, on the refuge issue, the 104th Congress did not have the bulk of U.S. citizens on their side. A poll conducted by Lake Research, Inc. for the Wilderness Society found that voters opposed drilling in the refuge by a margin of four to one. Nevertheless, Congress held firm. But President Clinton vetoed the budget bill on December 6 and promised to veto any other legislation that opens the Arctic National Wildlife Refuge to oil-and-gas development.

• **Endangered Species and Vanishing Ecosystems**: In July, President Clinton signed a compromise budget bill that rescinded certain funds that had already been appropriated in the last Congress. The bill helped to shrink government spending, but also included a rider with farreaching consequences for national forests and endangered species in the Pacific Northwest. This rider waived Endangered Species Act protections and all other environmental laws that might be applied to timber "salvage" operations in the national forests of the Pacific Northwest.

Amendment supporters argued that the waivers permitted dead and dying trees in national forests to be cleared quickly before rot renders them commercially useless. But the law defines salvage trees so broadly that it includes even healthy trees, that are merely susceptible to disease or insect infestation. "We've been joking that this salvage law only applies to trees that are made of wood," says a U.S. Forest Service biologist in Oregon. "But that's basically true. Even young, healthy stands are subject to disease."

The salvage-logging rider did not stop there. The legislation also contained direct assaults on endangered species. Tracts of old-growth forest that had been set aside previously as habitat for a threatened bird species, the marbled murrelet, were specifically included in areas to be logged even though the trees were healthy.

A rewrite of the Endangered Species Act, sponsored by House Resources Committee Chairman Don Young (R-Alaska) and Richard Pombo (R-California) and approved by the House Resources Committee, goes even further. It would redefine harming a listed species to mean only direct action against a plant or animal and would exclude losses due to habitat damage. In addition, more amendments designed to cripple enforcement of the act were slipped into other bills. Language on page 633 of the massive budget reconciliation bill would have eliminated a crucial requirement that federal agencies take endangered species into account before going forward with major plans such as designating areas to be opened to grazing or logging. According to John Kostyack, legal counsel in NWF's Conservation Division, this provision, later dropped, would have allowed irreversible damage to endangered species before alternatives to destructive federal plans were even considered.

Under an amendment to the Farm Bill introduced by Representative Wayne Allard (R-Colorado), the U.S. Forest Service would be forbidden to develop management plans designed to protect biological diversity. The Forest Service could act only when "the continued existence" of a species would be jeopardized, meaning that the health of forest species could not be considered in assessment of logging plans unless those species are on the brink of extinction.

*"The Forest Service could act only when 'the continued existence' of a species would be jeopardized..."*

Riders on the Interior Department appropriations bill would stop designation of critical habitat for listed species, exempt federal land-management plans from Endangered Species Act requirements and impose a moratorium on new listings of endangered species. That means that efforts to take action on the 200 candidates for listing would come to a standstill. And all of this is in addition to a 24 percent overall funding cut for endangered-species conservation.

Other measures Congress proposed:

• The Senate included a rider in the EPA funding bill that would end protection of groundwater from biological contaminants, such as the cryptosporidium bacteria that killed 104 people and sickened nearly half a million in Milwaukee in 1993 and that has prompted boil-water alerts in 35 states since then.

• A Senate amendment to the Interior Department appropriations bill called for increased logging in Alaska's Tongass National Forest, the largest remaining expanse of old-growth forest in the United States.

• A House amendment to the Transportation funding bill banned stricter fuel-efficiency standards for automobiles.

• A bill sponsored by House Majority Whip Tom DeLay (R-Texas) would repeal Clean Air Act rules designed to phase out production of ozone-depleting chlorofluorocarbons.

Some of these proposals died before they became law. This happened at least in part because the American people began to make it clear that they would not stand for undoing important environmental protections established during the past three decades. In the end, citizen voices could make a difference with this Congress.

In Texas, the Downwinders group turned up the heat on the two congressional representatives who promoted the cement-kiln rider—Democrat Jim Chapman, whose Texas district includes a hazardous-waste processor, and Republican Joe L. Barton, who represents Midlothian. Sue Pope confronted Barton at a town meeting, generating local press coverage of the heretofore little-noticed kiln amendment, and the group followed up with a barrage of faxes and letters asking every Texas congressperson to oppose the measure. The rider was among measures that died when Clinton, in part responding to citizen opposition to environmental deregulation, vetoed the EPA funding bill.

## MORE SKIN CANCER?

**Inside Congress:** House Majority Whip Tom DeLay (R-Texas) introduced legislation last year that would repeal Clean Air Act rules requiring phaseout of ozone-depleting chlorofluorocarbons and end U.S. commitment to the Montreal Protocol, an international agreement set to eliminate CFC use worldwide.

**Outside Congress:** Without the Montreal Protocol, Europe and North America will receive 35 percent more ultraviolet radiation than they do now. In one study, EPA estimated that failing to stem ozone depletion would yield 145 million cases of skin cancer and 2 million deaths by 2075.

## LAND THEFT?

**Inside Congress:** Senator Pete Domenici's (R-New Mexico) proposed Public Rangelands Management Act would require the Bureau of Land Management to manage its public lands primarily for the benefit of ranchers. Cattlemen could restrict all public access to land on which they hold grazing leases. The National Environmental Policy Act would no longer apply, putting an end to legal challenges over destructive grazing practices.

**Outside Congress:** Recent studies, including one by BLM itself, indicate that 60 percent of BLM arid western U.S. grasslands are in only fair to poor condition because of grazing impacts such as streamside erosion, compression of fragile soils and loss of vegetation. BLM lands receive more than 60 million recreational visits yearly. The BLM spends nearly $100 million yearly on range management but nets less than $15 million in rancher lease fees.

## UNSAFE DRINKING WATER?

**Inside Congress:** The House and Senate sought to curtail EPA development and enforcement of national standards for drinking-water contaminants.

**Outside Congress:** A variety of studies indicate that present federal standards for contaminant levels may not be strict enough to protect young children, pregnant women and the elderly. A 1995 EPA study concluded that 30 million Americans drink tap water from systems that violate one or more public health standards. A recent poll indicates that 76 percent of Americans who voted in the last election want Congress to strengthen safe drinking-water laws.

# The Takings Issue[2]

Imagine living in a place where farmers sue the government when deer eat their crops; where taxpayers pay developers to obey zoning laws; where regulators pay polluters not to pollute. If you're a sportsman, you undoubtedly find that shocking, but right now in Congress and in legislatures across the United States, lobbyists are pushing for laws requiring government to pay compensation for any regulation limiting what property owners can do with their land.

Advocates of this new legislation, known as "takings," ordinarily disguise their intent in language evoking images of the embattled farmer taking a stand against the forces of the king.

Of course, property-rights law already exists. It's called the fifth amendment, and it declares that "...no property shall be taken for public use without just compensation." This means that if the state wants to build a new road on your land, the state must pay you for property taken. Likewise, if you own valid existing mineral rights to a tract that later becomes a national park, you can sue the Park Service because your ability to exploit those mineral rights has been taken.

Those definitions of "takings" have been upheld by the courts time and again down through the years. But today's "property-rights" advocates want "takings" to be defined much more broadly, especially in regard to government-imposed regulations—in essence, they want to have the right to sue any agency that forces them to do anything they don't want to do.

If the idea sounds extraordinarily libertarian, that's because it is. Chicago law professor Richard Epstein actively promoted the concept in the mid-1980s, and former Attorney General Edwin Meese tried to employ it as a brake to slow federal and state regulatory efforts.

According to Charles Fried, the nation's solicitor general from 1985 to 1989, the Reagan administration's grand plan "was to make government pay compensation...every time its regulation impinged too severely on a property right—limiting the possible uses for a parcel of land or restricting or tying up a business in regulatory red tape." In other words, any regulation regarding property use would be considered as having taken the property in question.

A number of takings-based lawsuits were filed during Meese's tenure. The state of Alaska, for instance, filed a $29 billion suit against the United States, arguing that federally designated Wilderness Areas, Wild and Scenic Rivers, and other protected areas reduce state profits from mining and oil drilling.

In Wyoming, a group of ranchers sued the state, claiming that bag limits on deer and other wildlife had taken the landowners' ability to manage the land as they saw fit. On June 8, 1994, a federal judge

---

[2]Article by John McCoy, from *Field & Stream* 99:26+ Ap '95. Copyright © 1995 John McCoy. Reprinted with permission.

ruled against the ranchers, but the case has since been appealed. If the lower court's finding is overturned, the case could have far-reaching impacts on states' abilities to manage wildlife populations. June Rain, executive director of the Wyoming Wildlife Federation, said the ranchers' suit strikes at the very heart of a time-honored tradition—that a state's wildlife belongs to its people.

If history is any indication, the Wyoming suit won't be upheld, because wildlife accounts for just a fraction of the land's property value, and most Supreme Court judgments have held that property must lose its entire value before a "taking" can be said to have occurred.

Property-rights advocates disagree with this concept, and lobbyists for the "wise-use movement" and the Rocky Mountain Legal Defense Fund have crisscrossed the country, pushing for state and federal laws that can be interpreted more broadly. At the same time, they have been spreading their concept of property rights to regional, state, and local lobbying groups.

*"Courts historically have ruled that property owners must obey laws protecting others' property rights."*

Considered at face value, the arguments sound good—that property owners shouldn't have limits placed on their activities; that the Constitution guarantees owners the "highest and best," or most profitable, use of their land; and that any regulation that affects the value of that property is a taking of landowner rights.

But a closer look reveals a troubling picture. What would happen to the rights of neighboring property owners, or the community at large, if all land-use restrictions were canceled? Courts historically have ruled that property owners must obey laws protecting others' property rights. Zoning laws are a case in point. Without them, quiet residential areas could be invaded by factories, bars, massage parlors, or whatever a property owner chooses. Takings lobbyists leave this out when they woo lawmakers.

Bills have been introduced in Congress and in more than forty state legislatures so far. Takings-related language in H.R. 9, one of the first bills introduced in the new Republican-controlled House of Representatives, calls for compensation if a regulation has as little as a 10-percent impact on a property's potential value. Other bills would require governmental agencies to study all potential impacts on all possible landowners before putting any future environmental regulations into effect.

Congressional Republicans plan to push hard for "takings reform." Shortly after the election that swept the GOP into power, Sen. Phil Gramm (R-TX) called the property-rights debate the "principal item" on the party's environmental agenda. He since has introduced a bill, S. 145, that would compensate landowners for any regulation or *existing* law that affected property value by 10 percent or $20,000, whichever is less. A National Wildlife Federation lawyer, Glenn Sugameli, argued that landowners could employ Gramm's bill to avoid compliance with game laws. "If you wanted to, you could open a game ranch and charge someone $100,000 to come and shoot bald eagles, and Gramm's bill would allow it to happen, because the Eagle Protection Act would be considered a 'takings,'" Sugameli said.

Despite broad-based opposition from environmental, conservation, and sportsmen's groups, six takings bills have made it through state legislatures—in Delaware, Indiana, Utah, Washington, Arizona, and West Virginia. All but the West Virginia bill, which dealt specifically with regulations imposed by just one agency, require budget-busting studies on proposed environmental regulations.

Arizona's voters already have had second thoughts about the takings bill their legislators passed. Fearing a Pandora's box of lawsuits from conservationists and businessmen alike, 80,000 fiscally minded Arizonans rushed to sign repeal petitions. In a referendum held during last November's election, voters repealed the measure, 60 percent to 40 percent.

Idaho's legislature also passed a study-based takings bill in 1993. Gov. Cecil Andrus vetoed it. Andrus, a former U.S. interior secretary renowned for his proconservation views, minced no words in his veto notice.

"This bill is not concerned with the protection of property owners and the promotion of the social welfare of Idaho citizens," he wrote. "Instead, its central focus is the protection of select property owners (developers, polluters, etc.) to do what they want regardless of [the effects of] their actions on their communities and their neighbors."

Andrus's thinking closely parallels that of other governors. Early in 1992, the National Governors' Association issued an anti-takings policy.

"The governors believe that the interpretation of the Fifth Amendment of the Constitution is the appropriate province of the courts, and that legislative requirements are not warranted," read the statement.

Despite formidable opposition from such widely varied groups as the National Wildlife Federation, the National Urban League, the Alliance for Justice, the AFL-CIO, the Izaak Walton League, the Sierra Club, the Western States Land Commissioners Association, the Consumers Union, the National Education Association, and Trout Unlimited, the takings movement hasn't gone away. Its proponents continue to find sympathizers.

Public awareness of the issue hasn't begun to catch up with the political debate. NWF lawyer Sugameli lamented the public's ignorance on takings-related matters. "We need to do a better job of informing the public," he said. "Anyone who truly supports the idea of property rights for average citizens should oppose takings bills."

Sugameli said politicians, too are only now becoming aware of the implications of takings-related legislation. He predicted that as elected officials become familiar with the issue's political potential, debate will heat up considerably.

By all indications, the issue ultimately will be settled in the halls of Congress. Considering what's at stake, the final showdown could well become the environmental battle of the century.

# Natural Allies[3]

Every spring, when cowslips blaze yellow in Meadow Brook and peepers jangle around the marshy fringes of Poler's Pond, I lead an evening "woodcock walk" to the Grafton Conservation Area, 50 miles west of Boston. This year 20 participants and a reporter met at the trailhead at 7:15 P.M. and, while robins whinnied and song sparrows trilled, I read them Aldo Leopold's "Sky Dance." Then, in the orange explosion of a Yankee sunset, we hiked up the ancient cowpath and took our seats under a dogwood stand. The Conservation Area is a 52-acre sanctum for such suburban outcasts as foxes, owls, hawks, wild turkeys, and eastern coyotes—a place of shade and shine where meadow and woodland wildflowers bloom from early spring to late fall, where ruffed grouse thunder out of old orchards tangled with bittersweet, where butterflies dance through milkweed silk that sails on the summer breeze and the breath of school children.

*"Environmentalists don't reach out to sportsmen..."*

Eight years ago when a developer was poised to replace the living cloverleaves with the asphalt kind, to run a sewer line up the cowpath and gouge out foundations for 50 houses, my wife, Donna, and I organized a crusade to save our special place. Everyone, especially me, thought it was impossible. But we brought people here, showed them the wildlife and the beauty, and somehow convinced our frugal community of 12,000 to cough up $1.3 million to buy the land.

I like to bring my woodcock watchers here half an hour before curtain call so they can absorb the wildness of the place, listen to church bells from old-Grafton center and birdsong from hardwood groves, and gradually convince themselves that the woodcock isn't going to show. When, finally, he materializes out of the afterglow and utters his first nasal "peeent," the excitement is tangible. Sometimes I hear gasps when he launches into the azure sky, fluttering and twittering between Venus and the Moon, then warbling and falling like an oak leaf almost to our feet. When I explain to the woodcock watchers that I will hunt these birds in October with a 12-gauge shotgun and my soul mate, a 60-pound Brittany named Wilton, some of them are visibly shocked and disappointed.

More than 50 million Americans fish, and 15 million hunt, yet environmentalists have made scant effort to forge any lasting alliance with them to protect the land and water that sustain wildlife. "Environmentalists don't reach out to sportsmen," says Chris Potholm, a professor of government and legal studies at Bowdoin College in Maine. "If they did, they'd be invincible. Whenever sportsmen combine with environmentalists, you have 60 to 70 per-

[3]Article by Ted Williams, from *Sierra* 81:46-53 + S/O '96. Copyright © 1996 Ted Williams. Reprinted with permission.

cent of the population, an absolutely irresistible coalition."
Consider the alliance between the Rocky Mountain Elk Foundation
and the National Fish and Wildlife Foundation, an agency set up
and funded by Congress to leverage matching conservation grants
from the private sector. The latter is run by a former National
Audubon Society lobbyist; the former by elk hunters. Working
together (and with help from other sportsmen and environmentalists), the alliance has protected or restored 1.8 million acres north
of Yellowstone National Park.

Consider also Trout Unlimited, perhaps the most effective force
for environmental reform among sportsmen's groups. What has
made Trout Unlimited so successful is that it is run by people who
are not just sportsmen or just environmentalists, but both. On
endangered species, grazing reform, mining reform, hydroelectric
relicensing, clean water, forest practices, river dewatering—Trout
Unlimited is on the front lines, suing every exploiter in sight and
generally raising hell.

Such conservation-minded sportsmen predominate in Alaska,
though you'd never know it from talking to state officials. Only three
years ago the Alaska Department of Fish and Game hatched a plan
to generate more moose, caribou, and hunting-license revenue by
shooting wolves from aircraft. "We feel we are going to create a
wildlife spectacle on a par with the major migrations in East Africa,"
effused Fish and Game's wildlife director David Kelleyhouse, known
to his many critics as "Machine-gun Kelleyhouse" because he once
tried to requisition a fully automatic weapon for "wolf management." Supporting this 1920s-style theory of game production was
then-Governor Wally Hickel, who explained to me and other journalists at a Fairbanks "wolf summit" that "you can't let nature just
run wild." Most journalists reported that the state was responding to
Alaskan hunters. But, as usual, hunters got a bum rap; a statewide
poll revealed that only 36 percent of them were in favor. Since then
typical Alaskan hunters—who admire wolves and understand
ecosystems—have joined with environmentalists to try to ban aerial
wolf hunting permanently. The Wolf Management Reform Coalition,
as the alliance is called, has already gathered enough signatures to
get such an initiative on the November 1996 ballot, and Alaskans are
showing strong support.

Success stories of this sort don't raise Professor Potholm's eye-
brows. Sixteen years ago he founded the Potholm Group, a national polling and strategic-advice company that has engineered some
unlikely habitat victories in 55 state referenda. For example, it's
hard to imagine a more hopeless task for the Great Basin Nature
Conservancy than convincing the residents of that 83 percent federally owned bastion of property-rights fanaticism called Nevada to
pass a $47 million bond issue for the purpose of acquiring *more*
public land. Initial polls indicated that the 1990 referendum would
lose by a margin of four to one, but subsequent research established
that it could be won if both hunters and anglers were brought on
board. The Great Basin Nature Conservancy informed sportsmen

that the bond issue was important not just for endangered species but for game and public access. When the referendum came up in November—at the height of national-budget panic—it won with two-thirds of the vote. "We've won referenda in Nevada, New Mexico, Florida, Rhode Island, Maine, Minnesota, and Arizona because we were able to get environmentalists and sportsmen to cooperate," reports Potholm. "We can win environmental referenda anywhere if we can get environmentalists and sportsmen working together. I can get the cowboys in Montana to vote to save the black-footed ferret if the enviros will let them hunt elk on the land.... The biggest mistake enviros make is they always look to the Democrats first. If I can get the sportsmen on board, then I get them to bring the Republicans."

*"Hunters and anglers have a long history of protecting and restoring fish, wildlife, and habitat."*

Hunters and anglers have a long history of protecting and restoring fish, wildlife, and habitat. They saved game (and many species now classified as non-game) from commercial market hunting, a practice that had no more to do with sport hunting than gillnetting has to do with angling. At the beginning of the 20th century there were about 500,000 white-tailed deer in the United States; today there are 27 million. Only 41,000 elk survived in 1907; now there are a million. In 1910 antelope were down to 5,000; today there are at least a million. A century ago wild turkeys were close to extinction; last spring there were 4.2 million.

Our 92-million-acre national wildlife refuge system was started by hunter Theodore Roosevelt. And it was saved by hunter J. N. "Ding" Darling, the Pulitzer prize-winning political cartoonist of the *Des Moines Register* who, with his fellow waterfowlers, pushed through a law in 1934 to require duck and goose hunters to purchase a federal permit in the form of a stamp (to be pasted to the state hunting license that they also had to buy). Since that day duck-stamp money has gone to purchase national wildlife refuges.

In Darling's cartoons one of the bloated, cigar-chomping politicians commonly seen evicting bandaged, splinted birds and animals from their happy homes was President Franklin D. Roosevelt. Dumb, FDR was not; so he wrestled the camel's head inside the tent by hiring Darling to direct the Bureau of Biological Survey, progenitor of the Fish and Wildlife Service. When the president broke his promise to fund the new national wildlife refuge system, Darling conspired with Senator Peter Norbeck of South Dakota to tack a $1 million appropriation to the duck-stamp bill. The hugely popular Norbeck spoke in such a heavy Norwegian accent that when he asked for something, his colleagues preferred to just say "yes" rather than undertake the daunting task of translation. No sooner had Norbeck taken the Senate floor than he removed his false teeth and, as Darling loved to tell it, "asked, in words totally devoid of understandable articulation, for an amendment to the bill allocating six million dollars."

"Aye," said the Senate, uncertainly. Darling had told Roosevelt to watch for the bill and sign it. Somehow, it appeared on the president's desk just as he was hurrying out the door to go fishing. On returning to the White House, FDR sent Darling this note: "As I was saying to the Acting Director of the Budget the other day, 'this fellow Darling is the only man in history who got an appropriation through Congress, past the Budget, and signed by the President without anybody realizing that the Treasury had been raided.'"

To raise money for wildlife management, hunters and anglers have successfully lobbied for excise taxes on fishing tackle and ammunition. Today, they are joining with other nature lovers to push for new excise taxes on an even wider range of outdoor products (such as backpacks, tents, birdseed, and field guides) that would provide an additional $350 million a year for ecosystem management. Leading the charge are the state game and fish directors who call themselves the International Association of Fish and Wildlife Agencies. Their initiative, "Teaming with Wildlife," has been endorsed by more than 1,000 environmental and sportsmen's organizations and businesses.

Formation of such alliances, however, has been painfully, dangerously slow. A major obstacle is the ease with which hunters are body-snatched by their worst enemies. They, much more than anglers, are paranoid because they have been beaten up so savagely and so long—not just by the animal-rights advocates but by society in general. I cannot count the number of times I have been shrieked at by anti-hunters. Once I drove away with one slashing at me with her fingernails and literally hanging from my truck window. Now, when they demand to know if I have a hunting license, I ask them if they have a badge.

Hunting advocate Michael Furtman, writing in the April 1996 issue of *Midwest Fly Fishing*, offers this explanation: "After a decade of attacks by the animal-rights movement, defensive sportsmen were like a dog too long in its kennel—literally panting for kindly attention. Anyone that would pat us on the head would be rewarded with our undying friendship. That the person reaching out a hand—the wise-use movement—was intent upon taking that 'dog' to a medical research facility never occurred to most of us."

While environmentalists have been ignoring or alienating sportsmen, developers and their hirelings within the wise-use movement and Congress have been seducing them by dressing up in camouflage and flouncing around at photo ops with borrowed shotguns. For example, the 50 senators and 207 representatives of the Congressional Sportsmen's Caucus loudly profess to defend fish, wildlife, and sportsmen but consistently vote to destroy habitat. In the House, 83 percent of the CSC supported H.R. 961, the bill that would basically repeal the Clean Water Act. By contrast, only 34 percent of non-caucus members supported the bill. Last year CSC members voted for fish, wildlife, and the environment an average of only 23 percent of the time (as recorded by the League of Conservation Voters) compared with 43 percent for the entire House and 47 percent for the entire Senate.

Leading the CSC in the Senate are Conrad Burns (R-Mont.; LCV score 0), John Breaux (D-La.; LCV score 29), Richard Shelby (R-Ala.; LCV score 0), and Larry Craig (R-Idaho; LCV score 0). House leadership consists of Don Young (R-Alaska; LCV score 0); Pete Geren (D-Tex.; LCV score 31); Toby Roth (R-Wis.; LCV score 8); and John Tanner (D-Tenn.; LCV score 31). These voting records make perfect sense when you check some of the funders of the caucus's money-raising tentacle, the Congressional Sportsmen's Foundation: Alabama Power, Alyeska Pipeline Service, Chevron, Dow Chemical, International Paper, Weyerhaeuser, Champion International, Mead, American Forest and Paper Association, National Cattlemen's Association, Olin, and Phillips Petroleum.

Just before the last election Don Young—arguably the most vicious enemy of fish and wildlife in Congress—used his CSC connection to persuade *Outdoor Life* to ooze and gush about his self-proclaimed greenness. The 99-year-old publication told its 1.3 million subscribers that Young "is your kind of politician," that he "fights the good fight," and that "you'd be hard pressed to find a more fearless Washington advocate of the sportsman's life." There followed a lengthy interview in which Young berated the long-silent animal-rights activist Cleveland Amory and puffed and blew about the public's right to bear arms. This from the magazine that had produced Ben East—a giant in outdoor journalism, a heroic defender of wild things and wild places, and grandfather of Sierra Club executive director Carl Pope. (*Outdoor Life* is now under a new editor.)

Then there is the Wildlife Legislative Fund of America, a front for developers, wise-users, and right-wing ideologues that wangles voluminous space in outdoor media. When U.S. Fish and Wildlife director Mollie Beattie (now deceased) moved to control such incompatible and illegal activities on wildlife refuges as overgrazing and jet-skiing, WLFA told sportsmen to send money so it could stop her from also banning hunting and fishing—something she had never dreamed of doing. The hook-and-bullet press swallowed it hook, line, boat, and motor. *Wildfowl Magazine* reported that non-hunter Beattie was plotting "to abandon waterfowl management on the refuges," and asked its readers to confirm the rumor that she was "wearing spandex shorts to work" just like Mariel Hemingway, last seen in an Audubon TV special "strutting around the Chincoteague National Wildlife Refuge in her spandex biking shorts and whining [about hunting being 'controversial'] like some PMS poster child."

When Beattie added 15 hunting programs and six fishing programs on refuges (something she had planned to do all along), WLFA bragged that it had "bloodied" the service and saved the refuge system for sportsmen. At this point, WLFA's national affairs director, Bill Horn—who, as assistant secretary for fish, wildlife and parks under James Watt, had crusaded to open the Arctic National Wildlife Refuge to oil drilling and invited developers into the whole refuge system—set about drafting (or "helping to draft," as he prefers) H.R. 1675, the "National Wildlife Refuge Improvement Act," for Don Young. When Horn, a lawyer, isn't working for WLFA, he offers counsel to such clients as Washington State property-rights zealots trying to block a new wildlife refuge and Florida condo developers seeking to restore subsidized federal flood insurance in order to build more profitably on coastal habitats.

The bait Horn and Young set out, to attract sportsmen to their refuge bill, was the elevation of hunting and fishing (already permitted on refuges wherever possible and appropriate) from "uses" to "purposes," thereby changing the official mission of the refuge system from protecting biodiversity to pleasuring humans. In the same vein, the bill would waive restrictions on military uses of refuges and require the Fish and Wildlife Service to get congressional approval to buy any new refuge over 500 acres with land and water conservation funds. On April 24—the day the bill passed the House—Mollie Beattie called it "the beginning of the end of the National Wildlife Refuge System as we know it."

Basically, WLFA attributes its victory to me. "More than any other factor," writes Vice President Rick Story in a letter to the 2,000 members of the Outdoor Writers Association of America, my "diatribe against the bill [in the May 1996 issue of the association's magazine] provided that much-needed surge of adrenaline which helped motivate our staff to continue plugging through the arduous last stages of the campaign to ensure the bill's passage.... Sportsmen and sportswomen nationwide did a fabulous job communicating their concerns to Congress." For once I agree with Mr. Story, at least with the last sentence. It's just that the House, as usual, didn't listen. Under the inspired leadership of the National Wildlife Federation, the Izaak Walton League of America, Trout Unlimited, and local hunting-and-fishing clubs in Montana, sportsmen and sportswomen nationwide were and are working closely with the environmental community to kill the bill. Now it looks as if the alliance will prevail. The refuge bill is expected to run into major trouble in the Senate, and in the unlikely event that it makes it through, interior secretary Bruce Babbitt will ask the president for a veto.

*"The big green groups such as the National Audubon Society and the Sierra Club have never opposed hunting."*

Even as the frightened hunter hears monster stories from the Congressional Sportsmen's Caucus and the Wildlife Legislative Fund of America, some environmentalists oblige by acting the part of anti-blood-sport bogeyman. The big green groups such as the National Audubon Society and the Sierra Club have never opposed hunting. In fact, they recognize the sport as a legitimate and necessary wildlife management tool. But they are perceived as anti-hunting because of embarrassing behavior by some of their members. Take the position of certain state Audubon chapters on mourning-dove hunting. At the same time agribusiness destroys the habitat of upland gamebirds such as grouse, quail, and pheasants it produces vast swarms of grain-eating doves. Over 2 million hunters legally kill about 50 million doves a year in 37 states without even denting the population. In farming states like Indiana and Michigan there is every good reason to hunt mourning doves and no reason not to.

For any sober, practical champion of biodiversity, dove hunting is the quintessential non-issue. Yet when I explained this in the March 1985 *Audubon*, as part of an eyewitness report on Indiana's first dove hunt, the editor was deluged with mail and wound up printing 49 letters, 26 of them irate. "Are robins next?" demanded one reader. "I would not object to destroying Ted Williams," wrote an other. "We have an overpopulation of his breed." After 11 years I thought that *Audubon* chapters might have learned something, and maybe they have. But in 1995, when Michigan tried to legislate a hunting season for its superabundant doves, the Michigan Audubon Society (the second biggest chapter with 40 sub-chapters of its own) shouted the bill down. "Many, in these violent times, point to the irony of a proposed hunting season on the international symbol of peace," it seriously asserted.

"They didn't have to support the bill," remarks wildlife management supervisor Richard Elden of the Michigan Department of Natural Resources, "just remain neutral and it might have passed. Michigan Audubon said its position was not an effort to oppose hunting, but it truly was. We have plenty of doves. They just plain opposed expanding legitimate hunting opportunity."

Such behavior plays into the hands of those seeking to discredit the entire environmental movement. "There are people out there day in and day out telling the public and Congress that environmentalists are anti-hunting," declares Paul Hansen, director of the Izaak Walton League of America, a conservation group composed largely of hunters and anglers. "To my knowledge, the environmental groups haven't done a thing to clarify it. Some of their members might be anti, but institutionally none of them are—not Defenders, not Audubon, and not the Sierra Club. If there's one piece of advice I have for environmental groups it's this: Get right up front and say that you aren't anti-hunting."

The traditional refusal of most environmental groups to do this fuels sportsmen's paranoia and makes it difficult to educate them about environmental politics. I know because I've been attempting such education for 26 years. The very word "environmental" engenders suspicion in the hook-and-bullet set. Therefore, I am the "Conservation Editor" of *Fly Rod & Reel*. As "Senior Editor" of *Gray's Sporting Journal*, I took elaborate pains to explain how much gunpowder I've burned whenever I wrote something to augment the me-and-Joe stories. Even so, I received and published countless letters like the following: "Ted Williams has betrayed sportsmen everywhere" and "If you insist on bringing up controversial environmental issues, you do not become a sportsman's magazine but an environmental magazine. There are too many 'do gooder' magazines on the market today and few that give you the joy of remembering a good hunt or the one that got away. Please review your policy and let's keep *Gray's* a clean magazine." Or consider this, recently published in *Fly Rod & Reel*: "Dear Mr. Williams: You are a good writer, but I am getting tired of paying my money to hear your political agenda. From what little I know of the 'wise-use movement,' they appear to have taken a different (perhaps better) slant on managing our environment. Let me enjoy reading about your skillful exploits. Leave the politics alone."

Six years ago when Defenders of Wildlife tried to initiate dialogue with hunters by joining the Outdoor Writers Association of America, a large element of the association fantasized that Defenders was somehow anti-hunting and moved to throw it out. Such a prolonged stink was raised that Defenders voluntarily withdrew. "All we had in mind was an occasional exchange of views," read the good-bye letter. "Yours for diversity, biological and otherwise, M. Rupert Cutler, President." Joel Vance, who had just finished his term as OWAA's president, upbraided us in our magazine as follows: "For shame! We've run off a group that wanted to communicate with us...and we call ourselves communicators? Naah, we're just a bunch of hypocrites who can't stand a contrary view." So if environmentalists can excuse sportsmen for fleeing into the arms of their worst enemies, maybe sportsmen can at least understand why reaching out to them hasn't always been that easy.

But lately both sides have been doing a whole lot better. One of the brightest spots has been *Sports Afield* magazine, now in the hands of a fearless, enlightened editor named Terry McDonell, who has been educating his readers with such exposés as: "The Misguided War Over Refuges," "A Bad Deal for Sportsmen: What's Wrong with the Contract with America," and "A Spring Sermon...Or Siberia" (an essay on why sportsmen need to work with environmentalists). And yet only five years ago, under a different editor, the magazine contributed $24,375 to the Congressional Sportsmen's Foundation and ran a 15-page supplement (largely paid for by gun and booze companies) in which CSC members got to write articles on behalf of their campaign contributors, one of the more nauseating bearing Don Young's byline and entitled "Why Alaska Sportsmen Support Opening the Arctic National Wildlife Refuge."

A year ago the 600,000-member Bass Anglers Sportsman Society (B.A.S.S.)—a conservative, for-profit organization with strong ties to the Republican Party—took on a new role of environmental activist. Bruce Shupp, the respected biologist B.A.S.S. hired to run its conservation program, set about forging what promises to be a political juggernaut—a sportsman-enviro alliance called the Natural Resource Summit of America. The catalyst was the disastrous "clean water" bill and its mouthy House sponsorship, which made the costly error of referring to B.A.S.S. on national TV as "an environmental extremist group."

The summit's goals have evolved way beyond just saving the Clean Water Act to striving for solidarity on such fronts as environmental law and natural-resources and public-lands policy. The third meeting of the summit, on March 4, was attended by such diverse groups as the Sierra Club, the American Fisheries Society, the Izaak Walton League, the American Sportfishing Association, the Wilderness Society, the International Association of Fish and

Wildlife Agencies, and the Environmental Defense Fund. "The whole complexion changed yesterday," Shupp said on March 5. "We went in a new direction. We've got a product now. We're going somewhere. After 25 years of splitting apart we finally got our act together, and we're talking to each other."

Much credit for the new unity must go to the 104th Congress. For instance, Senator Pete Domenici (R-N.M.) has introduced a grazing bill so hideous as to accomplish the impossible—that is, forge an alliance not just between enviros and sportsmen, but between sportsmen and animal-rights advocates. Basically, the bill would reserve public lands in the West for the ranching industry. If agents of the Forest Service or BLM had to check compliance on a grazing lease, they would need permission of the permittee to set foot on the public's land. Eleven of the bill's 16 original sponsors are members of the Congressional Sportsmen's Caucus, but sportsmen haven't been fooled. Lonnie Williamson—vice president of the Wildlife Management Institute and past president of the Outdoor Writers Association blasted the CSC and Domenici, calling the legislation "the Rangeland Rape Bill." Urging opposition to the bill in a joint letter to members of the Senate are 155 unlikely collaborators, including the Sierra Club and eight of its chapters, 11 Audubon Society chapters, Defenders of Wildlife, National Wildlife Federation, Republicans for Environmental Protection, Humane Society of the United States, the Fund for Animals, People for the Ethical Treatment of Animals, Izaak Walton League of America, California Bowmen Hunters and State Archery Association, and Sportsmen's Council of Central California.

Assisting Domenici in forging this new unity has been Congressional Sportsmen's Caucus co-chair Senator Conrad Burns (R-Mont.), who in his last election bid raised over half a million dollars from energy, mining, and agriculture interests. Burns has introduced a bill that would promote the sale and development of public land managed by the Forest Service, the BLM, and the Bureau of Reclamation. But Montana sportsmen-enviros, marching under such banners as the Montana Wildlife Federation, Billings Rod and Gun Club, and Anaconda Sportsmen's Association, are exposing Burns with a media blitz called "Keep Public Lands in Public Hands." The coalition's stated mission: "Save Montana's hunting heritage from the clutches of Conrad Burns and his crazy attempts to sell off our public lands." Stung by the bitter opposition from a group that had bowed and scraped for him in the past, Burns charged that the Montana Wildlife Federation "has lied about the bill" and dubbed the organization a "front group for [the] Democratic Party."

Meanwhile, in Yankeeland, my sportsman-environmentalist friends are being called the same thing whenever they complain about a Contract-on-America bill that would squander our nation's real wealth. Most of them belong to the grand old party of Abe Lincoln and Teddy Roosevelt, but unlike some of the new Republicans who allegedly represent them, they have a right to call

*"Urging opposition to the bill in a joint letter to members of the Senate are 155 unlikely collaborators..."*

themselves "conservatives."

On John Muir's birthday last April, Donna, Wilton, and I met one of them trudging out of the Grafton Conservation Area. Behind him on the cowpath were four women and a small boy. They'd read the story about Friday's woodcock walk in the morning paper and had hoped to see the show for themselves; but they said the woodcock had stood them up.

"You're ten minutes too early," I said. With that, we all filed back up to the dogwood patch, took our seats under a crescent moon that flashed through fast, pink clouds and, to the score of peepers, field sparrows, and distant church bells, watched a spectacular double sky dance by dueling males.

In the old days I used to lecture my generally anti-blood-sport woodcock watchers about what bird hunting means to me, and the words would always come out wrong. Now I just tell them how this wild, magic place came to be saved. We get along fine.

# IV. Managing Ecosystems

## Editor's Introduction

As the articles reprinted in the previous section demonstrate, much of the legislation enacted to protect wildlife concerns the use and administration of public lands: national parks, refuges, wetlands, and other sanctuaries. In the United States, which contains 261 types of ecosystems, designated wilderness areas account for 100 million acres. The history of the American national park system is the subject of the first selection here, in which Dave Foreman, a director of the Sierra Club and the founder of Earth First!, discusses the analogy that has been made between islands and national parks. Noting that islands that are isolated or far from the mainland lose more species than those that are part of an archipelago or that are closer to the mainland, conservation biologists have suggested that our isolated pockets of national parks are also losing species, and for similar reasons. Foreman argues that parks need to be linked together by habitat corridors and surrounded by buffer zones if their largest, most wide-ranging species are to survive.

In the second selection, Will Nixon discusses the issues involved in sustainable forestry, which seeks to simultaneously manage ecosystems and conduct limited logging. The third selection, "The Call of South Africa," by Victoria Butler (who is also the author of the piece on Zimbabwe's CAMPFIRE program in the fifth section of this book), looks at South Africa's highly successful conservation efforts. Whereas African species are dwindling in many areas as their habitats are reduced, South Africa's wildlife habitat has increased, to almost six million hectares (14.82 million acres). Butler provides a "tour" of several South African parks. In the fourth selection, "New Defenders of Wildlife," Jeffrey P. Cohn describes the unlikely conservation role played by American military bases, which cover 25 million acres of land in the United States. The fifth selection, "Accidental Sanctuary," by the novelist and naturalist Peter Matthiessen, explores an even less likely haven for wildlife: the demilitarized zone between the two Koreas. Uninhabited by humans for over 40 years, the 150-mile-long DMZ, which is 2.5 miles wide and is buffered by a Civilian Control Zone of about the same size on the South Korean border, is home to white-naped cranes and red-crowned cranes.

# Missing Links[1]

Field biologists, with their stubbornly insistent focus on the minutiae of the living world, are unlikely people to be scaring the bejesus out of us.

But they were the first to see, beginning back in the 1970s, that populations of myriad species were declining and ecosystems were collapsing around the world. Tropical rain forests were falling to saw and torch. Ocean fish stocks were crashing. Coral reefs were dying. Elephants, rhinos, gorillas, tigers, and other "charismatic megafauna" were being slaughtered. Frogs everywhere were vanishing. The losses were occurring in oceans and on the highest peaks, in deserts and in rivers, in tropical rainforests and arctic tundra.

Michael Soulé, a population biologist who founded the Society for Conservation Biology, and Harvard's famed entomologist E[dward] O. Wilson pieced together these disturbing anecdotes and bits of data. By studying the fossil record, they knew that during 500 million years of terrestrial evolution there had been five great extinctions. The last occurred 65 million years ago when the dinosaurs disappeared.

Wilson, Soulé, and company calculated that the current rate of extinction is as much as 10,000 times the normal background rate documented in the fossil record. That discovery hit with the subtlety of a comet striking Earth: we are presiding over the sixth great extinction in the planet's history.

Wilson warns that one-third of all species on Earth could die out in the next 40 years. Soulé says that the only large mammals remaining after the year 2000 will be those that humans consciously choose to protect. "For all practical purposes," he says, "the evolution of new species of large vertebrates has come to a screeching halt."

Alas, this biological meltdown can't be blamed on something as simple as stray cosmic detritus. Instead, responsibility sits squarely on the shoulders of 5.5 billion eating, manufacturing, warring, breeding, and real-estate-developing humans.

The damage done in the United States is particularly well documented. According to a National Biological Service study released early this year, ecosystems covering half the area of the 48 contiguous states are endangered or threatened. The longleaf-pine ecosystem, for example, once the dominant vegetation of the coastal plain from Virginia to Texas and covering more than 60 million acres, remains only in tiny remnants. Ninety-nine percent of the native grassland of California has been lost. There has been a 90 percent loss of riparian ecosystems in Arizona and New Mexico. Of the 261 types of ecosystems in the United States, 58 have declined by 85

---

[1]Article by Dave Foreman, the founder of Earth First! and a director of the Sierra Club, from *Sierra* 80:52-55+ S/O '95. Copyright © 1995 Dave Foreman. Reprinted with permission.

percent or more and 38 by 70 to 84 percent.

If the United States had completely ignored its public lands, it might simply be getting what it deserved. But that's not the case. National parks and designated wilderness areas in this country make up the world's finest nature-reserve system. When President Clinton signed into law the California Desert Protection Act in 1994, the acreage of federally designated wilderness carved out of our public lands soared to more than 100 million acres, nearly half of which are outside Alaska. The acreage of the national park system jumped to almost 90 million, more than one-third in the Lower 48. That is much more than I thought we would ever protect when I enlisted in the wilderness wars a quarter-century ago.

But that's still not enough for Reed Noss, editor of the widely cited scientific journal *Conservation Biology* and one of the National Biological Service report's authors, who claims "we're not just losing single species here and there, we're losing entire assemblages of species and their habitats."

How is it that we have lost so many species while we have protected so much?

*"The answer, environmental historians tell us, lies in the goals, arguments, and processes used to establish wilderness areas and national parks over the last century."*

The answer, environmental historians tell us, lies in the goals, arguments, and processes used to establish wilderness areas and national parks over the last century. In his epochal study, *National Parks: The American Experience* (University of Nebraska, 1979), Alfred Runte discusses the arguments crafted to support establishment of the early national parks. Foremost was what Runte terms "monumentalism," the preservation of inspirational scenic grandeur like the Grand Canyon or Yosemite Valley, and the protection of curiosities of nature like Yellowstone's hot pots and geysers. Later proposals for national parks had to measure up to the scenic quality of a Mt. Rainier or a Crater Lake. Even the spectacular Olympic Mountains were initially denied national park status because they weren't deemed up to snuff.

A second argument for new national parks was based on what Runte calls "worthless lands." Areas proposed for protection, conservationists argued, were unsuitable for agriculture, mining, grazing, logging, and other productive uses. Yellowstone could be set aside because no one in his right mind would try to grow corn there; no one wanted to mine the glaciers of Mt. Rainier or log the sheer cliffs of the Grand Canyon. The worthless-lands argument often led park advocates to agree to boundaries gerrymandered around economically valuable forests eyed by timber interests, or simply to leave out such lands in the first place. Where parks were designated over the objections of extractive industries (such as at Kings Canyon, which was coveted as a reservoir site by California's Central Valley farmers), protection prevailed only because of the dogged efforts of the Sierra Club and allied groups.

When the great conservationist Aldo Leopold and others suggested that wilderness areas be protected in the national forests in the 1920s and 1930s, they adapted the monumentalism and worthless-lands arguments with great success. The Forest Service's enthusiasm for Leopold's wilderness idea was, in fact, partly an attempt to head off the Park Service's raid on the more scenic chunks of the national forests. Wilderness advocates also used utilitarian arguments in their campaigns: the Adirondack Preserve in New York was set aside to protect the watershed for booming New York City, and the first forest reserves in the West were established to protect watersheds near towns and agricultural regions.

The most common argument for designating wilderness areas, though, touted their recreational values. Leopold, who railed against "Ford dust" in the backcountry, wanted to preserve scenic areas suitable for roadless pack trips of two weeks' duration. Bob Marshall expanded the recreational theme, defending wild areas as "reservoirs of freedom and inspiration" for those willing to hike the trails and climb the peaks.

In the final analysis, though, most national parks and wilderness areas were (and are) decreed because they had friends. Conservationists know that the way to protect an area is to develop a constituency for it. We rally support for wilderness designation by giving people slide shows, taking them into the area, and urging them to write letters, lobby, or even put their bodies on the line in protest. If we're lucky, and not too many concessions are made to resource industries, we end up with wilderness that we can be proud of. The result is that wilderness areas tend to be spectacularly scenic, rugged enough to thwart resource exploitation (or simply lacking valuable timber and minerals altogether), and popular for non-motorized recreation.

But there's one problem: that's not necessarily what wildlife needs.

It's important to note that ecological integrity has always been at least a minor goal and argument in wilderness and national-park advocacy. In the 1920s and 1930s, the Ecological Society of America and the American Society of Mammalogists developed proposals for ecological reserves on the public lands. Aldo Leopold was a pioneer in the sciences of wildlife management and ecology, and argued for wilderness areas as ecological baselines. Even the Forest Service applied ecosystem thinking when it recommended areas for wilderness in its second Roadless Area Review and Evaluation (RARE II) in the late 1970s. Somehow, though, professional biologists and advocates for wilderness preservation drifted apart—far enough so that the Forest Service now lumps its wilderness program under its division of recreation.

*"Conservation could no longer be just about outdoor museums and backpacking parks."*

It took news of a global biological meltdown to shake up both biology and conservation. Biology could no longer be removed from activism. Conservation could no longer be just about outdoor museums and backpacking parks. Biologists and conservationists all began to understand that species can't be brought back from the brink of extinction one by one. Nature reserves had to protect entire ecosystems, guarding the flow and dance of evolution.

For insight, conservation biologists drew on an obscure corner of population biology called "island biogeography." In the 1960s,

E[dward] O. Wilson and Robert MacArthur studied colonization and extinction rates in oceanic islands like the Hawaiian chain. They hoped to devise a mathematical formula for the number of species that an island can hold, based on factors such as the island's size and its distance from the mainland.

They also looked at islands, places like Borneo or Vancouver, that were once part of nearby continents. When the glaciers melted 10,000 years ago and the sea level rose, these high spots were cut off from the mainland. Over the years, continental islands invariably lose species of plants and animals that remain on their parent continents, a process called "relaxation."

Certain generalities jumped out at the researchers. The first species to vanish from continental islands are the big ones—the tigers and elephants. The larger the island, the slower the rate at which species disappear. The farther an island is from the mainland, the more species it loses; the closer, the fewer. If an island is isolated, it loses more species than one in an archipelago.

*"In 1985, ecologist William Newmark looked at a map of the western United States and realized that its national parks were also islands."*

In 1985, ecologist William Newmark looked at a map of the western United States and realized that its national parks were also islands. The smaller the park and the more isolated it was from other wildlands, the more species it had lost. The first to go had been the large, wide-ranging creatures: gray wolf, grizzly bear, wolverine. Relaxation had occurred, and was still occurring. Newmark predicted that all national parks would continue to lose species. Even a big protected area like Yellowstone isn't large enough to maintain viable populations of the largest wide-ranging mammals. Only the complex of national parks in the Canadian Rockies is substantial enough to ensure their survival.

While Newmark was applying island biogeography to national parks, Reed Noss and Larry Harris at the University of Florida were studying the state's endangered panther and its threatened black bear, hoping to design nature reserves for these species that were more than outdoor museums. A small, isolated group of bears or panthers faces two threats. Because it has few members, inbreeding can lead to genetic defects. And a small population is more vulnerable to extinction ("winking out" in ecological jargon) than a larger one. If the animals are isolated, their habitat can't be recolonized by nearby members of the species. But if habitats are connected so that animals can move between them—even as little as one horny adolescent every ten years—then inbreeding is thwarted and a habitat can be recolonized.

Noss and Harris designed a nature-reserve system for Florida consisting of core reserves surrounded by buffer zones and linked by habitat corridors. Over the past decade this visionary application of conservation biology has been refined by the state of Florida, and now state agencies and the Nature Conservancy are using it to set priorities for land acquisition and protection of key areas. Once a pie-in-the-sky proposal, a conservation-biology-based reserve system is now the master plan for land protection in Florida.

Ecosystem theory has caused biologists to rethink the way they viewed large carnivores, too. Scientists had always considered the biggest animals perched atop the food chain to be sovereign species whose condition had little effect on the well-being of the flora and fauna down below. Until the 1930s, in fact, the National Park Service used guns, traps, and poison to exterminate wolves and mountain lions from Yellowstone and other parks. Early in his career, even Aldo Leopold beat the drum for killing predators.

Today, biologists know that lions and bears and wolves are ecologically essential to entire systems. For example, the eastern United States is overrun with white-tailed deer, which devastate trees with their excess foraging. If allowed to return, wolves and mountain lions would move deer from their concentrated wintering yards and reduce their numbers, thereby allowing the forest to return to more natural patterns of succession and species composition.

Even songbirds suffer when wolves and cougars disappear. The decline in populations of migrant neotropical songbirds such as warblers, thrushes, and flycatchers as a result of forest fragmentation in Central and North America is well documented. But the collapse is also partly attributable to the absence of large carnivores. Cougars and gray wolves don't eat warblers or their eggs, but raccoons, foxes, and possums do, and the cougars and wolves eat these midsize predators. When the big guys were hunted out, the populations of the middling guys exploded—with dire results for the birds.

In addition to being critical players in various eat-or-be-eaten schemes, large carnivores are valuable as "umbrella" species. Simply put, if enough habitat is protected to maintain viable populations of large mammals like wolverines or jaguars, then most of the other species in the region will also be protected.

A final piece in conservation biology's big-picture puzzle is the importance of natural disturbances to various ecosystems. To be viable, habitats must be large enough to absorb major natural disturbances (known as "stochastic events" in ecologist lingo). When Yellowstone burned in 1988, there was a great hue and cry over the imagined destruction. But ecologists tell us that the fire was natural and beneficial. Because Yellowstone covers 2 million acres and is surrounded by several million acres more of national-forest wilderness, the extensive fires affected only a portion of the total reserve area.

Things didn't turn out so well when the Nature Conservancy's Cathedral Pines Preserve in Connecticut was hammered by tornadoes in 1989. In this tiny patch of remnant old-growth white-pine forest, 70 percent of the trees were knocked flat, devastating the entire ecosystem. Had the tornadoes ripped through a forest of hundreds of thousands of acres, they instead would have played a positive role by opening up small sections of the forest to new growth.

Conservation biology's central tenets are not hard to grasp. For a natural habitat to be viable (and for a conservation strategy to succeed) there is a handful of general rules: bigger is better; a single large habitat is usually better than several small, isolated ones; large native carnivores are better than none; intact habitat is preferable to artificially disturbed habitat; and connected habitats are usually better than fragmented ones.

Too often, wilderness areas and national parks in the United States fail to qualify as viable habitat. They are pretty, yet unproductive. For the most part, the richer deep forests, rolling grasslands, and fertile river valleys on which a disproportionate number of rare and endangered species depend have passed into private ownership or been released for development. To make matters worse, the elimination of large carnivores, control of natural fire, and livestock grazing have degraded even our largest and most remote parks and wilderness areas.

Conservation biologists tell us we must go beyond our current national park, wildlife refuge, and wilderness area systems. What's needed are large wilderness cores, buffer zones, and biological corridors. The cores would be managed to protect and, where necessary, restore native biological diversity and natural processes. Wilderness recreation is compatible with these areas, as long as ecological considerations come first. Surrounding the cores would be buffer zones where increasing levels of compatible human activity would be allowed as one moved away from the center. Corridors would provide secure routes between cores, enabling wide-ranging plant and animal species to disperse and facilitating genetic exchange between populations.

*"What's needed are large wilderness cores, buffer zones, and biological corridors."*

Existing wilderness areas, national parks, and other federal and state reserves are the building blocks for this ecologically based network. While rarely extensive enough to protect habitat in and of themselves, these fragmented wildland chunks preserve imperiled and sensitive species. Had today's parks and wilderness areas not been protected through the tireless efforts of wilderness conservationists over the years, these species would be much more in danger than they are today, if they existed at all.

In the northern Rockies, groups such as the Alliance for the Wild Rockies and the Greater Yellowstone Coalition have been working to turn fragmented wildlands into viable habitat. They reckon that if Yellowstone isn't large enough to maintain healthy populations of grizzlies and wolverines, then we need to link the park with larger areas.

At a minimum that means treating the national forests around the park as integral to the park itself. Even grander ideas would link Yellowstone with the vast wilderness areas of central Idaho, the Glacier National Park/Bob Marshall Wilderness complex in northern Montana, and on into Canada.

These efforts produced the most expansive ecosystem-based legislation ever proposed in the United States. The Northern Rockies Ecosystem Protection Act (NREPA) would designate 20 million acres of new wilderness areas and identify essential corridors between them. The bill, endorsed by the Sierra Club, currently has 35 cosponsors.

Through its Critical Ecoregions Program, the Sierra Club is applying ecosystem principles to other large landscapes across North
America. But conservation biology's tenets can also be applied on a
traditional scale. Across the country, activists are helping shape the
next generation of national-forest management plans. They are iden-
tifying habitat for sensitive species, remnants of natural forest, and
travel corridors for wide-ranging species. They can then champion
the creation of wildlife linkages and expansion of existing wilderness
areas into ecologically rich habitats. In many places, they'll be able
to make the case that roads be closed to protect sensitive ecosystems, that once-present species like wolves and mountain lions be
reintroduced, and that damaged watersheds be restored.

But it gets even wilder.

In late 1991 a small group of scientists and activists married conservation biology and conservation activism on the grandest and
most visionary scale yet. The Wildlands Project has set itself the
all-encompassing goal of designing science-based reserve networks
that will protect and restore the ecological richness and native biodiversity of North America from Alaska to Panama.

At a time when legislators are handing out private rights to public lands like candy, such visions may seem like delusions. Congress
is dominated by zealots who would tear down decades of conservation policy and open public lands to the exploiters Teddy
Roosevelt fought almost a century ago. Senator Slade Gorton
(R-Wash.) does the bidding of the timber industry in trying to gut
the Endangered Species Act; just across the hall Representative Billy
Tauzin (D-La.) unleashes lies and demagoguery against wetlands
protection and the Clean Water Act. Lurching through the Contract
with America checklist, Congress threatens wilderness in the Arctic
National Wildlife Refuge, in the Northern Rockies, and in the slick-
rock canyons of Utah. Even the national parks aren't safe from legislators who know the price of everything and the value of nothing.

An understanding of conservation biology and a vision of ecologically designed wilderness cores, corridors, and buffer zones can
help stop the war being waged on the environment. First, conservation policies and arguments are strengthened by a grounding in
sound science. Second, a big-picture view allows activists to see
that they are not isolated, that their campaigns to protect local wildlands fit into a national, even continental plan.

And it is no small benefit that a vision of wilderness recovery
allows us to show what conservationists are for. Too often, activists
are dismissed as negative, whining doomsayers. By developing
long-term proposals for wilderness, we say, "Here is our vision for
what North America should look like. Civilization and wilderness
can coexist. By acting responsibly with respect for the land, we can
become a better people."

A management plan that treats Florida as an ecological whole, a
federal bill that crosses borders to protect wildlands throughout the
northern Rockies, and a continent wide proposal like the Wildlands
Project's wrest the fund from those who would gladly plunder our

natural heritage. Do we have the generosity of spirit, the greatness
of heart to share the land with other species? I think we do.

# Can We Make Our Forests Last?[2]

In a way "sustainable forestry" comes at an odd time in our history. "In the early 1800s one traveler from New York to Boston reported that he passed through only 20 miles of woodlands in 12 small tracts. Now you drive much of the trip through forests," says Doug MacCleery, an avid amateur historian who works in timber management at the USDA Forest Service.

In the eastern United States, which holds two-thirds of our forests, yellow poplars (tuliptrees) once again stand like giant masts in the woods, hickories and oaks shade the earth, and some red maples have grown old enough to seem like characters from early American folk tales with their shaggy bark and ghoulish trunk knots. Wildlife has returned, especially whitetail deer, wild turkeys, beavers, herons, egrets, and other animals once hunted for meat or feathers. A scraggly coyote was recently found living in a cemetery in the Bronx, fed pet chow and leftover Chinese food by a couple who figured that he was an abandoned dog.

Our nation's forests really hit bottom in 1920, after 70 years of clearing the land to feed an exploding population as well as livestock. (A third of the farmland—some 70 million acres—once raised animal feed.) The forests also fueled the industrial revolution, from factories to locomotives, steamboats to homes. And every year fires ravaged 30 [million] to 50 million acres, compared to three million to five million acres today. The owners of those destroyed acres simply gave up on their land, much as slumlords now abandon the burned hulks of ghetto real estate.

By the turn of the 20th century, says MacCleery, "The 'timber famine' was just over the horizon, it was widely believed, and it would bankrupt the country." So "sustained-yield" forestry took hold as an enlightened idea. Coupled with better agriculture and the rise of fossil fuels, it has turned the 19th century rout into a 20th century victory parade. "Since 1950, timber value has increased by one-third on all of our national forest land," he says. "In the East and South, it has almost doubled."

Yet "sustained-yield" forestry is a dying paradigm that is now being replaced by "sustainable forestry." The silviculture techniques that developed in this century were aimed largely at raising commercial tree species faster, better, and stronger to reassure us of a steady supply of timber over the long course of time: a "sustained yield." But those techniques don't answer much of what we need to know to maintain complete and diverse forest ecosystems full of wildlife, clean water, and plants and animals with no commercial value except for their part in the diversity of life on the planet. Sustainable forestry, on the other hand, aims to ensure that all of

---

[2] Article by Will Nixon, editor-at-large for *E Magazine* and contributor to other environmental publications, from *American Forests* 101:14-15 + My/Je '95. Copyright © 1995 Will Nixon. Reprinted with permission.

these elements survive and prosper.

MacCleery believes that this shift stems from the transformation of our agricultural nation to an urban one that simply wants different things from forests. But many ecologists have a less sanguine view. Though trees have spread in the Northeast and the southern Piedmont, says Reed Noss, a conservation biologist at Oregon State University, "These second-growth forests are nothing like the original old-growth forests in their structure and species complexity. No one knows how long these forests will take to regain their full biodiversity. Some estimate that it may take centuries, particularly for invertebrates and herbaceous wildflowers." Sure, the country looks greener, says Mike Scott of the National Biological Survey, but "Much of our forest cover is not native to the area, and a lot is in monoculture. Self-sustaining, natural systems" aren't the same thing as trees.

Scott and Noss recently collaborated on a survey of our nation's threatened ecosystems which noted that some forest types have all but vanished. The longleaf pine has disappeared from 98 percent of its original swath across the South, replaced by commercial plantations of slash and loblolly pine. The great sea of red and white pines across the north-central states has become tiny islands among the hardwoods. Ponderosa pine that once grew in open, parklike stands across millions of acres in the inland West have been swallowed up by thick forests of firs. In stamping out the grass fires that once pruned the ponderosa pine community every few years, Smokey Bear may have inadvertently sentenced an ecosystem to disappear.

"If you take a telescope up to the Blue Mountains in eastern Oregon, you can't see far enough to spot a live tree," says Robert Hendricks, an international policy analyst at the Forest Service. All of the ponderosa and lodgepole pines have died from an invasion of insects. The ridgetops of the Great Smokies in the South hold miles upon miles of gray, weathered spikes, the dead red spruce trees and fraser firs that may have succumbed to acidfog. In fact, there are troubling stories all around the country. And the wildlife species that have prospered are the "generalists" that have adapted to our changing forests, not the "specialists" that are losing their particular habitats. The spotted owl in the ancient forests of the Northwest is only the most famous example. As Mike Scott says, "Only 10 percent of the original old-growth acreage in the Pacific Northwest still exists."

In the 1990s, "sustainable forestry" has been approaching on many fronts. Inspired by green consumerism, independent certifiers such as Smart Wood and Scientific Certification Systems have established standards for wood harvested from "sustainably managed" forests and offered their seals of approval. But as Richard Donovan of Smart Wood says, these groups may wind up serving a role more like independent financial auditors than like *Good Housekeeping*. The public may pay extra for some green products, like fancy furniture, but basically they want to know that the companies are environmentally sound.

From a global standpoint, nations participating in the Earth Summit in 1992 signed a document of "Forestry Principles" and devoted one chapter of Agenda 21 to "Combating Deforestation." These early statements didn't venture much beyond endorsing "God and motherhood," says one observer, but European countries are negotiating through the "Helsinki Process" to agree to more concrete guidelines. The United States has joined the "Montreal Process" with nine other countries that hold much of the world's temperate and boreal forests, including China, the Russian Federation, Chile, Australia, and Japan. In February 1995 the group issued a "Santiago Declaration" that calls upon each country to gather the varied data that may reveal how sustainably their forests are doing.

In the U.S. the Forest Service's timber inventory, produced every 10 years, may be transformed into a sustainability review, says Hendricks. Ultimately this information could contribute to a "sustainability index," now being studied by the President's Council on Sustainable Development, that would be an environmental version of the gross national product.

*"Ecologists now view forests as dynamic systems, patchworks of old and new growth, closed canopies and open meadows."*

In June 1992 the Forest Service announced that the concepts of ecosystem management would guide its plans, and one year later the U.S. announced that our forests would be sustainably managed by the year 2000. ("The President says that," clarifies Chris Risbrudt, the agency's acting director of ecosystem management. "I don't know what he means." People in the field realize that true sustainability won't be proven for many years.) The Bureau of Land Management has adopted the policy, and President Clinton may sign an executive order to require all federal agencies to use it.

In some ways, ecosystem management repackages rules from the National Environmental Policy Act of 1969, which required the agency to study the environmental and human impacts of its actions across a landscape, not just in individual timber stands, and the National Forest Management Act of 1976, which asked it to protect biodiversity, including key species like the spotted owl, and promote the efficient economic use of its land. But in the past, the Forest Service performed these duties in the service of its major goal, "maximum timber production," says Risbrudt, while the new mission is "to keep the ecosystem functioning."

And what is a functioning ecosystem? "For the last 100 years we thought that if forests were left to themselves, they would grow into a steady state of old-growth," says Chad Oliver, a forestry professor at the University of Washington. No more. Ecologists now view forests as dynamic systems, patchworks of old and new growth, closed canopies and open meadows. Over time, fires, blights, and windstorms reweave these components of an ecosystem over the broad landscape. (In the early 1800s, for example, old-growth covered only 40 to 50 percent of the forest land on the Oregon and Washington coasts.)

Humans have also been shaping forest ecosystems for thousands of years: Native Americans burned tens of millions of acres of land across the United States to clear farm land, sprout new vegetation for game animals, or raise wild berries.

But ecosystems oscillate within limits. "There are thresholds," says Neil Sampson, executive vice president of *American Forests*. "If a system passes through one, it won't recover, or at least not in the same way." He offers a vivid example of a dry forest in the West that grew much too crowded from years without fire, until a blight swept through to kill every tree in sight. (Dry forests are the most vulnerable to catastrophe.) "We know from clearcuts in places that are too hot, that the forest doesn't grow back," he says, because the soil changes in the direct sunlight. "This dead forest might become something else for 1,000 years."

Ecologists don't really know the ecosystem thresholds, but they have a surprisingly good idea of the ranges of ecosystems over the past 10,000 years, taking cues from ancient pollen found in bogs and charcoal layers underground that reveal early fires. So experts like Risbrudt judge the "functioning" of an ecosystem by how well things match up with their historic patterns.

In the late 1980s and early 1990s, Risbrudt was a deputy regional forester for the Forest Service in Montana. Throughout the Inland West, Smokey Bear's success has changed forests, all of which relied on fires. Some tree communities like grand fir and whitebark pine that saw fires only every 80 to 200 years haven't yet felt the impact of our free-exclusion policy, but those that historically burned more often have changed dramatically, especially the ponderosa pine. So many fir trees have crowded among them and so much dead wood has collected on the ground that a fire today would leap into the crowns and kill the pines. "We have one-third more biomass there today than in the last 10,000 years," Risbrudt says. "It's not a practical alternative to let things be. They will disappear."

The Forest Service uses a new kind of timber sale to help these troubled forests. The cuts are larger and lighter, as loggers thin out the understory trees, cutting, say, 25 percent of the timber rather than the 95 percent of traditional sales.

"We calculate the number, size, and species of trees that we want to leave behind," Risbrudt says, "rather than how much volume we want to remove."

Clearcuts in the northern Rockies have dropped from 55 percent of the timber sales five years ago to about 10 percent today, and the cuts mostly remove stands hit by disease.

Loggers also drive new machines with long arms that snip trees 30 feet away, then strip the branches in front of the harvester to make a carpet so that the tires won't chew up the soil. They also can travel 2,000 feet from a road before needing to return, unlike the older ones that range 500 to 700 feet. "They'll reduce the number of roads by two-thirds or three-fourths," Risbrudt says. After a logging or two, the Forest Service can safely set an old-fashioned small fire on the site. And he adds that the managers are thinking this way around the country, especially in the Southeast, where they're setting fires to restore the longleaf pines.

The longleaf pine community depended on fires every five years or so to clear out the woody undergrowth and allow wire-grass to flourish. Otherwise, palmettos, gall-berries, and scrub oaks will crowd the open forest stands, becoming tinder for hot lutes on dry summer days that can reach the tree crowns and kill the pines. The understory species have no commercial value, so the Forest Service can't rely on timber sales to solve this problem. Instead, the agency will burn these areas once or twice in winter, when cooler fires simmer through the underbrush, and then return and set a safe fire in the early summer, when the longleaf pine traditionally burned.

"You can start with a woody understory that is six to 10 feet tall, and after two or three treatments you will get a sea of grass," says Ron Coats, acting director for fire in the Forest Service's southern region. To maintain the longleaf pine ecosystems, of course, the agency must keep burning them.

Under ecosystem management, the Forest Service gives top billing to longleaf pine on the high, dry, sandy land where this ecosystem once flourished. Across the South, landowners have replaced this tree with slash and loblolly pines that regenerate much faster, but as the Forest Service harvests these trees on its land through timber sales, it now replants the clearcut sites with longleaf pine.

The new timber sales mentioned above aren't perfect. Environmental groups still appeal them, forcing delays. (Gerald Gray, vice president for resource policy at *American Forests*, suggests that the new sales be called "Stewardship Contracts" to minimize the taint of timber.) And the sales can easily lose money. In one, says Risbrudt, "We painted blue dots on 30,000 trees. That cost an arm and a leg."

But the biggest weakness with ecosystem management may be people. In theory, sustainable forestry calls upon three disciplines— silviculture, ecology, and socioeconomics—but the third often feels like the odd one out. Told of the Forest Service's new machines, Jonathan Kusel, a sociologist at the University of California at Berkeley, groans: "That may be sustainable for machines, but it isn't for people." In his studies of rural communities in the Sierras, he finds that loggers themselves want sustainable forestry. "They are extremely upset at the Forest Service and the industry."

For "socioecosystem management" we should study human communities much the way we now study natural ones, suggests James Kent, a consultant in Aspen, Colorado, who has advised the Forest Service and the Bureau of Land Management. What worries him is that the current approach doesn't seem to get around to communities until it considers their "reactions" to the "impacts" of the new management plans. An ecosystem that ignores a community system will ultimately be as artificial as the zoning and government boundaries that have caused so many of our environmental problems today.

In 1985 the Bridger-Teton National Forest announced that it would dramatically reduce its timber supply to DuBois, Wyoming,

*"An ecosystem that ignores a community system will ultimately be as artificial as the zoning and government boundaries that have caused so many of our environmental problems today."*

which had relied on the local Louisiana-Pacific mill for 65 years. Kent, who speaks much like an ecologist, said that the town suffered from poor economic diversity. So Kent helped the local people plan new businesses—finding a woman who made clocks, for instance, and stacked them in the garage because "she didn't know how to market them. Another lady sewed. As they felt more independent, they looked at the resources beyond their trailer. They were in the middle of bighorn-sheep country. So they started a museum." The Forest Service decided to cut back on the timber over the course of three years to give this new economy time to grow. "We moved from a big company and a national market to family enterprises and service markets," Kent says, a trend in these communities across the West.

In October 1994 the American Forest & Paper Association adopted a broad set of "Sustainable Forestry Principles" that had been 18 months in the making. The group was responding to a crisis that wasn't in the forests, says John Heissenbuttel, the assistant vice president for forest resources, but in the industry's public image. Try as they might to explain the sound silviculture of clearcutting, for example, industry foresters met deaf ears in focus groups and telephone surveys. "The public told us that they didn't want to hear explanations, they wanted to see changes," he says. "That was hard for a lot of our members to take." But the AF&PA, which represents 425 companies and organizations that own 90 percent of the industrial forestland in the country, set about changing its reputation.

The public picked the name of the new initiative. Heissenbuttel says, "We tested several themes—Sustained Yield, Multiple Use, Ecosystem Management, and Sustainable Forestry. The last one was far and away their favorite." (The federal government might take notice.) And the public helped set the agenda, asking for better protection of wildlife, wilderness, and waters, and greater reassurance that "future generations will enjoy the same benefits from forests that we do today." They also liked the idea of outside experts monitoring the industry's work.

Sixty senior managers from member companies drafted principles, which were discussed at regional workshops with upwards of 2,000 people and finally approved by the AF&PA board of directors. The member companies must now meet these guidelines by the end of this year or be dropped from the association. "It's a stretch, as it should be," Heissenbuttel says. "We hope to isolate the 5 percent who are the bad actors and highlight the 95 percent of the industry that operates in a respectable fashion."

The companies must now replant harvested sites within two years, invite outside experts to review their efforts to protect lakes and streams, and follow Oregon's "green up" rule that young trees on a former clearcut site must be three years old or five feet tall before adjacent land can be logged.

"What concerns the public is the 'ugly' in clearcuts," Heissenbuttel says. Companies must now limit these cuts to 120 acres, a dramatic drop from the 250- to 300-acre clearcuts that can be found in the South and the Northeast. They must also leave buffer zones along highways and quit "checker-boarding" the landscape by cutting in more varied patterns that follow the terrain.

"A lot of these practices will be new to a lot of companies," he says.

Lastly, the companies must report on their progress to the AF&PA, which will release annual reports on the industry's performance. Heissenbuttel claims that the organization has now jumped three or four steps ahead of the federal programs.

Neil Sampson agrees: "The largest companies have the best science in the land and the flexibility to make quick decisions to use new methods. The Forest Service has access to the best science and no flexibility."

One group remains absent from the sustainability equation: the seven million people who own 59 percent of our forest land, often in small woodlots of 100 or 150 acres, They are known by the acronym PNIF, for private nonindustrial forestland owners. Their very diversity may be good for ecosystems, says Neil Sampson, because they treat their property so differently. "A lot of them never even cut it," he says. "It's their birdwatching or hunting patch, or they leave it for their kids."

But people who log their land unwisely can wreck havoc. Many states have no laws controlling private-land forestry, offering voluntary guidelines instead. And professional foresters oversee less than 20 percent of the harvests from these private woodlots.

Mistakes aren't hard to find. "You see pretzel-logic skidder trails that chewed up the ground," says Richard Donovan, "and trunks scarred where the skidders banged into them." Good forestry starts as simply as walking the property beforehand to mark trees and map routes so that the skidder won't wind up playing demolition derby.

The AF&PA Principles in effect sidestep the owners and work with the loggers, who promise to be an easier-to-reach and more receptive audience than landowners. "Bad things happen out of ignorance," says Heissenbuttel. "If they know better, they'll do better."

In 1995 the Association's members will help to arrange logger-training programs to explain the principles, the laws, and the best management practices that many state foresters have established, although they're usually voluntary. These sessions will cover everything from road building to replanting to worker safety. In 1996 AF&PA will begin tracking the timber that its members buy from trained and untrained loggers. "Let's say the industry average for wood harvested by trained loggers is 75 percent," Heissenbuttel explains. "The CEO of a company with a percentage much lower than that will have some tough questions for his procurement people." This approach of education and voluntary incentives in the marketplace appeals to Gerald Gray, since new laws can be expensive to enforce. "Loggers are the people on the ground," he says. "Their practices really make the difference in how the harvest is done." Some states now certify loggers, and the U.S. Department of Agriculture's Extension Service offers its own Logger Education to

Advance Professionalism Program.

State foresters bear the responsibility for extending good forest management to private lands, although they often have no legal authority over logging practices. So they must deploy good advice and small incentives. In Missouri, 250,000 people own 85 percent of the state's forestland, which since 1972 has grown by one million acres to cover 14 million acres today. Many are farmers with woodlots beside their fields, while others are absentee owners. State Forester Marvin Brown reports that his agency works with 2,000 people a year on forest stewardship plans.

"They come to us after a logger has seen their property, knocked on the door, and asked to buy the trees for lumber. They call us and say, 'I don't know what I've got out there—would you help me?'" Or they may want to change their woods to attract more deer and turkeys.

*"State foresters bear the responsibility for extending good forest management to private lands, although they often have no legal authority over logging practices."*

With the help of the Forest Service's Forest Stewardship Program, the state gives some of these owners cost-sharing grants for planting trees, building brushpiles for turkey nests, fencing out grazing cows, or placing rocks in streams for fish habitat. Brown is now toying with the idea of turning this effort into a state certification program. "I wouldn't want to guarantee that certification will increase the value of their wood, because it's not true right now," he says. "But as the notion of sustainable forestry catches on in five, 10, or 15 years, their wood might have a higher value. The time to plan for it is now."

Will sustainable forestry work? The humbler ecologists offer cautions. "We don't even have a precise answer to how much dead wood and how many live trees to leave after a harvest for an ecosystem to thrive for long periods of time," says Reed Noss. We have turned away from our worst practices—clearcutting and high-grading (cutting all the best trees and removing the deformed ones that happen to be the best wildlife habitat). But Noss doesn't know if "promising experiments" in new forestry techniques will work on "the scale necessary to supply the wood products we are used to getting."

Others are anxious to get started. "We've gotten people to the moon and back on best guesses," says Chad Oliver. "The forests won't sit still and wait for us to find perfect answers. Most people in the field know enough to get going."

# The Call of South Africa[3]

A lumbering beast emerges suddenly from the South African bush. Standing in the center of a dirt road, the antediluvian creature eyes us, two intruders, and blocks our way. The sight of the sharp, curved horns sweeping majestically off its snout sends thrilling shivers down our spines. Nature photojournalist Michael Freeman and I have come to see South Africa's famous wildlife, and this is a promising beginning. The southern white rhinoceros is one of the world's most endangered animals.

In contrast with the rest of the African continent, South Africa's animal kingdom has been steadily increasing, its habitat expanding over the last 50 years. Nearly six million hectares are set aside for conservation, and indigenous species are thriving in a growing network of public and private reserves. KwaZulu Natal province, which we are visiting, boasts more than 50 such refuges.

A century earlier the picture was quite a different one. By the 1870s huge herds of zebras, elephants, giraffes, and antelopes, as well as rhinos, had been decimated by hunters, herders, and farmers. A rinderpest epidemic that swept Africa in 1896 devastated the ruminants. In this century, a disastrous 40-year campaign was mounted to wipe out the tsetse fly, carrier of nagana, a wasting cattle disease. Hundreds of thousands of wild animals, suspected of being carriers of nagana after contact with the fly, were destroyed.

South Africa's wildlife recovery began in the late 19th century when Paul Kruger, president of Transvaal province, grew alarmed that his country's once bountiful game populations had become seriously depleted. Kruger proposed a large parcel of land, later to become part of Kruger National Park, to be set aside as a wildlife area.

Meanwhile, in 1895, British authorities in Natal declared as wildlife parks Hluhluwe and Umfolozi, the traditional royal hunting grounds of the Zulu kings. (The Corridor Reserve that now links Hluhluwe and Umfolozi was proclaimed in 1989.)

Conservation efforts continued to gain momentum and by the 1940s some animals that had faced extinction began to rebound. Since 1960 a national commitment to conservation, coupled with the realization that wildlife prosper where cattle do not, has spawned private conservancies, wildlife parks, and game ranches. Today South Africa has more than 10,000 private game farms in addition to some 350 government controlled game reserves, nature reserves, national parks, state forests, and wilderness areas.

We began our trek at Itala Game Reserve in northeast KwaZulu Natal, a four-hour drive east of Johannesburg, South Africa's main industrial city. Twenty-five years ago the Natal Parks Board (NPB) reclaimed 30,000 hectares of overutilized, barren land to create

*"In contrast with the rest of the African continent, South Africa's animal kingdom has been steadily increasing, its habitat expanding over the last 50 years."*

---

[3]Article by Victoria Butler, from *Wildlife Conservation* 99:38-43 Ja/F '96. Copyright © 1996 Victoria Butler. Reprinted with permission.

Itala. The wildlife had long been gone, the vegetation destroyed. Today, waterfalls, pools, and gorges flank dense thickets of riverine forest falling to a plain of sharp thornbush.

Itala park officials have reintroduced 25 animal species since 1973, including elephants, rhinos, and cape buffalos as well as giraffes and various antelopes. The reserve boasts 65 black rhinos and 130 southern white rhinos.

On an early morning drive we spotted princely giraffes and scampering warthogs. We heard turtle doves and flushed a flock of guinea fowl. We passed herds of zebras and wildebeests. Rounding a curve in the dirt road, we came face to face with a white rhino (*Ceratotherium simum simum*), the largest land mammal after the elephant. White rhinos are known as "gentle giants." Nevertheless, we kept a respectful distance from this two-ton fellow. Finally he ambled off.

Itala, like many South African parks, offers guided wilderness walks. During a three-hour hike over rocky terrain, a Zulu guide introduced us to the "bush." We touched various acacias, including the sweet thorn and the scented thorn favored by black rhinos. We stood by mountain aloes that had been munched on by elands and examined a Stamford tree that produces a sour fruit eaten by monkeys, baboons—and people. Black whartley, olive, and marula trees provided patches of shade and wild thyme scented the air. We followed game trails and listened to the "go away" cry of a gray lourie, as the crested bird wailed in the treetops above us.

With the sun sinking across the horizon, we topped a hillock and headed home, only to be stopped in our tracks by a group of grazing white rhinos. It's one thing to follow rhinos in a car and quite another to meet them on foot. The guide circled around, trying to outflank the rhinos; but these giants followed along. We moved; they moved. One animal stared in our direction through small, beady eyes. Rhinos are notoriously shortsighted and it could not see us. But it could hear us, and its keen sense of smell picked up our scent. We retreated in a wide arc and crept to the road some distance away.

Most of the animals in Itala came from the great Hluhluwe/ Umfolozi Park in northern KwaZulu Natal, our next destination. We arrived there in late afternoon, when the African sun casts a golden spell on the land. We drove through savanna woodlands, past a waterbuck enjoying his evening drink at a stream, and up steep, grass-covered slopes. As the sun dropped in an orange blaze behind the mountains, an elephant trumpeted the day's end.

The next morning we drove to the bomas, or game pens, to meet Keith Micklejohn, head of the game-catching unit of NPB. White rhinos, black rhinos, and giraffes had been captured and the pens were full. Bomas on the other side of the park held hundreds of zebras and antelopes. Micklejohn explained that an auction was about to take place.

Six years ago George Hughes, director of the Natal Parks Board, defied conventional wisdom and decided to auction off a breeding group of five black rhinos to a large private sanctuary that would protect the animals. Hughes saw the auction, which has become an annual event, as a way to bring in much-needed revenue for conservation and at the same time disperse surplus animals rather than cull herds. Today NPB earns about $1.5 million a year by selling animals to game reserves and zoos.

Actually, NPB began moving white rhinos out of Hluhluwe/Umfolozi in 1962. Nearly 4,000 white rhinos have been translocated from this park to other reserves. "Every southern white rhino you see, anywhere in the world, comes from here," Micklejohn says with pride. "Since the mid-1960s we've caught more than a hundred thousand animals of 41 species. We've helped restock South Africa."

Along with 1,800 white rhinos and 350 black rhinos, Hluhluwe has 170 elephants. With a young park ranger to guide us, we set out to find some of them. The best times to see elephants are at dawn or late in the afternoon, when they are looking for water. The elephant is a thirsty beast—an adult drinks about 84 quarts of water a day. It is not unusual to see 25 or so elephants walking slowly in single file to a water hole. The newborn calves in the line are half-hidden from view—they walk under their mothers' bellies for protection. Some elephants raise their trunks: They're testing the air, alert to changes in the environment that could signal danger.

We sense that there are animals everywhere, although often we have to look into the bush to spot them. In a clearing, Burchell's zebras mingle peaceably with giraffes. Zebras are also seen in the company of antelopes—impalas, nyalas, and wildebeests. Each zebra's pattern of stripes is unique. A Burchell's zebra is distinguished from other species of zebras by a faint shadow stripe between the black stripes on its hindquarters. This is the animals' world and in the magic of Hluhluwe, we are their guests.

Some of that magic, no doubt, can be attributed to the ceaseless conservation efforts of NPB and Hughes, its innovative head. Under Hughes, NPB has upgraded park facilities, encouraged rangers to become involved in development programs with indigenous people living in the communities that border wilderness areas, and supported the creation of private reserves in areas surrounding the parks.

*"Across South Africa, land developers and environmentalists are converting unprofitable farms into game ranches and wildlife reserves."*

These private reserves may be the wave of the future. Across South Africa, land developers and environmentalists are converting unprofitable farms into game ranches and wildlife reserves. Conservation Corporation, a private ecotourism company, bought 17 run-down farms covering 14,000 hectares in far northern KwaZulu Natal, let the area go wild, and renamed it Phinda Izilwane, which in Zulu means "return of the wildlife." Elephants, which had not been seen in the region for more than a hundred years, are back. So are kudus, nyalas, and impalas.

Keven Leo-Smith, a director of Conservation Corporation and manager of Phinda, insists that the wildlife offers an economically viable alternative to cattle-raising. As a rule of thumb, game farms generate 800 rand per hectare as compared with 80 rand per hectare for cattle farms. "The land here is as poor as it gets," Leo-Smith points out. "Ecotourism could bring in more cash than cattle grazing." He adds, "Animals will survive in Africa only if they can produce value to people. People are employed here because elephants, rhinos, and lions are here."

Phinda offers tourists a glimpse of the Big Five—lions, leopards, elephants, cape buffalos, rhinos—as well as a look at where they fit into the whole ecosystem. We watched a cheetah mother and her four frolicking cubs. A family of newly translocated elephants rumbled through the acacia forest. "Paradise lost and paradise regained," says Leo-Smith. "That is the story here." If conservationists in South Africa have their way, it is a story that will be retold many times, in many places in their beautiful wild country.

# New Defenders of Wildlife[4]

James Bailey stands on the banks of Romney Creek, a broad but short tidal stream that flows through the U.S. Army's Aberdeen Proving Ground and into the Chesapeake Bay north of Baltimore. Here, on a sunny fall day, an eastern deciduous forest sheds its autumn leaves quietly not far from a site where army engineers test weapons, munitions, and other military equipment.

A short distance upstream, some 30-40 roosting bald eagles eye the water for signs of fish. Downstream, great mounds of dried guano on Pooles Island in the Chesapeake Bay attest to the 600 pairs of great blue herons that nested there over the summer. At a nearby pond, some 2,000 ducks and other migrating waterfowl rest on cool fall nights.

"If we weren't here, this land would be all marinas and condominiums," says Bailey, an army wildlife biologist at Aberdeen. Instead, Aberdeen's 79,000 acres hold a healthy deer herd, beaver ponds, turkey vultures and black vultures, red-tailed and marsh hawks, and the largest bald eagle population on the northern Chesapeake. "We are a de facto wildlife sanctuary," Bailey says.

When one thinks of natural lands with abundant wildlife, protected endangered species and research opportunities, images of national parks, wildlife refuges, and other preserves usually come to mind. One rarely thinks of military bases, like Aberdeen.

Yet, the US Department of Defense (DOD) manages more than 25 million acres of land nationwide. Among government agencies, that amount of area is second only to the Department of the Interior. Within that department, the Bureau of Land Management holds 270 million acres, the US Fish and Wildlife Service (USFWS) has 92 million acres of national wildlife refuges, and the National Park Service has 83 million acres of national parks.

Some DOD facilities encompass more land than most national parks or wildlife refuges. Eglin Air Force Base near Pensacola, Florida, for example, totals 464,000 acres. The Naval Air Weapons Station at China Lake, California, has 1.1 million acres, and the Army's White Sands Missile Range in New Mexico 2.2 million acres. The latter is equal in size to Yellowstone National Park in Wyoming, the largest park in the continental United States.

"We've got more endangered species per acre than any other federal land management agency," says Philip Pierce, an army natural resources officer in Arlington, Virginia. "Our bases are islands of protected species. They probably hold more species today than when we acquired them."

The reason: Most land on military bases remains largely natural. More than 90 percent of the 850,000 acres at the army's Yuma

*"Some DOD facilities encompass more land than most national parks or wildlife refuges."*

4 Article by Jeffrey P. Cohn, a Washington, D.C.-based science writer who specializes in conservation issues, from *BioScience* 46:11-14 Ja '96. Copyright © 1996 American Institute of Biological Sciences. Reprinted with permission.

Proving Grounds in southwestern Arizona is undeveloped. At Avon Park, Florida, the air force uses only 3,000 acres of a 106,000-acre base and bombing range south of Lake Kissimmee. And, at Fort Sill in Lawton, Oklahoma, where the army artillery trains, 86,000 of the base's 94,000 acres are wild.

Large expanses of land are needed as safety or security zones, says Lieutenant Colonel Tom Lillie, an air force program manager for natural and cultural resources at the Pentagon. They are also needed, the army's Pierce adds, to train troops in environments similar to those US forces might face in future wars.

## Limiting Access on Bases

Not only is land preserved on military bases, but public access is often limited. "Military installations are not national parks or zoos," says Junior Kerns, a wildlife biologist at the Yuma Proving Ground. "We can close off areas without going through public hearings."

Military personnel may also be prohibited from entering environmentally sensitive areas on bases. At Camp Pendleton, the Marine Corps' amphibious warfare training center halfway between Los Angeles and San Diego, a sign warns people to keep out of a particular beach "by order of the base commander." One-fifth of all California least terns, an endangered subspecies, nest from May to August at Pendleton along the coastal estuary where the Santa Margarita River flows into the Pacific Ocean. The sign is obeyed because "marines are used to taking orders," explains Slader Buck, natural resources manager at Pendleton.

On the other hand, natural does not mean unused, especially where ground troops operate. "All of our land may be used for training," Buck says of Pendleton's 126,000 acres, the last large reservoir of California chaparral and coastal scrub between Mexico and Los Angeles. "That's our mission. We're not a national park. It's not vacant land to us."

Nor does natural, in most cases, mean pristine. Some bases, like the Army's Fort Benning near Columbus, Georgia, were once heavily logged. Others, like the Rocky Mountain Arsenal near Denver, now a thriving national wildlife refuge, contain leftover chemical wastes and toxic pollutants. Elsewhere, troops conduct training maneuvers, drive tanks and other heavy vehicles over the ground, fire live artillery shells, and drop bombs.

Still, large, mostly natural lands with restricted human access and abundant wildlife in a variety of habitats from coast to coast provide diverse opportunities not only for wildlife conservation, but also research. "Our military bases are natural laboratories," says the Army's Kerns, president of the National Military Fish and Wildlife Association, a group for DOD wildlife biologists.

For years, the only DOD money available for wildlife conservation and research came from selling logging, farming, or grazing rights on military lands. The Sikes Act of 1960 extended that concept by authorizing DOD to collect fees for hunting and fishing on military bases. The act also required DOD to cooperate with USFWS and state wildlife agencies.

In 1991, Congress created the Legacy Resource Management Program. Until recently, the legacy program provided $50 million a year to fund projects aimed at managing wildlife and other natural, anthropological, or cultural resources on military lands. It had been viewed as a "godsend," Kerns says, because it provided money that was specifically targeted to wildlife research. (At press time, the program was facing budget cuts from Congress of 80 percent.)

Even with funding for research and conservation programs, DOD has sometimes had problems with managing natural resources. In 1992, three civilian army employees at Fort Benning were charged with conspiracy to violate the Endangered Species Act, a felony. They had designated some of the base's extensive pine forests for clear-cut logging, including habitat for the endangered red-cockaded woodpecker.

Under the terms of a pretrial agreement, two of the employees were fined. One was reassigned to other duties, and the other retired. Charges against the third were dropped. Although the Fort Benning case involved civilians, it "sent a message through the military [that] this is not the way to do business," says Philip Laumeyer, a field supervisor in the USFWS's Brunswick, Georgia office.

Another case involved the commander and another officer at Fort Monroe in Hampton, Virginia. They were officially reprimanded in 1994 for ordering base workers to destroy yellow-crowned night heron nests. The birds were not harmed, but their nests were knocked down because heron droppings defiled lawns, roads, and cars. The birds are not endangered, but they are protected under the Migratory Bird Treaty Act.

Beyond civil penalties, such reprimands can affect an officer's military standing. "It could end a career, especially during times of downsizing," Kerns says. "Officers can't afford even a hint of blemish on their record."

Most military personnel now seem to understand the need to obey wildlife laws. "We hammer home the message that you need to consult with us," says Tom Campbell, a biologist at the navy's China Lake weapons station. "Some don't like it, but they have bit the bullet. We have the commander's support, so people pay attention."

## Navy Changes Practices

The attention shows in conservation and research projects on military bases from coast to coast and sometimes beyond. For starters, the navy redesigned its tugboats and other small craft. The change came after a female manatee and her calf were killed by a ship's propellers at the navy's submarine base at Kings Bay, Georgia. The new design adds metal shields to prevent the manatees from being drawn into ship propellers. No manatee is known to have been killed by propellers since the navy made its changes.

The navy's conservation efforts at Kings Bay extend into the Atlantic Ocean. Navy biologists are working with the Coast Guard and federal and state wildlife agencies to protect a right whale calving area off the Georgia and Florida coasts. Navy biologists survey the whales and monitor their movements. The information is then fed to local shippers and recreational boaters to help them avoid collisions at sea.

## Habitat Conservation Is Under Way

Habitat conservation and restoration has become a major focus at other military bases as well. At Barksdale Air Force Base in Shreveport, Louisiana, for example, base land managers built controls and a pump on existing canals to reflood drained wetlands along the Red River. The result: Approximately 2,000 acres of re-created wetlands now attract 6,000 nesting white ibises, little blue herons, and other wading birds to an area that had few if any before.

*"Smith hopes eventually to restore 5,000 acres, including 2,000 acres of white cedar, on formerly clear-cut land at the Dare County range."*

Some 2,300 miles away, the navy protects 225 acres of old-growth forest at the Jim Creek Radio Station north of Seattle. The area, a key communications link between naval shore commands and US submarines at sea, holds one of the Pacific Northwest's last stands of virgin Sitka spruce, Douglas fir, cedar, and western hemlock.

Yet other large trees are the focus of a habitat restoration project at Dare Country Air Force Bombing Range in North Carolina. Forester Scott Smith has planted Atlantic white cedar trees on a 15-acre test plot in an attempt to reestablish the species. Only 10 percent of Atlantic white cedar habitat, which once stretched along the coast from New Jersey to Louisiana, remains. Smith hopes eventually to restore 5,000 acres, including 2,000 acres of white cedar, on formerly clear-cut land at the Dare County range.

Elsewhere, near Lawton, Oklahoma, the army has set aside 2,000 acres around an artillery firing range at Fort Sill. The protected area contains the largest chunk of ungrazed tall-grass prairie in the West, says James Gallagher, an army wildlife biologist. The preserve provides habitat for white-tailed deer, scissor-tailed flycatchers, and the largest wintering population of northern harriers in the United States.

Habitat protection is particularly difficult at Fort Sill and at Fort Knox, the army's tank headquarters, south of Louisville, Kentucky. At both bases, heavy tanks, howitzers, rocket launchers, and other vehicles chew up the ground, dig deep ruts, and add to soil erosion. At Fort Knox, where forests rather than prairies prevail, the heavy equipment and weapons also bowl over trees and bushes.

The army has launched active land-restoration programs at both sites. Bulldozer crews have restored natural contours on 1,000 acres at Fort Knox since 1991, says Albert Freeland, the base's chief environmental manager. Ditches, some eight feet deep, have been filled, and trees and other native vegetation have been planted.

## Working with Individual Species

Besides protecting and restoring habitat, DOD biologists also are concentrating on individual species. For instance, the navy is recreating habitat for the endangered red-cockaded woodpecker at the Naval Weapons Station at Charleston, South Carolina. The small black-and-white birds, named for the males' red head tufts, usually nest in cavities in the trunks of mature pine trees. However, the birds have disappeared from large areas in the southeastern United States because pine forests have been heavily logged.

Navy biologists have affixed 16 nest boxes, modified to keep other birds away, to pine trees. The boxes replaced tree cavities lost when mature pines were destroyed during Hurricane Hugo in 1989. The biologists also have drilled holes in trees to give the woodpeckers a head start in building a nest cavity, which can take two years to complete, and they have planted pine seedlings on 385 acres to promote new growth.

The woodpecker's habitat is also protected at Fort Benning and at a dozen other military bases. One base where red-cockaded woodpeckers appear to be doing well is Fort Bragg near Fayetteville, North Carolina. Home of the army's 82nd Airborne Division, Fort Bragg trains 40,000 troops a year. The fort also houses approximately 300 woodpecker clusters, a series of pine trees inhabited by groups of birds.

At Fort Bragg, nearly a dozen biologists study and monitor red-cockaded woodpeckers, especially during breeding season, says army wildlife biologist Alan Schultz. To aid the woodpeckers, the biologists burn undergrowth and remove hardwood trees that make the habitat unsuitable for the pine trees the woodpeckers need for nesting. They also band the birds for population and genetic studies. Fort Bragg biologists keep tracked vehicles out of cluster sites and have closed some firing lanes to protect the birds.

To protect a butterfly species, the navy halted construction on a pipeline at a fuel depot in San Pedro, California, 25 miles south of downtown Los Angeles. In 1994, workers discovered the Palos Verdes blue butterfly there. Thought extinct in the early 1980s when their last known habitat was bulldozed, naval biologists at San Pedro have found 270 PV blues, as the butterfly is known. Navy biologists are surveying the fuel depot for other butterflies, monitoring the population, and restoring the coastal scrub habitat that the species requires, says Dawn Lawson, a navy botanist.

Further south, wildlife biologists at Camp Pendleton are helping conserve the least Bell's vireo. Once common in riparian forests from northern California to Baja, the least Bell's vireo was listed as endangered in 1986 when the population dropped to only 300 pairs in California. Now, the bird is making a comeback at Pendleton.

For 15 years, marine biologists and land managers have protected the Santa Margarita River and its riparian woodlands, says Pendleton's Buck. More important here, they have also trapped and removed brown-headed cowbirds, which are recent arrivals in California.

Female cowbirds lay their eggs in vireo and other birds' nests, fooling the latter into raising cowbird chicks often at the expense of their own. The least Bell's vireo numbers at Pendleton have risen from 14 in 1980 to an estimated 350 today, nearly half the species total US population.

The Marine Corps also provides money and habitat for a study of how habitat changes and fragmentation affect mountain lions in rapidly urbanizing areas adjacent to Camp Pendleton in southern California. Paul Beier, assistant professor of wildlife ecology at Northern Arizona University in Flagstaff, spent four years studying Pendleton's pumas.

Approximately 20 mountain lions wander nearly 1,300 square miles of woodlands, chaparral, and coastal scrub that characterize Pendleton and the Santa Ana Mountains to the east. Beier has found that the big cats rapidly adjust to the burning of chaparral and coastal scrub at Pendleton caused by exploding bombs and artillery shells. The mountain lions may temporarily lose the cover they need to ambush deer and other large prey, but they switch readily to raccoons, beaver, opossums, and other small animals.

Beier also learned that corridors connect separate mountain lion habitats around Pendleton. The corridors, one of which is on the base, are especially important for young mountain lions, which use them to disperse from their mother's home range. The young lions can find and use the corridors, he learned, if they contain sufficient woody cover, road underpasses, and only low-density development.

*"The Marine Corps has set aside 6,000 acres for desert tortoises and adopted a management plan for the rest of Twentynine Palms."*

Further inland, in California's Mojave Desert, four military bases—the navy's China Lake, the Marine Corps' Twentynine Palms, Edwards Air Force Base, and the army's National Training Center at Fort Irwin—total 2.6 million acres of some of the nation's best desert habitat. They protect the desert tortoise, one of the three land tortoises in the United States. The animal is a threatened species. North and west of the Colorado River, desert tortoise numbers have dropped due to habitat loss, the destruction of its burrows by off-road vehicles, and a fatal upper respiratory disease spread by pet tortoises freed by well-meaning owners.

"We want to protect the tortoise and its habitat," says Roy Madden, a natural resources officer at Twentynine Palms, a 600,000-acre Marine desert training facility. "It's an important species in the desert. Military training and tortoise recovery are not mutually exclusive."

The Marine Corps has set aside 6,000 acres for desert tortoises and adopted a management plan for the rest of Twentynine Palms. The designated site contains the highest tortoise density on the base. Off-road vehicles are prohibited, speed limits of 25 miles per hour have been set, and aerial bombing sites have been moved. Madden has also begun a four-year, $40,000 test project aimed at reestablishing native plants and restoring tortoise habitat.

East of Twentynine Palms, the air force has designated 60,000 acres at Edwards as critical desert tortoise habitat. Mark Hagen, a natural resources manager, surveys the base to identify areas requiring tortoise management and to locate burrows. He uses the information to remove any of the reptiles living near pads used to test rocket engines. The tortoises are carefully returned to their burrows following the tests.

Similarly, the navy has established a 200,000-acre protected zone for desert tortoises at China Lake. Not only must vehicles stay on marked roads, biologist Tom Campbell says, but all work within the area is closely monitored and restricted to approved places. When necessary, Campbell also monitors weapons tests to ensure any effects on tortoise habitat are minimal and any leftover explosives or other debris are cleaned up afterwards.

Meanwhile, back at Aberdeen Proving Ground, the bald eagles are the subject of research on the importance of the base for recovering endangered species. On contract with the army from 1983 to 1992, James Fraser, a professor of wildlife sciences at Virginia Polytechnic Institute in Blacksburg, studied eagles along the northern Chesapeake Bay. During that period, he followed some 300 eagles and radio tagged 154, including 22 at Aberdeen.

Fraser learned the Chesapeake acts as a meeting ground for three separate bald eagle populations. One comprises birds that breed or were hatched along or near the bay. A second group includes eagles that migrate to the bay each fall from northern New England and eastern Canada. The third is the birds that come north each spring, then return south in the fall. More important, perhaps, Fraser found that bald eagles prefer the undeveloped forests and shorelines still available at Aberdeen and some other sites along the Chesapeake. They avoid places used by people, such as areas around roads, buildings, and marinas. At Aberdeen, the eagles prefer areas down-range from artillery and tank firing zones because, he says, "shooting keeps people away."

## Will the Legacy Continue?

Whether such research and conservation efforts on military bases continue depends on the budget-slashing atmosphere in Washington. Republicans in Congress have criticized nonmilitary programs in DOD, and, insiders say, the legacy program remains unpopular with some military leaders because it forces them to spend time and money on nonmilitary activities.

At the same time, some military bases lack enough biologists and resource managers to run research programs. At White Sands Missile Range in New Mexico, the army currently has only three natural resource managers for the base's 2.2 million acres. "There are so many projects that we have been unable to do," says David Anderson, White Sand's land manager. Nevertheless, the outlook for research and conservation on military bases remains good. "We still have the habitat," says Buck. "We don't have anything you can't find elsewhere, we just have more of it. We have wild places that don't exist for many species on the outside."

# Accidental Sanctuary[5]

In the late autumn of 1950, small flocks of migrating red-crowned and white-naped cranes were flared from their winter feeding grounds in the border region between North and South Korea by immense and scaring bursts of light and noise. The War of June 25, as the South Koreans called it—after the date when North Korea invaded the South through the Panmunjom Valley—was well under way, in all its uproar of explosives and artillery. For conspicuous, large, wary birds like the wild cranes, which require large reaches of silent, open country and clean water, the war made the Koreas all but uninhabitable. The armistice signed at Panmunjom in 1953 established a frontier between the Koreas that was roughly defined by the narrow waist of the peninsula, and this time the border was consolidated by a so-called demilitarized zone which was heavily fortified by mines and tank traps, huge embankments, and formidably high barbed-wire fences. Zealously enforced by the hard-nosed soldiery on both sides, these barriers forbade all access, to a zone as much as 2.5 miles across, extending from the Yellow Sea all the way east to the Sea of Japan. In addition, this DMZ was buffered on the South Korean side by a CCZ, or Civilian Control Zone, of comparable width, where controlled farming—but no habitation—was permitted.

What was created in this no-man's-land was a wildlife refuge, several miles across and 150 miles long (about 375 square miles altogether), with streams and springs that remained open all winter—the most fiercely protected, and most peculiar wildlife sanctuary anywhere on Earth, and an accidental paradise for the great cranes.

A region from which *Homo sapiens* is excluded is inevitably hospitable to other species, but since a bird sanctuary was scarcely what the combatants had in mind, the return of the great cranes passed as unremarked as had their wartime disappearance from the country. Not until November 1961 did Ben King, a U.S. Army lieutenant stationed in South Korea, report that a flock of some 2,300 white-naped cranes, apparently en route to Japan, had rested a few days on the mudflats in the estuary of the Han and Imjin rivers, at the Yellow Sea. In the years that followed, both the white-naped crane (*Grus vipio*) and the red-crowned crane (*G. japonensis*) were reported in the winter months along the Imjin and in the nearby Panmunjom Valley. But not until the early 1970s were there reports that both species were overwintering in the Cholwon Basin, in the central mountains, after migrating south from the Amur River watershed in northeastern China and far eastern Siberia. By an astonishing irony, the Han-Imjin and the Cholwon—perhaps the two regions most bitterly contested during the war—had become

---

the most significant winter crane habitat left in Korea.

Today, after four decades of peace, the no-man's-land is seriously threatened, less by the ever-escalating military activities than by grandiose plans for industrial and municipal development, because the economic boom in the new Asia has changed the entire face of South Korea and has drawn attention to the former war zone as the last large tract of undeveloped land on the peninsula. Due to its military rule and restricted location, the border region is well behind the rest of South Korea in its economy. Also, Koreans on both sides are aware that from a financial point of view (the near-unanimous point of view in the new Asia), a valuable resource is being "wasted." And so, increasingly, there is talk of large-scale development of the buffer zone, whether or not the two countries heal their differences.

The threat to two of the rarest and most beautiful of the earth's creatures—not in the name of human welfare but of commerce—is real and imminent. Were their last Korean wintering grounds to be eliminated, the prospects for red-crowned and white- naped cranes might suffer severely. This possibility is alarming to conservationists, especially to George Archibald of the International Crane Foundation (ICF), in Wisconsin, who in the winter of 1996 made a journey to the DMZ with some concerned Korean friends, seeking ways to avert such a calamity. Dr. Archibald was kind enough to invite me to join him, and on January 27 he met me at the Seoul airport, accompanied by Kim Sooil, an assistant professor of environmental biology at the Korean National University of Education and an adviser to the Ministry of the Environment. Escorting them was Chung Kwang-Joon, a Seoul businessman who, like Dr. Kim, is a charter member of the Korean Association for Bird Protection (KABP), founded in 1980.

*"The threat to two of the rarest and most beautiful of the earth's creatures...is real and imminent."*

All but destroyed during the Korean War, when it was still a small provincial city, modern Seoul, viewed from the air at night, is a vast, radiant display of colored lights set about the inky reaches of the great Han River. Due to congested traffic caused by new construction on all sides, the trip into the city is a long one. Korea is sometimes called the Land of the Morning Calm, and the peaceful doorbell of my Seoul hotel room simulated birdsong, but it was clear on that first evening that this vestigial longing for harmony with the natural world could only be quaint and elegiac in the new Korea.

Early next morning we set out for the Cholwon in the glad company of 10 or 12 KABP members, all of them males in winter plumage of black-and-white—checked caps with black earflaps, suitably emblazoned with an insignia of *turumi*, the red-crowned crane. Friendly and boisterous, they wave a white banner honoring the ICF and hail Dr. Archibald as "Archie" while referring formally to one another as "Mr." So-and-so.

In Kim Sooil's opinion, and George Archibald's, too, the KABP represents at the very least the beginning of a shift in South Korea's national consciousness in regard to wildlife, and it has already established a winter feeding program for the cranes at Cholwon. "We are not yet a scientific society," admits Dr. Kim, an informed and dedicated conservationist and the only professional naturalist in the KABP. "We are still working with the heart rather than the brain."

Before we depart, Mr. Chung leans forward and pinches my leg in several places—as it turns out, merely to satisfy himself that I am wearing long johns, for the Cholwon Basin, scene of so many bitter winter battles, is one of the highest and coldest regions in South Korea.

I travel north in the good company of Kim Sooil, who teaches me a good deal about crane history in this country during the drive. In former days, the red-crowned crane especially was a favored companion of sages, scholars, and musicians, who are commonly portrayed in communion with the elegant *turumi*—in many cases, as tall as their human companions. As in Japan, when one speaks of "the crane," it is this species one refers to. In both countries, the white-naped crane is referred to as "the gray crane," an entirely inadequate name for a splendid silver-gray, black, and white bird with a gold eye and a fiery red disk on the side of the face—perhaps the one rival to *turumi* as the most beautiful of the world's 15 crane species. Despite their reverence for these birds, says Dr. Kim, the pragmatic Koreans commonly killed cranes and sold their plumage as souvenirs to the Japanese, especially during the Japanese Occupation of 1910–1945, and there are reports that *turumi* are now killed by poachers for the international trade in animal parts that is also threatening such species as the tiger.

*"Only a few years ago the Naktong flock of hooded cranes was estimated at 250 birds..."*

In 1986 the presence of a third rare crane—the hooded crane (*Grus monacha*)—was confirmed in the vicinity of the Naktong and Kumho rivers, to the south. But by that time, the economic boom that would make this country the wonder of Asia was under way, and today a vital staging area and winter habitat for this shy woodland species of north China and Siberia is being devastated by land reclamation and construction. Only a few years ago the Naktong flock of hooded cranes was estimated at 250 birds; this year perhaps 80 pick disconsolately around the proliferating domes of white vinyl greenhouses, while two of this small country's seven automakers build new factories on the last open land across the river.

"*Grus monacha* has lost," Kim Sooil pronounces gloomily. "There is no more hope for our hooded crane." Passionate about wildlife since boyhood, he makes no attempt to disguise his sorrow over the almost total destruction of Korea's birdlife, including the waterbirds common in his youth along the Han, where the last wetlands and marshy edges were tidied up with concrete embankments for the 1988 Summer Olympics.

From Seoul to the Cholwon Basin is no more than 70 miles, but the going is slow due to remorseless traffic as well as icy roads and snow, which makes the road more perilous as it gains altitude. Beyond the old post–World War II frontier, two-thirds of the way to Cholwon, army check-points and military vehicles increase, with a grim shift in atmosphere that intensifies all the way north to the

Civilian Control Zone.

The flat plain of the Cholwon Basin, with its rich and very valuable volcanic soil, runs straight across the border, penetrating deep into North Korea, which is why this region, known in the Korean War as the Iron Triangle, was so fiercely contested in the weeks preceding the armistice accord of 1953. The plain is broken and surrounded by small, sudden mountains—the odd, picturesque rock eruptions seen in the mists of so many Oriental paintings—that because they became strategically important were often the scenes of the worst loss of life.

"The crane," says Kim Sooil, "is well known to bring long life and good fortune, and crane images are seen everywhere at the New Year, when we make our wishes. And now—because they are most numerous in this border region, where so many thousands of men died before the armistice—the crane is our symbol of peace. And that is because reunification is our dream."

I note that Mr. Chung refers to Mount Paektu, in North Korea, as "the highest mountain in our country." Like many older Korean people—he is 62—he has not reconciled himself to the partition of Korea imposed by the superpowers after World War II, which extended the humiliating misery caused by 35 years of Japanese occupation.

Dr. Kim's parents were born in what is now called North Korea and are still heartbroken by the separation. Kim Sooil himself grew up under the dictatorship of the late South Korean president Park Chung Hee, who often used the ideological dispute between Communism and the West to oppress his people, much as the North Korean government does today. Paranoia exists on both sides, inflamed by the North's chronic acts of terrorism, and despite vain efforts by a National Board of Unification, most of these men think reunification is far away.

Since the two Koreas have never signed a peace treaty, they remain in an official state of war. In early April, nine weeks after our departure, North Korea accused the South of deploying weapons in the DMZ, which it said it would no longer respect, and for the next three days it sent armed troops into the zone in what were described as "self-defensive measures." These actions preceded elections in South Korea as well as a visit by President Bill Clinton, and probably they represent no more than the latest in a long series of provocations. Because of the repeated threats, however, the South lives in a nervous state of perpetual preparedness, ever strengthening and upgrading its defenses, even though virtually everyone believes that North Korea is on the brink of economic implosion and self-destruction. As recently as 1993, North Korea withdrew from the Nuclear Non-Proliferation Treaty and seemed to be preparing for renewed war, and what is feared here is a last, desperate military adventure, even a nuclear or chemical attack, designed to take the Enemy down with it.

As the road ascends into the central mountains, the country changes, but in fact there is no real country to be seen, only clusters of white vinyl greenhouses crowded between dry, stubbled rice paddies and small, pinched yards and habitations, all the way north to the Civilian Control Zone. There is new construction everywhere the sore eye turns. The only wild things are the street-smart black-billed magpie and the tree sparrow, and even these tough city birds are few.

Entering the CCZ, one has a brief illusion of farm landscape, but army bases and fortifications are everywhere in evidence, and on every hill are sentry posts and bunkers. Near the first anti-tank barriers is the somber, ruined shell of what was once the North Korean Communist Headquarters, and the meager woods—thin fringes of second growth on rocky outcrops and along the roads—are surrounded by barbed wire strands hung with inverted red triangles marked LAND MINES, some of which—but by no means all—are left over from the Korean War. At one checkpoint, an ominous sign reads, "Obedience Is Equivalent to Life," which Dr. Kim, who served three years in the South Korean Army (North Korean boys, he says, serve 10), interprets cheerfully to mean "Obey or Be Killed."

The snow diminishes and the sun comes dimly through the winter fog shrouding the paddies, and over a hill beyond the hollow, war-burned building, two white-naped cranes cross the winter morning in misty silhouette. Farther on, a family of three *turumi*, whiter than the snow, share a paddy with white-fronted geese; not far beyond, three white-naped cranes inspect a snowy corn patch on a rock-knoll hillside, ignoring its decrepit scarecrow as they pick unhurriedly among the scattered stalks. Soon numerous cranes of both species start to appear in fields and along embankments, most of them in small family parties, keeping a safe distance from the road.

In the Cholwon region of the DMZ, the extensive rice fields of the CCZ, reconstituted in the 1970s, are especially critical to the wintering birds, which depend on waste grain in the harvested paddies for their primary food. Before the war, these fields were harvested by hand, and any waste grain was taken by the ducks and chickens that were turned out into the paddies by the peasants, so the wintering cranes were probably very few. Today the human inhabitants are gone and the fields are machine harvested, and for the cranes, which appear after the harvest in late October and November, the paddies offer a rich gleaning of waste grain, together with plentiful mudfish, frogs, and snails.

In addition to food, the open, treeless fields provide protection for the wary birds, which require an unobstructed view in all directions. Easily disturbed by soldiers, farmers, DMZ sightseers, eagles, or vultures, the cranes may quit the CCZ during the day to take refuge in the DMZ. Toward dusk they return to the fields to feed and roost, preferably in shallow water, where the approach of any predator is easily heard. At this time of year, when the water may be frozen, the birds resort to the open ice on the reservoir.

In a bare rice paddy lies a dead water deer, attended by huge cinereous vultures and carrion crows and a white-tailed sea eagle.

As if attracted to the scene, though not sharing in the feast, a northern harrier courses the brown paddies and a rough-legged hawk sits hunched on a dead tree, mobbed by five magpies, which for magpie reasons—no doubt astute—ignore the eagle that is perched nearby. Both eagle and rough-leg are endangered species in this country, and Dr. Kim observes sadly that all raptors are now rare throughout South Korea, and presumably in the North as well. In effect, he says, the wildlife throughout the peninsula is all but gone.

In the center of the valley is a high and heavily fortified earth wall overlooking the demilitarized zone. The wall severs and extinguishes the former rail line that, like a spinal cord, connected the Koreas. At the foot of the wall, the old railroad station is still intact, but the last train, blasted by war, lies in rusted ruin. On the wall itself stands a large tower with a top-floor observatory fitted with tourist telescopes and a diorama depicting what lies in the forbidden territory off to the north. Beneath the tower are two high steel fences with rolled barbed wire on the top, then an open strip, close-cropped and mined, and finally the woods and undergrowth of the DMZ itself. Though second growth and of little apparent interest (except as a potential study area of a half-century of natural plant succession), the DMZ was the only undeveloped land I saw in South Korea.

*"The zone can also claim the last red foxes in this battered country."*

The water deer—a small, rufous, long-haired species whose males lack antlers but are fitted out with tusks—is abundant in the DMZ, and a few roe deer and wild goats—gorals—are still found at higher elevations. The zone can also claim the last red foxes in this battered country. (There are even rumors of a few surviving Asian leopards, which were common throughout the peninusula until systematically poisoned after the war, but nobody cares to test the hair triggers of the soldiery by entering the DMZ in search of tracks.) And there are birds, which venture out into the CCZ—rustic, yellow-breasted, and Siberian meadow buntings, green finches and a northern shrike, turtledoves and the common buzzard, in addition to what I sometimes call requiem birds—magpies and crows—which prosper everywhere in the wake of man's disruptions.

At the observatory snack bar, we warm chilled bones with kimchi (pickled cabbage) and hot noodle soup. Dr. Kim introduces us to Sunwoo Young-Joon, director of the Ecosystem Conservation Division of the Ministry of the Environment. Mr. Sunwoo, a tall, open young man, is sincere and hard-working in his job, Dr. Kim assures us, and indeed he takes extensive notes as Dr. Archibald explains why this unspoiled zone is so critical to the future of South Korea's "bird of peace"—far more important than any of the proposed alternative uses, such as a new "Cholwon City," or some sort of North-South university, or a nuclear-waste site for the country's 10 or 12 reactors, or yet another Hyundai auto factory.

As Dr. Archibald points out to Mr. Sunwoo, the *turumi* here at Cholwon represent almost a quarter of all known red-crowned cranes on the Asian mainland. As for the gray cranes, which rest only two or three days at most Korean staging areas during migration, they depend on this valley for four to six weeks before traveling on to Japan. No other area in Korea, North or South, is so critical for crane conservation.

Because of pressure from Cholwon farmers, the boundary of the CCZ has crept steadily northward, narrowing the feeding territory of the cranes, and what Archibald and the Korean Association for Bird Protection are urging is some sort of crane sanctuary with an area closed to motor vehicles, where the birds can feed undisturbed. Ideally the feeding grounds could be viewed and enjoyed from an observatory and tourist center for the 11 tour buses a day that come to view the DMZ; the army sentry posts might serve as blinds for wildlife observation. Most important is continuing the CCZ ban on construction of vinyl greenhouses, which eliminate the birds' main source of food. This "dry-ground agriculture"—with its year-round utility and its fast-moving specialty crops such as green vegetables and cut flowers—is simply more profitable than the old-time rice paddies, and the ban is being contested by the owners, who naturally resent any conservation strictures that might devalue their land.

What Dr. Archibald has in mind, he tells Mr. Sunwoo, is an eco-tourism in which local people must have a share right from the start—not a strict reserve or refuge but a sort of park that also allows for private use of the good farmland. Like all enlightened conservationists, Dr. Archibald knows that parks and sanctuaries work best when the local people's interests and opinions are considered. Because Cholwon claims Korea's finest rice, grown in unpolluted water and clean air, the rich soil of the valley floor is worth billions of dollars, and its local owners, forced to live outside the buffer zone, will never relinquish it without a fight, which could include a vengeful slaughter of the cranes.

Doubtless Mr. Sunwoo is aware that by 1970, the red-crowned, white-naped, and hooded cranes had been granted official designation as Natural Monuments 202, 203, and 228, respectively. Since then, Cholwon itself—125 acres of it, at least—has become Natural Monument 245, and the Han estuary, 250. It is a first step only, since this status protects neither the birds nor the habitat from development. In any case, Mr. Sunwoo assured us before leaving that the Ministry of the Environment was seriously considering alternatives to industrial and municipal development. Dr. Kim said he believed that Mr. Sunwoo was sincere, and despite mistrust of bureaucrats and politicians, this was our impression too, perhaps because we wanted badly to believe him.

Over the landscape in the winter evening comes an insensate blare of amplifiers and weird martial music—the propaganda hurled by both encampments at each other's heads, in a horrid babel of hollow voices accompanied by a tinny din of soulless music. A church on the South Korean side has joined in this Orwellian barrage, erecting an empty House of God with a mighty cross that is visible from near and far, as if to demonstrate to those godless

Communists across the border that the merciful Lord who permitted such slaughter in this place remains undaunted.

I drive back to Seoul with Suh Il-Sung, a journalist turned free-
lance photographer, who, like most if not all of the KABP members
in our party, understands very well the long-term significance of the
DMZ, remarking of his own accord that no comparable "wilderness" may be found in South Korea. It is evening now, long after
dark, yet heavy road traffic with its blare and fumes plagues us all
the way into the city. Though Mr. Suh has surely grown inured to
these conditions, he finally voices what he knows this visitor to his
country must be thinking. "Too many people, too many cars," he
sighs. In Seoul, he tells me, there are now 11 million people, with
500 new mouths every day.

Next day we head north along the Han River on the Freedom
Highway, another expression of the Korean yearning for reunification. Opened to traffic in 1992, the new highway is strongly fenced
and heavily guarded by Republic of Korea (ROK) soldiers against
invasion or infiltration from the river and its estuary. In consequence, a wide area along the riverside is inaccessible to
humankind, serving the same purpose as the DMZ. Between the
river and the road lie bottomlands where the huge new Ilsan City
was created to take care of Seoul's overflowing population. The rest
of this vast floodplain is covered by white greenhouses proliferating
like pale fungi, thousands upon thousands, mile after square mile,
with no room for a sparrow in between.

*"Opened to traffic
in 1992, the new
highway is
strongly fenced
and heavily
guarded by
Republic of Korea
(ROK) soldiers...."*

Near the confluence of the Imjin River and the Han, the mountains of North Korea rise from the morning mist, and a flock of 12
to 15 white-naped cranes crosses to the riverbottoms of the Imjin
Delta. In recent years the resting area for these cranes in this great
estuary has been much degraded due to high salinity caused by barrage construction up the river, with invasive reed grasses replacing
the sedges that formerly supplied the migrant flocks with abound-
ing tubers. The increase in this species at Cholwon since the 1970s
seems mostly attributable to habitat deterioration and disturbance
in the Imjin and also in the Panmunjom Valley, to the north.

At Imjingak, where North Korean refugees living in the South
come to send prayers and pay reverence to their lost homeland, our
party must show special passes before crossing the Imjin River into
the Civilian Control Zone. After so many miles of traffic and construction, this country of fields mixed with scrub woods is a great
relief, though the poor woods are second growth and heavily
mined. At one place where we stop along the way, the kind KABP
men, unable to see the farm track I am using, yell in alarm when I
step off the tarred road ahead, seeking to identify a bird.

Farther north, at a United Nations checkpoint manned in part by
U.S. soldiers, is the only point along the border where outsiders
may enter the DMZ itself. Here our party is taken in hand by a hard-
faced ROK military policeman wearing prominent side arms and a
hand grenade. With an official blue pennant fluttering from the car

window, we proceed north to Taesongdong, a token village within the DMZ, where after more paperwork we are permitted to climb to the ROK Army observation tower overlooking Panmunjom Valley. In the tower, young soldiers in camouflage greens overturn clipboards to protect their top-secret contents from our prying eyes and warn us with rough gestures against taking pictures. Even our viewing of the empty valley is treated with frowns of professional suspicion, since they cannot know—and would never understand—that these foreign devils have not come to ferret out their defenses but to look for cranes. When we leave the observation tower a few minutes later, the soldiers jump up with warlike shouts and fierce salutes.

Taesongdong is known as Freedom Village; the blue- and orange-trimmed North Korean housing directly across the no-man's-land, on the far side of the valley, is named Peace Village. Unlike Freedom Village, Peace Village appears devoid of human life, and even the mountains beyond it are denuded, stripped bald of trees, apparently to eliminate the last cranny where some counterrevolutionary or capitalist running dog might seek to hide. Peace Village claims the highest flagpole in the world—high as a radio tower, which it resembles—and it flies a gigantic North Korean flag, red, white, and blue. Here at Freedom Village, the pole is somewhat smaller, but the flag is bigger—the biggest in Korea, Dr. Kim assures us.

Below Taesongdong is a sort of pagoda in a grove of pine and cedar, marking the place where uncounted thousands of young soldiers—much like these watching us, I can't help thinking—fought and screamed and died. Beyond the pagoda are more walls and more fortified steel fences, and I am astonished by a water deer that crosses an embankment and vanishes into the scrawny trees around a bunker, like the last remnant of departed wildlife.

The complex of fortifications descends to the valley floor, the only place where patrolled farming within the DMZ is now permitted. The oxcart that lumbers along under the eyes of so many armed men is incongruous indeed, as a crane would be were we to find one in such a setting, for the fallow wetlands of the DMZ are being obliterated here by draining and cultivation. Inevitably, the cranes are missing, and George Archibald shakes his head, ready to leave. From 1974 to 1979, before this war atmosphere resumed and the rearming escalated to the point of lunacy, he made four journeys to the DMZ to research the newly discovered flocks of wintering cranes, and he is disheartened by their absence from this valley where 20 years ago he recorded 10 families of *Grus japonensis*—about 40 birds altogether—accompanied by several hundred *G. vipio*.

Our permit allows a visit to Panmunjom village, where the official border neatly bisects the table on which the armistice was signed and where one may visit a North Korean museum erected to commemorate American atrocities. However, we decline this opportunity, electing to go birdwatching instead. With two armed ROK guards marching behind, we walk along the south edge of the DMZ, over dirt roads that might resemble country lanes were it not for that amplified blare of propaganda echoing across the landscape from both sides. At one point—because one of our armed guards has retraced his steps a little ways to direct a car, leaving our official escort one man short—we are halted by a roving patrol led by a large, leashed dog. In this clear military emergency, the patrol of 20 men actually unlimber their automatic rifles and squat on the road shoulder in full combat alert until their missing comrade catches up with us.

Oblivious to all this martial nonsense, a water deer fawn scrambles over a grassy bank and flocks of pretty parrotbills forage busily in the sedges, as does a great spotted woodpecker, a few raptors, and fair numbers of doves and pheasants. Later a Daurian redstart is seen, as well as a flock of Naumann's thrushes, blowing in fits and starts through the bare winter trees.

Searching in vain for the lost cranes, we make our way down an embankment path toward the Imjin River. In a corner of the snowy fields, the brave men of the KABP, bright checked caps flashing, discover mist nets set for songbirds by the local people. One net is twisted by the struggles of two buntings and a parrotbill that their captors have not bothered to retrieve, and our men break up the bamboo net poles with excited shouts. Across the field, they come upon a poisoned goose that apparently reached this ditch before it died. Dr. Kim says that cranes, too, die from poisoned grain set out for geese and pheasants; last year five poisoned white-naped cranes were found dead on these mudflats. No shooting is permitted in the CCZ, but man is never at a loss when it comes to killing. "What a species we are!" Dr. Archibald exclaims after this long morning—less in judgement than in awe of human ways. There is nothing to be done about the goose, but the next day, just north of Inchon, the KABP performs a citizen's arrest on a man caught hunting ducks illegally.

Across the Imjin, which is clogged with chunks of dirty ice, the terrain is torn up and raw, marred by the dead, chemical colors of earth moving machines and plastic sheeting, flapping like shrouds in the winter wind. In this place, a mile upriver from the old Freedom Bridge at Imjingak, the South Koreans are building a new bridge for another new highway to the closed border, against the day of their reunion with the North. Despite these grim environs, the ice upriver from the bridge is a roosting place for thousands of bean geese and white-fronted geese, and stalking the paddies on the river bench above, on the very edges of the bridge approaches, is a flock of 26 white-naped cranes. Though as many as 2,000 of these cranes still pass through Korea on their way to southern Japan, about half of them now use Cholwon as their main staging area; only about one-eighth of the migrating birds will winter along the DMZ.

The wintering cranes of the Han Imjin region are thought to come south from the Zhalong Reserve, in northeast China, whereas those at Cholwon may follow a more easterly flyway, from breeding grounds in the Amur drainage and Lake Khanka, on the Russian-Chinese border. Since the total number of red-crowneds in the wild is perhaps half that of hoodeds or white-napeds, it might be assumed that the loss of Korean wintering grounds would be the most serious for this species. But Dr. Archibald points out that winter habitats of the red-crowned crane along the China coast remain more or less intact, whereas all the main wintering grounds of the white-naped crane—in southern Japan and south-central China as well as in Korea—are now threatened (in China, by the construction of the huge Three Gorges Dam across the Yangtze River). Thus the loss of their Korean refuge might be even more critical for this species.

Before leaving the CCZ, we locate a few more *Grus vipio* and four *G. japonensis*, all feeding in the vicinity of some new bunker construction where little chimneys for aeration of the *Homo sapiens* beneath stick up like weird red-metal mushrooms out of the ground. At Imjingak, a large flock of ruddy shelducks and spot-billed ducks and mallards has gathered in dry rice fields just below the bridge, and farther down the estuary are thousands of waterfowl of many species. But since these wetlands are fenced off, the only people who can enjoy them are the numerous patrols of soldiers in green camouflage garb, faces daubed with artificial mud and metal helmets stuck with humble straw, all set to repel those landings along the Han that in all likelihood will never take place.

Weather is sudden in Korea, and a blizzard sweeps in from the Yellow Sea over vast gray mudflats laid bare in a great rise and fall of outgoing tide. The *turumi* especially like to probe these saline mudflats for crustaceans, but any chance of locating the white cranes is swirled away in the thick snow. Today we have seen very few cranes in the Han-Imjin, even fewer than expected, and there seems small doubt that their numbers are diminishing.

With the Naktong marshlands all but destroyed, and the Han-Imjin under such stress, it appears that the last refuge of the cranes may be at Cholwon, where for the moment their numbers appear stable—about 275 red-crowneds and 350 white-napeds. But even at Cholwon, the South Koreans, despite the good intentions of the Korean Association for Bird Protection, may lack the resolve to stem the rush toward ever more development. The week after we left South Korea, the nation's seven automakers announced their ambition to spend a combined $5.31 billion on capital investment—up 32 percent in a single year—with more than $1.3 billion from Hyundai alone. (Between 1990 and 1994, carbon emissions rose 44 percent in South Korea, as opposed to 13 percent in China and 24 percent in India.)

Yet it is heartening to learn that in a recent poll of 1,500 South Koreans by the government-funded Korea Environmental Technology Research Institute, an astonishing 85 percent of the respondents worried that pollution was getting worse each year, and 90 percent cited "habitat loss" as the greatest environmental problem after the pollution of air and water. Eighty-five percent of those polled also stated that the environment was more important than economic development.

*"...it appears that the last refuge of the cranes may be at Cholwon, where for the moment their numbers appear stable— about 275 red- crowneds and 350 white-napeds."*

Two days ago at Cholwon, toward dusk, we observed the largest crane flocks of our trip at a point just north of Yangji-ri, or Sapsulbong, an abrupt little mountain less than 700 feet high that stands by itself in the middle of the basin. Sapsulbong acquired its present name of Ice Cream Mountain during the Korean War, perhaps because of the cone shape that resulted from relentless battering by the artillery on both sides. Not far to the west, in the mountain cirque, rises Porkchop Hill, another notorious slaughter ground. According to Kim Sooil, the small, nondescript Sapsulbong changed hands 14 or 15 times in the fierce fighting that took place in the last weeks of the war, before the new boundaries that would leave it in South Korea could be hammered out at that table in Panmunjom. After the war, peasants excavating the rubble around its base to make new rice fields unearthed a pit of skulls and bones several feet deep.

Watching these great and ancient birds flying and calling through these mists in a damp cold where so many young soldiers crouched in fear and misery, watching them striding in calm elegance across these fields laced with so much human blood, one is beset by somber, confused feelings. As George Archibald remarks quietly, watching the birds drift over the silent land in the dimming sun, "I feel all the more blessed that I can see such beautiful creatures, knowing the horrors other men had to endure here years ago." And we agree how fitting and respectful it would be to those who had to die here if the cranes were honored and protected as harbingers of peace and morning calm.

The wary cranes might be perceived as emblematic of true wilderness, of clean water and clean air and the expanses of clean earth required to sustain the cycles of their ancient seasons. To see such magnificent creatures in these sullen borderlands, skirting barbed wire fences and embankments, highway construction and utility poles in a hard-hammered landscape fraught with unnatural noises and disturbance, is deeply saddening. One can only marvel at the endurance of wild things and their strong instinct toward survival, which offer hope that these beautiful creatures may persist long enough for mankind to appreciate what might be lost and make some room for them.

# V. New Directions in Wildlife Conservation

## Editor's Introduction

Whereas the traditional role of wildlife conservationists, which has centered on habitat protection, has expanded to include habitat restoration, the role of zoos has also been changing. The first two selections in this final section examine the transformation of zoos from glorified museums and amusement parks, whose main function was to attract spectators, to internationally renowned centers with strong programs in captive breeding (in which endangered species are bred in captivity) and an emphasis on public education about wildlife conservation. Among the recent developments in the zoo business identified by Tom Arrandale are "landscape immersion" exhibits that strive to replicate the natural environment, scientific experiments in breeding techniques, and joint efforts with other organizations involved in international wildlife conservation. Although more Americans attend zoos than other sporting events combined, zoos' budgets have become increasingly tight as cities and municipalities are forced to cut back on expenditures across the board. Contemporary marketing strategies and clever fund-raising activities seek to garner the resources necessary for the zoos to accomplish their new missions. In the second selection, Edward R. Ricciuti explores the reasons for the success of the Providence, Rhode Island-based Roger Williams Park Zoo in meeting some of these challenges.

In the third selection, Victoria Butler describes the Communal Areas Management Program for Indigenous Resources (CAMPFIRE), a controversial effort to simultaneously conserve wildlife—including elephants, buffalo, antelope, lions, and leopards—and promote community development in Zimbabwe by allowing communities to sell hunting rights to safari companies. Another controversial industry with implications for wildlife conservation is ecotourism. (See Perri Knize's article in Section II.) In the fourth selection here, two writers for *Newsweek* examine the unintended consequences of ecotourism projects everywhere from Africa to South America. They conclude that despite the problems inherent in many ecotourism endeavors, the affected wildlife is nonetheless better off than it had been before ecotourism arrived. The solution, the authors suggest, lies in reform. Thus conservationists in all areas, from conservation biology to legislative activism, from managers of national parks and military bases to directors of zoos and ecotourist agencies, have arrived at comparable stages in the human race's efforts to conserve wildlife for future generations.

# The Zoo Biz[1]

When Martin Chavez was elected mayor of Albuquerque, he didn't build his platform around working with the People's Republic of China to save snow leopards and Manchurian cranes. But if tax-payers approve a bond issue this fall, a few years from now the city's Rio Grande Zoological Park will be running a $5 million cap-tive-breeding and exhibit facility for some of China's most threat-ened wildlife. The Chinese government will send the animals, but Albuquerque will pay the bills.

The planned breeding facility certainly would enhance the Albuquerque zoo's prestige. But city officials think it would also make a big contribution to the zoo's bottom line, drawing another 300,000 or so visitors a year to what is already New Mexico's third-largest public attraction. Those visitors will pay $4.25 each to get in, not to mention the money they will leave behind for soft drinks and T-shirts.

Preserving Chinese species might seem ambitious for a city gov-ernment whose 385,000 constituents live in the New Mexico desert halfway around the world from Beijing. The Chinese wildlife facili-ty is still in the planning stages, and Chavez has scaled back initial funding for the project. But over the past 15 years, Albuquerque has been building a first-class zoo that's already playing a role in inter-national wildlife conservation. "For a city our size, we have a phe-nomenal zoo," Chavez says. "It makes a really strong statement about our city."

In many cities, maintaining a zoological park has long been a matter of municipal pride. But as public interest in wildlife con-servation has grown, those venerable public institutions are taking on new roles in conserving endangered wildlife and educating the public about environmental problems. Over the past two decades, city and county park agencies have spent millions of dollars to rehabilitate aging zoos and aquariums and launch conservation and education programs. At the same time, zoo managers have been turning to savvy marketing campaigns and other money-mak-ing promotions to cover the rising costs of breeding and maintain-ing wild animals.

Baltimore and Chattanooga are among the cities that have built modern aquariums to help anchor urban redevelopment efforts, while other communities have begun investing heavily in upgrad-ing their zoos by building naturalistic "landscape immersion" exhibits, experimenting with scientific breeding techniques and joining international wildlife conservation campaigns.

The new zoo mission is admirable, but it also may be beyond the

---

[1]Article by Tom Arrandale, from *Governing* magazine 8:38-40 Jl '95. Copyright © 1995 *Governing* magazine. Reprinted with permission.

means of some municipal governments that are struggling to come up with funds just to mow the grass and replace tennis court nets at other parks and recreation facilities. At the San Francisco Zoological Gardens, for instance, attendance plunged over the past five years because city officials had let Depression-era displays corrode and crumble even before the 1989 earthquake damaged a monkey island exhibit built in 1937. "The city's priorities are elsewhere," says Peggy Burks, the San Francisco Zoological Society director. "It had not been able to provide for the zoo for many years."

Around the country, zoo-keeping costs have risen apace just as taxpayer revolts sharply limited what city and county governments have been willing to spend on upgrading zoo facilities. With municipal budgets so tight, "it's just very difficult for a traditional zoo to get enough resources to compete," notes J. Michael Rice, an architect and planner for Zoological Planning Associates, a Wichita, Kansas, consulting firm. Breeding and caring for rare and vulnerable wildlife can be a round-the-clock task, and animals don't usually get sick or give birth at times that fit into the eight-hour days that government work rules dictate.

Cumbersome government purchasing procedures can sometimes interfere with taking good care of animals. Several years ago, when a giraffe developed an overgrown hoof, San Francisco zoo officials realized that the animal would be lame before the city could complete the six- to eight-month-long procurement process and build a chute to hold the animal so the condition could be treated. At the city's request, the zoological society took on the task and got it done in six weeks.

These days, a community can get a black eye if it tries to simply maintain an old-fashioned zoo with a few concrete and steel cages housing "postage stamp" collections of everything from anteaters to zebras. A decade ago, embarrassed Atlanta officials forced the municipal zoo director out after Twinkles, a popular but arthritic 12-year-old elephant, died after being sold to a traveling circus. Reports also surfaced that employees had dined on surplus animals. When things like that happen, it's no wonder many environmentalists and animal-rights activists condemn keeping wild creatures in captivity just so families can entertain their children on Sunday afternoon with an outing at the zoo.

Not that there isn't plenty of demand for that kind of entertainment. Altogether, American zoos draw more than 110 million visitors a year—more than the combined annual attendance at baseball, football and basketball games. More and more, however, zoos are competing with sports, movies, amusement parks, public museums, civic symphonies and privately owned wildlife "safari" parks for the public's support and the consumer's spare-time dollars.

Big-time zoos and affiliated zoological societies now augment their budgets by publishing magazines, conducting summer camps, organizing concerts and other events, and guiding wildlife viewing safaris to Africa and South America. Many are courting support

*"Altogether, American zoos draw more than 110 million visitors a year—more than the combined annual attendance at baseball, football and basketball games."*

from local businesses and civic groups and inviting prominent citizens to join zoo society boards of directors. "They've become more like a symphony, an opera, or an art museum as places you can put your effort," says Phoenix zoo director Warren Iliff, who formerly headed the Dallas zoo.

Even such venerable attractions as Chicago's Brookfield and Lincoln Park zoos, the Smithsonian Institution's National Zoological Park in Washington, D.C., and the Bronx Zoo in New York City have mounted sophisticated marketing campaigns to draw more visitors and their dollars. The heavily promoted San Diego Zoo hosts three million visitors a year, ranking third behind Disneyland and Universal Studios as a Southern California tourist attraction.

That's how the zoo pays most of its bills. The Zoological Society of San Diego, a nonprofit organization, operates the city's 100-acre zoo in Balboa Park and an affiliated 1,800-acre Wild Animal Park 30 miles away at Escondido. It costs $90 million a year to run both facilities, and a city property tax levy enacted in 1935 covers just 3 percent of the budget. Another 10 percent comes from donations and membership fees, so the society must make up the remaining $78 million from $13 admission fees, special promotions, food and drink sales, T-shirts, animal trading cards and other merchandise. The San Diego Zoo licenses a top-selling CD-ROM computer game about wild animals, and officials are trying to renegotiate the royalty agreement to boost revenue beyond the $50,000 the zoo took in last year from sales of the game.

Only a handful of zoos cost as much as San Diego's to run. But the time is ending when many city park agencies could afford to operate zoos free of charge for the pleasure of their residents. Just 11 U.S. zoos, including the popular parks in St. Louis, Chicago and Washington, D.C., still offer free admission. Overall, zoos now depend on government appropriations to cover less than half of their operating costs. In many cities, nonprofit zoological societies have begun shouldering the load of raising the funds to upgrade outmoded facilities, add new attractions and undertake ambitious wildlife conservation projects.

Going a step further, nonprofit societies have taken over day-to-day management of some the country's most notable municipal zoos. The New York Zoological Society has long run the Bronx Zoo; two years ago, the San Francisco board of supervisors agreed to turn management of the city's troubled zoo over to the local zoological society under a five-year lease arrangement. Massachusetts Governor William F. Weld pushed through state legislation in 1991 that set up a Commonwealth Zoological Corporation to manage two Boston zoos and raise funds for a $45 million capital improvements program.

In a typical arrangement, the city government keeps ownership of the zoo and its facilities and helps cover operating expenses. The nonprofit zoological society or corporation owns the animals, keeps gate receipts and concession revenues, and drafts plans for zoo improvements. San Francisco provides $4 million a year to help operate its zoo, and the city has also issued $26 million in bonds to replace earthquake-damaged pipes and make other improvements in the zoo's utility systems. The society has taken on the job of raising $30 million for renovating displays. "Our first priority was getting our cats out of an awful shabby row of cages," Burks reports, and the society last fall opened a new $2 million exhibit for lions, tigers and other big cats. It is demolishing the damaged monkey island and replacing it with a new exhibit depicting cloud forests and other South American habitats.

*"For badly rundown zoos, going private may offer the only hope for renewal."*

For badly rundown zoos, going private may offer the only hope for renewal. Atlanta's 40-acre zoo got lost in the shuffle in the 1960s while the city parks agency built a stadium for new pro baseball and football teams. Fixing Atlanta's zoo threatened another drain on the city budget, so in 1985 the city turned it over to Zoo Atlanta, a nonprofit corporation that began thoroughly overhauling the facility. Terry Maple, a renowned primate specialist, was brought in as the zoo's president and chief executive officer. Attendance has quadrupled, and membership in the organization has grown tenfold. The Zoo Atlanta budget has jumped to $9.3 million from $850,000 a year, while a $1.4 million annual operating subsidy from the city was terminated two years ago.

But even some scientifically trained curators and other zoo professionals have reservations about nonprofit management. Some zoos learn to operate effectively within government bureaucratic constraints, they say, while zoological society volunteers are more likely than mayors and city council members to meddle in management decisions. "Some people get on the board for 10 or 15 years and they think they know how to run a zoo," complains one zoo curator from the Midwest.

Some municipal governments split management with zoological societies; others have shifted control from parks departments to special zoo agencies. Topeka, Kansas, is considering a proposal to create an independent zoo agency modeled on airport authorities. Four years ago, when Montgomery, Alabama committed $5 million in bond money to expand its six-acre zoo to 40 acres, the city created a separate zoo department that finances most operations through an enterprise fund that channels gate receipts and other revenues directly back into management.

That arrangement "makes the people who work in the zoo a lot sharper," says the zoo's director, Bill Fiori. Employees can see that caring for animals and keeping the grounds clean pay off by drawing more visitors, thus increasing the funds they have to operate with. The number of annual visitors has jumped from 140,000 to 300,000 since the zoo expansion was launched in 1990, and visitor revenues cover $1.6 million of a $2 million annual budget. When Fiori surveys the zoo parking lot, half of the visitors come from other Alabama counties and from Georgia and Florida.

Albuquerque's zoo now draws 700,000 visitors a year. Zoo managers figure that building the proposed eight-acre Chinese breeding facility, designed to resemble a rural Chinese village, could boost annual attendance beyond a million people and draw even more tourist dollars to the city. This fall, Chavez' administration plans to ask city voters to approve selling $500,000 in bonds to get the project started.

Around the country, zoos remain popular enough that cities have had little trouble in recent years persuading taxpayers to finance improvements. But to keep attendance growing, zoo managers figure they need to add new exhibits every few years that will draw previous visitors back. That's often beyond the fiscal reach of some small and even medium-sized communities, so officials may need to rethink what they want to accomplish with their zoo collections. Davenport, Iowa, has considered a proposal to turn its zoo into an outdoor classroom operated jointly with an adjacent natural history museum. The Peoria, Illinois, Park District recently ruled out moving its cramped seven-acre Glen Oak Park zoo, but is drafting a $2 million plan that directors believe will give visitors more insight into wildlife and conservation issues. "We don't want to be a St. Louis or a Chicago zoo," says Jan Schweitzer, who has managed the Peoria zoo for the past 13 years. "What we're trying to do is make ours unique, where people can get up close and personal with the animals."

But zoo experts say some communities that are unwilling to spend the time and money to upgrade their zoos might be better off shutting them down altogether. Few zoos earn enough to cover all expenses, and zoo planners say a facility must serve a market with at least 500,000 people to have a chance to ever become self-supporting. "There are some zoos that have lost their base," notes Rice, the Wichita zoo consultant. "The zoo-going public has gotten a lot more sophisticated, and they're less willing to put up with what would have been acceptable just a couple of years ago."

New London, Connecticut, closed its shabby zoo a decade ago. When Bridgeport, Connecticut, faced bankruptcy during the 1980s, officials considered closing the city's decrepit 30-acre Beardsley Zoological Gardens, the only remaining zoo in the state. But the Connecticut Zoological Society, the zoo's volunteer affiliate, persuaded the state legislature to chip in $4 million for new rain-forest and hoofed-animal exhibits, and officials began working closely with Bridgeport teachers to integrate field trips into local school curriculums. Attendance has climbed from 150,000 to 200,000 visitors a year, and improved facilities qualified the park for accreditation from the American Zoo and Aquarium Association.

Operating the Beardsley zoo still costs the city $1.2 million a year, and that's only partly offset by charging adults $4 and children $2 for admission. Even so, "no one is talking about closing the zoo now," says Lisa Tryon, who was hired six years ago as the Connecticut society's first paid director. "Every city in the country has financial problems, but zoos have to find ways to work around them."

# Big Little Zoo[2]

Good Old Yankee ingenuity is alive and well in the Ocean State, particularly at Roger Williams Park Zoo. New Englanders are expert at doing a lot with a little, and the staff of the Providence, Rhode Island-based zoo is no exception. A stockade of cut utility poles, for example, surrounds the Plains of Africa, and the exhibit entrances are roofed with limbs from dead trees. This relatively inexpensive woodwork provides a rustic backdrop for elephants, cheetahs, zebras, and giraffes. The antiquated Elephant House, built in 1930, has been gutted and transformed into a tropical American rain forest for free-flying birds, anacondas, and Brazilian giant cockroaches, which are a great hit with young boys but occasionally "gross out" more-sensitive visitors.

There are no graphics in the rain-forest building. "We want people to feel as if they are really in the rain forest and there are no labels there," explains zoo director Anthony Vecchio. As they enter the display, visitors can pick up large laminated cards that identify the jungle animals.

Another unobtrusive and realistic touch is an aerial walkway designed to resemble a swinging, rope-railed jungle bridge. It sways slightly when you walk on it, not much, just enough.

Its visitor-friendly atmosphere plus achievements in wildlife conservation and research, as well as a touch of showmanship, garnered this vest-pocket zoo in the country's smallest state national media attention in 1995. The *New York Times* called it "one of the best zoos in the country for its conservation efforts," and the *Boston Globe* named it "New England's great zoo." Not bad for a 40-acre facility and a staff of about 30.

From a low point in the late 1970s, the zoo—with help from the city, the Rhode Island Zoological Society, and special grants—has undergone a major makeover. New or renovated exhibits have sprouted like mushrooms after a rainstorm: an underwater viewing area for Asian small-clawed otters, an expanded garden for native butterflies, a wildlife of Madagascar complex, and a walk-through aviary for Australian birds. The zoo also unveiled the pint-size "African Kopje, Smaller Wonders of the Plains," with porcupines, dik-diks, and bat-eared foxes. In a passageway through the rocks, which is easily negotiated by children, the triggering of an electric eye sets off sounds of lions roaring, zebras fleeing, and hyenas cackling.

Much of last year's media coverage, however, centered on a single event. On July 1, a family of cottontop tamarins was released in a wooded area within the zoo grounds. Until fall the five mini-monkeys roamed freely over and around an existing walkway, which was called the Tamarin Trail. Zoo visitors could even tell the primates apart; the white shock of fur atop the head of each eight-inch monkey was dyed a different color. That's the same technique that Anne Savage, the zoo's director of research, uses to identify individuals in the rain forest. She spends several weeks a year in Colombia, tracking tamarins and trying to help preserve their shrinking habitats. Savage also coordinates the Species Survival Plan for cottontop tamarins, a long-term effort among members of the American Zoo and Aquarium Association to save the species.

Because the small monkeys are not always easy to see in the foliage, plush-toy tamarins were placed out on branches where they could be spotted. In Colombia, Savage trades similar toys to youngsters in return for the slingshots they often use to wing stones at tamarins in the trees.

Speaking of trees, "we have a two-for-one policy," says Vecchio. "If we have to cut down one tree, we plant two somewhere else." Greenery camouflages fences, buildings, walls, even roofs. It's easy to forget that the zoo sits at the edge of a state capital and cheek-by-jowl with Interstate 95.

Plenty of open space remains, including a marsh that is one of the best spots in Rhode Island to observe wood ducks. According to Vecchio, some of the zoo's open space (not the marsh) will house new exhibits, such as the Marco Polo Trail, which will display animals from some of the places reached by the great explorer.

Vecchio credits Providence Superintendent of Parks Nancy Derrig for supporting the resurgence of Roger Williams Park Zoo. You would think that all of the zoo's fans would be excited over where it is heading. Apparently not. "This summer," says Vecchio, "four people complained to me that we were starting to look like a big zoo."

# Is This the Way to Save Africa's Wildlife?[3]

Three years ago, John Tendengdende, headman of Dete village in Zimbabwe, watched helplessly as his maize seedlings, cotton plants and chili bushes shriveled and died during the country's worst drought in living memory. Tens of thousands of other subsistence farmers in the Zambezi River valley lost their crops. At the bleakest moment, Tendengdende and his people stood on the threshold of starvation, all maize stocks gone, and the future hinging on whether enough rain would fall to nurture the next crop.

Then an innovative wildlife conservation program gave the villagers a lifesaving windfall. "For the first time we got money for our wild animals," explains Tendengdende. "I used my money to buy 50 kilograms (110 lbs.) of corn meal. That's how we survived."

The program that helped to save the Dete villagers is the Communal Areas Management Program for Indigenous Resources (CAMPFIRE). Not only does it add a new dimension to wildlife conservation in Zimbabwe by helping to make wildlife valuable to local people, but it also offers a management model that other nations are examining closely.

Under CAMPFIRE, the government has transferred ownership of wildlife on communal lands to the communities, which sell hunting or photographic concessions to safari companies. The money goes to the communities, whose members decide how it will be spent. Zimbabwe's Department of National Parks and Wildlife Management sets the hunting quotas and trophy fees in each communal area, while local authorities, with support from the department, bear responsibility for wildlife protection and management. Wildlife is perhaps the greatest treasure of the Zambezi River valley, a 900-kilometer (560-mi.) swath of acacia thornbush that stretches across Zimbabwe from Victoria Falls in the northwestern corner of the nation to the border with Mozambique in the east. The valley covers some of south-central Africa's most remote and rugged landscape and produces large herds of elephants, buffalo and antelope as well as populations of lions, leopards and other wildlife. Consequently, about half of the valley's 56,230 square kilometers (21,710 sq. mi.) have been set aside in national parks, reserves and forests to protect wildlife.

The other half is divided into tribal communal lands, where some 325,000 people subsist on crops of maize, cotton and a few vegetables. The thin, gray top-soil, rocky terrain and inadequate rainfall make for uncertain crops, but about 20 percent of the communal lands also produce significant amounts of wildlife.

---

[3]Article by Victoria Butler, from *International Wildlife* 25:38-43 Mr/Ap '95. Copyright © 1995 Victoria Butler. Reprinted with permission.

Ironically, the people of Dete and other villages in northern Zimbabwe's Hurungwe District did not value the animals until the drought ravaged their crops and threatened them with destitution. Then, the influx of funds from CAMPFIRE, which they had recently joined, showed the villagers that their wildlife could be vitally important to them.

The program also is important to wildlife conservation. Many communal holdings border national parks, state forests and reserves, which cover 14.5 percent of the country. For years, people have settled illegally on protected lands. Poaching has been a persistent problem as people killed wildlife to supplement income or to provide food for the pot.

But thanks to CAMPFIRE, a new era is dawning in the Zambezi valley. The $13 that each of the 574 heads of household in his village received in the year of the drought has changed local attitudes toward wildlife, says Arius Chipere, a member of a village wildlife committee. "Ten years ago, we liked the animals, of course," he explains. "But now we like them more because we are getting money for them."

*"The $13 that each of the 574 heads of household in his village received in the year of the drought has changed local attitudes toward wildlife..."*

Every CAMPFIRE village has an "animal reporter" who monitors wildlife movements and reports poachers. "Local poaching is a menace," complains Champion Machaya, chairman of Dete's wildlife committee. "We have people from other areas coming in and taking our animals. But our people have stopped poaching. They understand that a buffalo is worth much more if it is killed by a foreign hunter."

Ray Townsend, the 35-year-old boss of a safari camp, sees a shift in community attitudes since CAMPFIRE started. "We're looking at a slightly reduced poaching problem, and people are starting to complain that they don't have enough animals," he says.

CAMPFIRE is rooted in the 1980s, when the limited resources available for the fight against encroachment on protected areas forced officials of Zimbabwe's Department of National Parks and Wildlife Management to consider new ways to conserve the country's animals and plants. With the support of the Worldwide Fund for Nature (WWF), the United States Agency for International Development (USAID), the Zimbabwe Trust, and the University of Zimbabwe's Center for Applied Social Sciences, they settled on CAMPFIRE.

The program started officially in 1989, when the parks department granted two districts authority over their wildlife. Since then, nearly half of Zimbabwe's 55 local districts have signed on. In 1993, 12 districts nationwide, with a combined human population of nearly 400,000, earned $1,516,693 in trophy fees. They received an additional $97,732 from tourism, culling and from problem animals that had to be shot.

Though the idea that hunting can help save wildlife may seem ironic, hunting and conservation have a long history of mutual support. In the United States, for example, some of the earliest efforts to protect vanishing species such as bison, elk and deer were initiated by hunters who, at the close of the 19th century, feared they would lose the animals that offered them sport. Under modern management, careful monitoring helps ensure that hunted populations remain stable or increase.

The Zimbabwe government regulates sport hunting by setting local quotas based on annual wildlife surveys. All foreign sportsmen must be accompanied by a professional hunter licensed by Zimbabwe after completing a rigorous apprenticeship and passing state exams. A national-parks game scout accompanies all hunters to ensure that quotas are observed. Hunting is banned between dusk and dawn.

Most hunters book safaris months in advance. Safari operators meet their clients at the airport and whisk them away to bush camps that boast varying degrees of luxury in the wild. Some camps offer tents, some thatch huts and some lodges of natural stone. In all camps, a staff of cooks and waiters attends the clients, who happily pay up to $1,000 a day to hunt in the African bush. A single hunter can spend more than $40,000, with half going to local communities.

*"One concern ever on the minds of CAMPFIRE advocates is the increasingly vociferous anti-hunting lobby in western countries."*

One concern ever on the minds of CAMPFIRE advocates is the increasingly vociferous anti-hunting lobby in western countries. Although Jon Hutton—an ecologist and director of Africa Resources Trust, a nongovernmental organization for conservation and human development—is encouraging the development of photo-safaris and other nonconsumptive uses of wildlife, he says it will be a long time before communal lands will have the infrastructure to cater to large numbers of tourists. "Hunters have a different view than tourists," explains Hutton. "They just need a bush camp and a fire, without all the fancy facilities."

Zimbabwean ecologists argue that hunting is both good conservation and sound financial sense. The Zambezi valley, for example, supports at least 22,000 elephants with an annual population growth rate of 4 to 5 percent. The valley's eight communal districts have a combined quota of only 58 elephants, roughly 5 percent of the growth rate in 1993. Hurungwe was entitled to seven, but foreign hunters shot only six, yielding $54,825 to the district. The safari operator distributed all meat to local villagers. The Department of National Parks and Wildlife Management, in contrast, periodically culls elephants to maintain an ecological balance in wilderness areas. Although villagers get the meat, they do not receive any money.

WWF estimates that CAMPFIRE has increased household income in communal areas by 15 to 25 percent. At the end of 1992, the 31,000 people in Hurungwe District received $119,342 through CAMPFIRE. In 1993, they received $145,519.

Each village decides at year's end how it will use the income. Some villages divide it equally among heads of household. Some put it into community projects, such as schools, grinding mills, beekeeping or clinics. Others split it between projects and household cash dividends.

In many villages, the money goes to pay children's school fees.

For financially strapped villages, this can be the difference between education and ignorance. Sign Chawabvunza and his wife, Semia, have lived in the Chundu area of Hurungwe District all their lives. They grow maize, groundnuts and sorghum on 3.6 hectares (9 acres). Five of their 11 children live at home. "Before CAMPFIRE we did not have enough money to buy seeds, fertilizers and pay school fees," says Chawabvunza. In 1993, Chawabvunza received $54 from CAMPFIRE. "I used some of the money to pay school fees, and the rest I used to buy food for the family," he said. "Before CAMP-FIRE, no one assisted us. We had to struggle to make ends meet."

The success of CAMPFIRE has engendered some hard feelings, primarily because not everyone shares the program's financial rewards. Only villages with wildlife resources can participate. Moreover, each village's share of the spoils depends on which animals are shot on its land. Dete, for example, received $3,534 in 1993, while the neighboring village of Chikova earned four times as much because it has more wilderness area and higher-priced animals, including elephants, buffalo, lions, leopards and sable antelope.

Villages with no wildlife resources receive no CAMPFIRE funds. Margaret Taodzera, chairperson of the wildlife committee in Hurungwe's Chitindiva village, is an outspoken critic of the CAMP-FIRE program. "We do not have any animals in this area. We are surrounded by other villages. So, we get nothing," she complains. "Every household in this district should get a share. We are all under one chief. The animals belong to God, not to this village or that village. No one is feeding those animals. The money should go to projects, not to households."

In an attempt to address such grievances, neighboring villages that received money from CAMPFIRE recently gave Chitindiva funds to buy a grinding mill. Nevertheless, people living on communal lands with wildlife argue that they deserve their compensation since they bear the sometimes heavy costs imposed by the animals. Every year crocodiles, hippopotamuses and elephants kill people in communal areas.

The animals also destroy crops. In Chikova, where nearly one-third of the land remains a wilderness, elephants, baboons and bushpigs regularly raid fields. Kenyas Dzokamushure grows maize and groundnuts. "I have major problems with elephants, because when they come into the fields, they completely destroy them," he says. The elephants come at night to feed. "I start a fire and the whole family beats tin cans and buckets throughout the night to scare them off." Sometimes this doesn't work, and the lost crops mean no food and more debt.

In Hurungwe, CAMPFIRE does not reimburse farmers for losses, but it does put money into their pockets while offering some protection. As part of his deal with the Hurungwe District Council, which allows him to bring clients onto communal lands, professional hunter Ray Townsend agreed to help communities handle problem animals. Every year, at least one elephant develops an appetite for maize. Before reacting, district as well as park officials

*"The success of CAMPFIRE has engendered some hard feelings, primarily because not everyone shares the program's financial rewards."*

assess the extent of the damage. If they determine that an elephant has become a menace, they turn it over to Townsend. He tries to sell the animal, often at a reduced price, to a client, ensuring the greatest return for the community.

CAMPFIRE has sparked interest throughout Africa, and conservationists from many neighboring countries have visited Zimbabwe to assess the program. All are trying to devise ways for local communities in their own countries to benefit from national parks and reserves. Simon Metcalf, a development expert with the Zimbabwe Trust, says that while CAMPFIRE probably will not be duplicated, other countries may borrow some of its features.

Richard Leakey, former head of the Kenyan Wildlife Service and an outspoken conservationist, is less enthusiastic. "It works perfectly well on the communal lands in Zimbabwe, but I don't think it would work anywhere else in Africa in the same way. The communal land structure in Zimbabwe is unique."

Leakey also has doubts about sport hunting as a sustainable source of income, particularly for highly remunerative species such as elephants, which each yield at least $7,000 in trophy fees. "Sport hunting of elephants is obviously an alternative to the ivory trade at the moment, but whether it is viable in the long term, I seriously doubt. I personally believe that attitudes about elephants have and will continue to change, making it more and more likely that killing elephants will become increasingly antisocial."

For the moment, however, Dete residents are tapping the benefits of CAMPFIRE. In 1993, the villagers voted to use CAMPFIRE income to finish a desperately needed clinic. Before the clinic was completed, pregnant women, the sick and the injured walked, went by ox cart or caught an irregular bus to the nearest clinic 18 kilometers (12 mi.) away. "A few months ago a child died on the bus on the way to the clinic," says David Mutara, a 62-year-old maize farmer.

His frown melts into a smile as he points at the clinic being built in the center of the village. "I'm very happy about what CAMPFIRE did," he says.

# Beware of the Humans[4]

Back in the bad old days, the Ugly American would fly to a tropical paradise in a pollution-spewing jet and loll about a hotel whose sewage killed the coral reef at its doorstep. How 1980s. In the enlightened 1990s, tourists can still do all that—*but save the Earth at the same time*. Or so goes the theory of "ecotourism." Locally controlled and environmentally sensitive, ecotourism promised to be the greatest thing for travelers since frequent-flier miles, a way to vacation amid unspoiled beauty, to meet rare animals up close and personal, and to do it all under a green halo. But the law of unintended consequences is still on the books, and ecotourism isn't always working as planned. From whale watching off Baja California to photo safaris in Kenya's game parks, says Emily Young, professor of geography at the University of Arizona, ecotourism is "fast becoming tourism without the eco."

*"...ecotourism is 'fast becoming tourism without the eco.'"*

It was supposed to be more than a vacation with a politically correct name. Ecotourism was based on the realization that some people (usually poor Africans, Asians and Latin Americans) live in places surrounded by precious living things that other people (well-off Americans and Europeans) want to preserve. The idea was to enable people in the developing world to earn more by preserving nature than by using it up; people would put down their machetes and harpoons and pick up laundry and trays. "It's simple," says Juan Rodriguez, 43, who captains a tourist skiff in Baja. "As long as we don't eat the whales, we eat more."

But now ecotourism is beset by eco-troubles. For example, vacationers throng Mexico's Pacific coast to watch sea turtles lay their eggs on moonlit beaches; tourism seemed the perfect way to lure locals away from poaching. But the beachfront hotels cast such bright light that the turtles become disoriented as they lumber ashore, and fail to lay eggs. In the Mexican highlands, butterfly lovers flock to the pine-scented winter home of millions of orange-and-black monarchs; but the pressure to deforest a little here and a little there—for tourist facilities—keeps growing. In the Canary Islands off Spain, where tens of thousands of Europeans descend every year to ogle pilot whales, tourist boats charge their quarry as if they were in an oceanic rodeo. The frightened whales dive underwater for so long they risk suffocating (though biologists have not recorded any deaths).

Off Australia's east coast, dolphin-feeding expeditions were introduced to replace the reckless net fishing that snared dolphins. But the feeding reduces the ability of young dolphins to find their own food. And in Kenya's Masai Mara, where locals have been promised a cut of the park's revenue in exchange for turning their land into

---

game reserves, the tourist boom is driving away human-phobic cheetahs, according to John Waithaka of the Kenya Wildlife Service. "The cheetahs left in the park have had their reproductive capability lessened," he says, due to inbreeding.

Nowhere did ecotourism seem more promising than in the whale-watching waters off Baja California and Argentina's Valdez, into whose warm lagoons hundreds of gray and southern right whales migrate every winter to breed. Before the 1980s, vast overharvesting by commercial fishermen and whale hunters was turning the waters into dead zones. So environmentalists persuaded skiff owners to roll up their nets and roll out the red carpet for Americans with Leicas and dollars. Presto: groupers, lobsters and scallops proliferated, and gray whales—which have a dolphinlike affinity for human contact—continued their comeback from extinction's edge.

*"Now manatees are being mangled by the propellers of speedboats rushing tourists to Tortuguero..."*

But there's only so much watching that whales can take. This season 20,000 tourists are expected in Baja. "Travel agents now promote whale *petting*," says Jose Varela of Kuyima Eco-Turismo in Baja. And in Valdez, where tourist boats have been known to separate mothers and calves, whale counts have dropped in the 1990s and scientists have launched a study to see whether birthrates have been affected.

**Squirrel monkey:** Costa Rica embraced ecotourism early and earnestly, creating an ecotourism institute and a faculty of ecotourism at its Latin American University of Science and Technology. The industry brings in almost $500 million a year, second only to banana exports. But some of Costa Rica's most charismatic animals are struggling to survive this bright idea. Squirrel monkeys swing through treetops to eat, mate and otherwise survive (they are too shy and delicate to traverse the cruel earth). But so many hotels and restaurants now dot the jungle that the tiny primates have been virtually weeping in confusion as they swing from tree branch...to hotel roof.

And Costa Rica's manatees, sleek mammals that long ago inspired sailors to spin tales of mermaids, have the bad luck to live in the rivers and lagoons behind Tortuguero, the last nesting beach of the endangered green sea turtle. Now manatees are being mangled by the propellers of speedboats rushing tourists to Tortuguero, says Bernard Nietschmann of the University of California, Berkeley. (Tortuguero's turtles, however, are thriving now that villagers think of them not as soup ingredients but as tourist attractions.)

Ecotourism has fallen short of its economic goals, too. Locals were promised prosperity—or at least a living wage—in exchange for laying down their harpoons. But Arizona's Young and Serge Dedina find that while tourism in Baja's Magdalena Bay took in $4.7 million in 1994, only $33,000 found its way into local salaries and businesses. The rest went to tour companies, most based in California. "Ecotourism doesn't leave much for the locals except low-level jobs," says Mexican author and environmental activist Homero Aridjis. "Before ecotourism, these people were dignified loggers or fishermen. We shouldn't be turning them into busboys."

Even if whales are harassed by tourist boats and turtles can't breed in peace, the animals are now better off than when they were destined for blubber factories and jewelry shops. So instead of pronouncing ecotourism a failure, governments and guides are trying to reform it. "The best regulatory measure we can take," says consultant Erich Hoyt, "is to require that tourists be taught about the whales before they get on a boat. The key is to make them troubled by any abuses." Last month the Canary Islands decided to limit the number of whale-watching vessels that can clog the seas and require a marine naturalist on board each excursion to prevent harassment of the whales. Costa Rica is spacing hotels farther apart to minimize environmental damage and devising ways to let visitors enjoy nature without trampling it. Literally: one plan is to run cable cars over the jungle. The monkeys may not be able to hang from them, but at least the humans will be out of the way.

# Bibliography

*An asterisk (\*) preceding a reference indicates that an excerpt from the work has been reprinted in this compilation.*

## Books and Pamphlets

Adams, Jonathan S. & McShane, Thomas O. The myth of wild Africa: conservation without illusion. Norton '92.

Alvarez, Ken. Twilight of the panther: biology, bureaucracy, and failure in an endangered species program. Myakka River '93.

Anderson, David S. & Bridge, David R. Focus on Africa: wildlife, conservation, and man. Bridgewood Productions '94.

Ballou, J. D., Gilpin, Michael E. & Foose, Thomas J., eds. Population management for survival and recovery: analytical methods and strategies in small population conservation. Columbia Univ. Press '95.

Bean, Michael J., Fitzgerald, Sarah G. & O'Connell, Michael A. Reconciling conflicts under the Endangered Species Act: the habitat conservation planning experience. World Wildlife Fund '91.

Benedick, Richard Elliott. Ozone diplomacy: new directions in safeguarding the planet. Harvard Univ. Press; published in collaboration with the World Wildlife Fund and the Conservation Foundation '91.

Benirschke, Kurt & Warhol, Andy. Vanishing animals. Springer-Verlag '86.

Berger, Joel & Cunningham, Carol. Bison: mating and conservation in small populations. Columbia Univ. Press '94.

Bergman, Charles. Wild echoes: encounters with the most endangered animals in North America. McGraw-Hill '90.

Bissonette, John A. & Krausman, Paul R., eds. Integrating people and wildlife for a sustainable future. (Papers presented at the first International Wildlife Management Congress, San Jose, Costa Rica, 19-25 September 1993.) Wildlife Society '95.

Bonner, Raymond. At the hand of man: peril and hope for Africa's wildlife. Knopf '93.

Bookhout, Theodore A., ed. Research and management techniques for wildlife and habitats. (5th ed.) Wildlife Society '94.

Braun, Elisabeth. Portraits in conservation: eastern and southern Africa. North American Press; published in collaboration with the International Wilderness Leadership Foundation '95.

Breen, Kit Howard. The Canada goose. Voyageur '90.

Brown, Bruce. Mountain in the clouds: a search for the wild salmon. Collier Books '90; Univ. of Washington Press '95.

Brown, Michael H. & May, John. The Greenpeace story. (2d ed., new & revised.) Dorling Kindersley '91.

Burgman, Mark A., Ferson, S. & Akcakaya, H. R. Risk assessment in conservation biology. Chapman & Hall '93.

Buskirk, Steven W., ed. Martens, sables, and fishers: biology and conservation. Comstock '94.

Byrne, Peter. Tula Hatti: the last great elephant. Faber & Faber '90.

Cadieux, Charles L. Wildlife extinction. Stone Wall '91.

Carr, Susan & Lane, Andrew. Practical conservation: urban habitats. Open University; Hodder & Stoughton; published in collaboration with the Nature Conservancy Council (Great Britain) '93.

Carty, Winthrop P. & Lee, Elizabeth. The rhino man and other uncommon environmentalists. Seven Locks '92.

Chadwick, Douglas H. The fate of the elephant. Sierra Club '92.

Chandler, William J., ed. Audubon wildlife report, 1989-1990. Academic Press; published in collaboration with the National Audubon Society '91.

Chase, Alston. In a dark wood: the fight over forests and the rising tyranny of ecology. Houghton Mifflin '96.

Clark, Tim W., Reading, Richard P. & Clarke, Alice L., eds. Endangered species recovery: finding the lessons, improving the process. Island '94.

Cox, George W. Conservation ecology: biosphere and biosurvival. Brown, W. C. '93.

Craighead, John J., Sumner, Jay S. & Mitchell, John A. The grizzly bears of Yellowstone. Island '95.

*Cronon, William. Uncommon Ground: Toward Reinventing Nature. Norton '95.

Cubitt, Gerald S. & Mountfort, Guy. Wild India: the wildlife and scenery of India and Nepal. MIT Press '91.

Davis, William E. Dean of the birdwatchers: a biography of Ludlow Griscom. Smithsonian Institution '94.

DeBlieu, Jan. Meant to be wild: the struggle to save endangered species through captive breeding. Fulcrum '91.

Dietz, Tim. The call of the siren: manatees and dugongs. Fulcrum '92.

Dingwall, P. R., ed. Progress in conservation of the Subantarctic Islands: proceedings of the SCAR/IUCN workshop on protection, research, and management of Subantarctic Islands, held in Paimpont, France, 27-29 April 1992. International Union for Conservation of Nature and Natural Resources—The World Conservation Union; published in collaboration with the International Council of Scientific Unions/Scientific Committee on Antarctic Research '95.

DiSilvestro, Roger L. The African elephant: twilight in Eden. Wiley '91.

DiSilvestro, Roger L. The endangered kingdom: the struggle to save America's wildlife. Wiley '89.

*DiSilvestro, Roger L. Reclaiming the last wild places: a new agenda for biodiversity. Wiley '93.

Dunlap, Thomas R. Saving America's wildlife. Princeton Univ. Press '91.

Ehrenfeld, David, ed. The landscape perspective. Blackwell Science; published in collaboration with the Society for Conservation Biology '95.

Ehrenfeld, David, ed. Wildlife and forests. Blackwell Science; published in collaboration with the Society for Conservation Biology '95.

Fergus, Charles. Swamp screamer: at large with the Florida panther. Farrar, Straus & Giroux '96.

*Flader, Susan & Callicott, J. Baird, eds. The River of the Mother of God and Other Essays by Aldo      Leopold. Univ. of Wisconsin Press '91.

Foreman, Dave. Confessions of an Eco-Warrior. Crown '91.

Foreman, Dave & Wolke, Howard. The Big Outside. Harmony '92.

Gaston, Kevin J., New, T. R. & Samways, Michael J., eds. Perspectives on insect conservation. Intercept '93.

Gibbons, Edward F., Jr., Durrant, Barbara S. & Demarest, Jack, eds. Conservation of endangered species in captivity: an interdisciplinary approach. State Univ. of New York Press '95.

Gipps, J. H. W., ed. Beyond captive breeding: reintroducing endangered mammals to the wild: proceedings of a symposium held at the Zoological Society of London, 24-25 November 1989. Clarendon Press; Oxford Univ. Press; published in collaboration with the Zoological Society of London '91.

Goddard, Donald Letcher, ed. Saving wildlife: a century of conservation. Abrams; published in collaboration with the Wildlife Conservation Society '95.

Gordon, Nicholas. Ivory knights: man, magic, and elephants. Chapmans '91.

Grosse, W. Jack. The protection and management of our natural resources, wildlife, and habitat. Oceana '92.

Grove, Noel & Krasemann, Stephen J. Preserving Eden. Abrams; published in collaboration with the Nature Conservancy '92.

Hansen, Kevin. Cougar: the American lion. Northland Pub.; published in collaboration with the Mountain Lion Foundation '92.

Harris, Esmond & Harris, Jeanette. Wildlife conservation in managed woodlands and forests. Blackwell '91.

Hawley, Alex W. L., ed. Commercialization and wildlife management: dancing with the devil. Krieger '93.

Heintzelman. Donald S. Wildlife protectors handbook. Capra '92.

Heyning, John E. Masters of the ocean realm: whales, dolphins, and porpoises. Univ. of Washington Press; published in collaboration with the Natural History Museum of Los Angeles County '95.

Homewood, K. M. & Rodgers, W. A. Maasailand ecology: pastoralist development and wildlife conservation in Ngorongoro, Tanzania. Cambridge Univ. Press '91.

Hudson, Wendy E., ed. Nature watch. Falcon Press; published in collaboration with Defenders of Wildlife '92.

Huntington, Henry P. Wildlife management and subsistence hunting in Alaska. Univ. of Washington Press '92.

Istock, Conrad A. & Hoffmann, Robert S., eds. Storm over a mountain island: conservation biology and the Mt. Graham affair. Univ. of Arizona Press; published in collaboration with the Smithsonian Institution '95

Jacobson, Susan K., ed. Conserving wildlife: international education and communication approaches. Columbia Univ. Press '95

Jayewardene, Jayantha. The elephant in Sri Lanka. Wildlife Heritage Trust of Sri Lanka '94.

Keiter, Robert B. & Boyce, Mark S., eds. The greater Yellowstone ecosystem: redefining America's wilderness heritage. Yale Univ. Press '91

Kerasote, Ted. Bloodties: Nature, Culture, and the Hunt. Random House '93.

Kellert, Stephen R. The value of life: biological diversity and human society. Island '96.

Kiss, Agnes, ed. Living with wildlife: wildlife resource management with local participation in Africa. World Bank '90.

Knight, Richard L. & Gutzwiller, Kevin J., eds. Wildlife and recreationists: coexistence through management and research. Island '95.

Koebner, Linda. Zoo book: the evolution of wildlife conservation centers. Doherty Assocs. '94.

Landau, Diana & Stump, Shelley. Living with wildlife: how to enjoy, cope with, and protect North American's wild creatures around your home and theirs. Sierra Club Books; published in collaboration with the California Center for Wildlife '94.

Littell, Richard. Controlled wildlife. (2d ed., revised & updated.) Association of Systematics College '93.

Littell, Richard. Endangered and other protected species: federal law and regulation. Bureau of National Affairs: Washington, D.C. '92.

Lowe, David W., et al., eds. The official World Wildlife Fund guide to endangered species of North America. Beacham '90.

Lunney, Daniel, et al., eds. Future of the fauna of western New South Wales. Royal Zoological Society of New South Wales '94.

Luoma, Jon R. A crowded ark: the role of zoos in wildlife conservation. Houghton Mifflin '87.

Lutz, Richard L. & Lutz, J. Marie. Komodo: the living dragon. DIMI '91.

McCullough, Dale R. & Barrett, Reginald H., eds. Wildlife 2001: populations: proceedings of the International Conference on Population Dynamics and Management of Vertebrates (Exclusive of Primates and Fish), held in Oakland, Calif., 29-31 July 1991. Elsevier '92.

MacDonnell, Craig A. New Massachusetts Endangered Species Act. Massachusetts Continuing Legal Educ. '92.

McIntyre, Rick, ed. War against the wolf: America's campaign to exterminate the wolf. Voyageur '95.

McNeely, Jeffrey A., ed. Expanding partnerships in conservation. Island Press; published in collaboration with the International Union for Conservation of Nature and Natural Resources '95.

Malcolm, Stephen B. & Zalucki, Myron P., eds. Biology and conservation of the monarch butterfly. (Papers from the Second International Conference on the Monarch Butterfly, 1986.) Natural History Museum of Los Angeles County '93.

Mann, Charles C. & Plummer, Mark L. Noah's choice: the future of endangered species. Knopf '95.

Mares, Michael A. & Schmidly, David J., eds. Latin American mammalogy: history, biodiversity, and conservation. Univ. of Oklahoma Press; published in collaboration with the Oklahoma Museum of Natural History '91.

Matthiessen, Peter. Shadows of Africa. Abrams '92.

Matthiessen, Peter. Wildlife in America. (Revised & updated.) Penguin '95.

May, John, ed. The Greenpeace book of dolphins. Sterling '90.

Mighetto, Lisa. Wild animals and American environmental ethics. Univ. of Arizona Press '91.

Mitchell, Joseph C. The reptiles of Virgina. Smithsonian Institution '94.

Moore, H. D. M., Holt, W. V. & Mace, G. M., eds. Biotechnology and the conservation of diversity: proceedings of a symposium held at the Zoological Society of London, 4-5 September 1990. Clarendon Press; Oxford Univ. Press; published in collaboration with the Zoological Society of London '92.

Mordi, A. Richard. Attitudes toward wildlife in Botswana. Garland '91.

Morris, David B. Earth warrior: overboard with Paul Watson and the Sea Shepherd Conservation Society. Fulcrum '95.

Murphy, James B., Adler, Kraig & Collins, Joseph T., eds. Captive management and conservation of amphibians and reptiles. Society for the Study of Amphibians & Reptiles; published in collaboration with the Herpetologists' League '94.

Musgrave, Ruth S. & Stein, Mary Anne. State wildlife laws handbook. Government Insts.; published in collaboration with the Center for Wildlife Law at the Institute of Public Law, Univ. of New Mexico '93.

New, I. R. Introduction to invertebrate conservation biology. Oxford Univ. Press '95.

Norris, Kenneth S. Dolphin days: the life and times of the spinner dolphin. Norton '91.

Norton, Bryan G., et al., eds. Ethics on the ark: zoos, animal welfare, and wildlife conservation: papers from a workshop held in Atlanta, March 1992. Smithsonian Institution Press '95.

Olney, Peter J. S., Mace, G. M. & Feistner, A., eds. Creative conservation: interactive management of wild and captive animals. Chapman & Hall '94.

Orenstein, Ronald I., ed. Elephants: the deciding decade. Sierra Club '91.

Otaishi, Noriyuki & Sheng, Ho-lin, eds. Deer of China: biology and management: proceedings of the International Symposium on Deer of China, held in Shanghai, China, 21-23 November 1992. Elsevier '93.

Owens, Delia & Owens, Mark. Survivor's song: life and death in the African wilderness. HarperCollins '93.

Patton, David R. Wildlife habitat relationships in forested ecosystems. Timber '92.

Payne, Neil F. Techniques for wildlife habitat management of wetlands. McGraw-Hill '92.

Payne, Neil F. & Bryant, Fred C. Techniques for wildlife habitat management of uplands. McGraw-Hill '94.

Payne, Roger. Among whales. Scribner '95.

Peters, Robert L. & Lovejoy, Thomas E., eds. Global warming and biological diversity. Yale Univ. Press '92.

Peterson, David. Racks: the natural history of antlers and the animals that wear them. Capra '91.

Peterson, George L., ed. Valuing wildlife resources in Alaska. Westview Press; published in collaboration with the Alaska/Division of Wildlife Conservation and the Rocky Mountain Forest and Range Experiment Station (Fort Collins, Colo.) '92.

Pollard, E. & Yates, T. J. Monitoring butterflies for ecology and conservation: the British butterfly monitoring scheme. Chapman & Hall; published in collaboration with the Institute of Terrestrial Ecology and the Joint Nature Conservation Committee '93.

Porter, Douglas R. & Salvesen, David A., eds. Collaborative planning for wetlands and wildlife: issues and examples. Island '95.

Reiger, John F. Gifford Pinchot with rod and reel: trading places, from historian to environmental activist: two essays in conservation history. Grey Towers '94.

Reynolds, Jane, Gates, Phillip & Robinson, Gaden S. 365 days of nature and discovery. Abrams '94.

Robinson, John G. & Redford, Kent Hubbard, eds. Neotropical wildlife use and conservation. Univ. of Chicago Press '91.

Rudloe, Jack. Search for the great turtle mother. Pineapple '95.

Samways, Michael J. Insect conservation biology. Chapman & Hall '94.

Schaller, George B. The last panda. Univ. of Chicago Press '93.

Sigler, William F. Wildlife law enforcement. (4th ed.) Brown, W. C. '95.

Simon, Noel. Nature in danger: threatened habitats and species. Oxford Univ. Press; published in collaboration with the World Conservation Monitoring Centre '96.

Sinclair, A. R. E. & Arcese, Peter, eds. Serengeti II: dynamics, management, and conservation of an ecosystem. Univ. of Chicago Press '95.

Swanson, Timothy M. & Barbier, Edward, eds. Economics for the wilds: wildlife, diversity, and development. Island Press; Earthscan '92.

Terbough, John. Where have all the birds gone? essays on the biology and conservation of birds that migrate to the American tropics. Princeton Univ. Press '89.

Tudge, Colin. Last animals at the zoo: how mass extinction can be stopped. Island '92.

Tudge, Colin & Flint, A. R. P. Science for conservation: the research of the Zoological Society of London. Zoological Society of London '91.

Turbak, Gary. Survivors in the shadows: threatened and endangered mammals of the American West. Northland Pub. '93.

Wagner, Frederic H. & Sax, Joseph L. Wildlife policies in the U.S. national parks. Island '95.

Ward, Geoffrey C. & Ward, Diane Raines. Tiger wallahs: encounters with the men who tried to save the greatest of the great cats. HarperCollins '93.

Waterman, Laura & Waterman, Guy. Wilderness ethics: preserving the spirit of wildness. Countryman '93.

Western, David & Pearl, Mary C., eds. Conservation for the Twenty-first Century. Oxford Univ. Press; published in collaboration with Wildlife Conservation International, a division of the New York Zoological Society (which is now the Wildlife Conservation Society) '89.

Wiese, Robert J. & Hutchins, Michael. Species survival plans: strategies for wildlife conservation. American Zoo and Aquarium Association '94.

*Wilson, Edward O. The Diversity of Life. Harvard Univ. Press '92.

Yaffee, Steven Lewis. The wisdom of the spotted owl: policy lessons for a new century. Island '94.

Yeager, Rodger & Miller, Norman N. Wildlife, wild death: land use and survival in eastern Africa. State Univ. of New York Press '86.

# Additional Periodical Articles with Abstracts

For those who wish to read more widely on the subject of wildlife conservation, this section contains abstracts of additional articles that bear on the topic. Readers who require a comprehensive list of materials are advised to consult *Readers' Guide Abstracts, General Science Abstracts, Biological and Agricultural Index,* and other Wilson indexes.

**Healthy habitat for howlers.** Chris Mackey. *Americas* 47:2-3 My/Je '95

The Community Baboon Sanctuary in Belize is demonstrating that it is possible to balance wildlife needs with human needs. This fifteen-square-mile area is home to howler monkeys, who reside in the rain forest treetops. Ethologist Robert Horwich and plant ecologist Jon Lyon developed a conservation plan with landowners, whom Lyon said had already been conserving monkey habitat through their land-use practices. The landowners are supplementing their income by providing food and lodging for ecotourists, and Lyon says that the howler population has grown about 18 percent since the sanctuary's establishment.

**Rescuing urban wetlands.** Michele Wolf. *Audubon* 97:89-90 N/D '95

The New York City Audubon Society's effort to clean up the Dubos Point Wetlands Sanctuary on Jamaica Bay in Queens has been a challenge. Formerly an industrial site, the sanctuary served as a dumping ground until 1988, when it was transferred to the city's parks department and New York City Audubon started managing it. As researchers work there to document its wildlife and to monitor water quality and assess coastal geology, car parts are still being removed from the site, according to the project's former director. David L. Burg, conservation chair of New York City Audubon, hopes that the Dubos restoration project will serve as a management model for a natural area in an urban setting.

**What's killing the manatees?** Jon R. Luoma. *Audubon* 98:18+ Jl/Ag '96

This spring, a mysterious, fatal respiratory syndrome that some termed a plague beset Florida's manatee population. The plague started in early March, and by the middle of the month 30 manatees had died. The reason for the deaths remained a mystery, however, and the pneumonia-like condition itself—characterized by red, inflamed, and bleeding lungs—resisted scientists' attempts to categorize it. By mid-May, with no reported deaths from the mystery disease in three weeks, it appeared that the epidemic might be over. Even if this is the case, the plague has provided a potent warning of the risks that small populations of endangered species such as the manatee face from forces beyond the control of any wildlife biologist or government agency.

**Conserving wildlife in tropical forests managed for timber.** Peter C. Frumhoff. *BioScience* 45:456-64 Jl/Ag '95

Conservationists concerned with forest biodiversity have generally focused on areas that are protected from logging, but they should also seek to preserve near-natural assemblages of plants and wildlife within tropical forests that are managed for timber. This goal is important because of the vast geographic scale of current and projected logging in the tropics. Moreover, there are increasing opportunities for conservation biologists to collaborate with tropical foresters. The article presents guidelines for protecting wildlife within tropical forests that are being managed for timber.

**Implementing the Endangered Species Act.** Andrea Easter-Pilcher. *BioScience*
46:355-63 My '96

The Endangered Species Act (ESA), signed into law on December 28, 1973, is sweeping
in its mandate of protection and conservation of endangered and threatened species and
the ecosystems on which they rely. In recent times, however, many people have come to
view the perceived and real economic and social costs of species and habitat conservation to be greater than any potential benefit from conservation. The regulations that guide
the implementation of the ESA must therefore be greatly improved. Moreover, as the ESA
is being considered for reauthorization, the distinction between the strong statute that is
the ESA and the regulations that guide its implementations must be clearly delineated to
allow effective assessment of the act. The writer attempts a quantitative assessment of
U.S. Fish and Wildlife Service decisions to list species as endangered or threatened.

**Come winter, a greener Hill?** Susan B. Garland. *Business Week* 66-7 Ap 15 '96

Encouraged by a public backlash against Republican attacks on environmental laws led
by House Speaker Newt Gingrich, eco-activists are preparing their biggest ever
voter-turnout effort this autumn. Bipartisan support for the environment ended in 1994,
when Republicans gained control of the House and battled to weaken laws protecting
water, air, and wildlife. The 24 GOP lawmakers who supported these moves are the
greens' main targets. The environmentalists, however, confront a challenge from business
groups that support endangered Republicans and set up the debate differently: Reasonable
safeguarding of the environment has to be weighed against a need to trim unreasonable
regulations. Politically active groups like the League of Conservation Voters and the Sierra
Club are collaborating with local groups to build grassroots support and increase voter
turnout in November.

**In the valley of death.** Graham Boynton. *Conde Nast Traveler* 30:158-63 + O '95

The writer describes a journey through southern Africa to assess the state of wildlife conservation in various countries and to judge the effectiveness of anti-poaching measures and
bans placed on the trade of rhino horn and elephant ivory. He says that many things have
changed since his last visit in 1989 as the world becomes increasingly aware of the plight
of African wildlife, but he concludes that the changes have not often been for the better.

**Dollars and sense in saving vicunas.** Andrea Mandel-Campbell. *E: the Environmental
Magazine* 6:17 N/D '95

In Peru, the legalization of live wool shearing of the vicuna is expected to help protect
this endangered species. In June the National Society of Vicuna Herders struck a $2.7 mil-
lion deal to sell vicuna wool to an international textile consortium. Previously, the
Convention on International Trade in Endangered Species of Wild Flora and Fauna's ban
prohibiting trade in vicuna meant that only poachers were able to benefit from the lucra-
tive market for vicuna wool. These heavily armed poachers are thought to be largely
responsible for the dramatic decrease in the animal's population over the last three years.
The deal could also save Peru's indigenous people from extreme poverty—as many as 700
communities could profit from the renewed trade in this extremely expensive wool.

**Common ground.** George Reiger. *Field & Stream* 100:12 + Je '95

Liberals should try harder to appreciate the many positive values that hunting provides to
both society and nature. In the recently reprinted *The New State of the Earth Atlas*, liber-
al author Joni Seager argues that sportsmen endanger wildlife. She falsely claims that

recreational hunters have pushed hundreds of species to the brink of extinction and supports this falsehood by citing credible sources like the International Union for the Conservation of Nature, the World Wildlife Fund, and the U.S. Fish and Wildlife Service, from whose publications she has extracted and distorted many of her "facts."

**Urban oasis.** Jerome B. Robinson. *Field & Stream* 100:28-9 S '95

The Eagle Bluffs Conservation Area, the first project in the world to use effluent from a sewage treatment plant to create habitat for waterfowl and other wildlife, demonstrates how environmental dilemmas can be solved by enhancing natural processes rather than by trying to subvert them. The Columbia, Missouri, project is attracting visitors from as far away as Egypt and is being hailed as a model for other municipalities.

**End of the ark?** Fiona Sunquist. *International Wildlife* 25:22-9 N/D '95

The basic mission of the zoo is changing from one of breeding and saving endangered species to one of protecting rare species in their native habitat. The captive-breeding program that zoos have focused on for the past 25 years or so will no longer be the main thrust; instead, zoos' new focus will link exhibits with zoo-sponsored conservation programs in the wild. Captive breeding will reportedly still play a role in the modern zoo, but more energy will be expended on field conservation, education, and research. The article discusses the history of the zoo, reasons behind the new change in philosophy, Species Survival Plan breeding, and the adopt-a-park concept being pioneered by certain zoos.

**NWF celebrates conservation win in 1996 farm bill.** *International Wildlife* 26:6 Jl/Ag '96

The Farm Bill recently passed by Congress marks an important triumph for NWF and the wildlife community, which formed an alliance of various groups to fight for conservation measures. Victories for the coalition include $1 billion in funding to continue the Conservation Reserve Program, which pays farmers to keep 36.4 million acres of sensitive lands out of production; continuation of "Swampbuster," an effective program that denies farm program benefits to farmers who destroy wetlands on their property; and reauthorization of the Wetlands Reserve Program, which provides government payments to farmers who voluntarily agree to restore and protect wetlands.

**Gentle gorillas, turbulent times.** George B. Schaller. *National Geographic* 188:58-71 O '95

Conservationists fear that Rwanda's instability could endanger the survival of the mountain gorillas of Africa. The Volcanoes National Park in Rwanda is home to more than a hundred of the world's 600 mountain gorillas, whose decline into extinction has been halted by years of conservation efforts in Rwanda, Zaire, and Uganda. During Rwanda's recent civil war, soldiers of both factions traversed the forests where the gorillas live. Despite the turmoil, however, the gorillas have not been decimated. Indeed, the Rwandan Patriotic Front expressed public concern for the gorillas' safety while it was engaged in battle. For his part, Rwandan prime minister Faustin Twagiramungu has affirmed his country's commitment to the apes, a remarkable declaration given Rwanda's urgent and crushing social needs.

**Ndoki: last place on earth.** Douglas H. Chadwick. *National Geographic* 188:2-45 Jl '95

The Ndoki watershed in Africa is one of the world's last undisturbed natural sanctuaries. Hosting perhaps the greatest abundance of wildlife on the continent, the region is teeming with leopards, golden cats, gorillas, elephants, chimpanzees, nine types of monkeys, and a variety of other species that range from forest hippos to genets, night-roaming carnivores related to the mongoose. The region is threatened by loggers and poachers, however, and a coalition of organizations led by the Wildlife Conservation is attempting to save it. In December 1993, nearly one million of the watershed's roughly three million acres became the Nouabale-Ndoki National Park. The writer recalls his expedition to the area as part of an effort to find out more about the region's elephant herds.

**On the brink: Hawaii's vanishing species.** Elizabeth Royte. *National Geographic* 188:2-37 S '95

Hawaii's feral pig has become a flash point in a conflict between hunters who want to maintain a sizable population for food and sport and conservationists who want to eradicate pigs in certain areas to protect native plants and animals. At least a thousand creatures that once enlivened Hawaii's landscape have vanished since Polynesian villagers first arrived on the islands some 1,500 years ago. Having evolved in isolation, native species were not equipped to withstand the onslaught of predators and competitors introduced with human arrival. The biggest threat to native rain forest species today, according to conservation biologists, is the pig, which sows seeds of alien plants in its droppings. Those seeds grow into dense thickets that crowd out native trees. Conservationists say that the loss of even one species may contribute to the decline of entire ecosystems and that native flora and fauna contain genetic information that could lead to new foods and medicines.

**Katmai at a crossroads.** Bill Sherwonit. *National Parks* 70:28-33 My/Je '96

Anticipating potential mishaps, the National Park Service is considering better ways to manage Brooks Falls in Katmai National Park and Preserve, Alaska, where increasing numbers of visitors flock for a close-up view of Alaskan brown bears. For years, bear experts have predicted that the area is an accident waiting to happen, given the constant, frequently unmonitored comings and goings of visitors and bears. As well as this safety issue, researchers have determined that camp facilities and crowding in the area have intruded into critical bear habitats, harassing and displacing the animals. In addition, Brooks Camp sits on one of the region's most significant archaeological sites, and some damage has already been done by the crowds. For all these reasons, the Park Service has developed a plan that will radically alter the way in which the Brooks River area is managed. The Development Concept Plan is discussed.

**Asking people first.** William W. Howard. *National Wildlife* 34:6 D '95/Ja '96

The National Wildlife Federation (NWF) has come up with a plan to replace the Endangered Species Act (ESA) with a revised law that increases citizen involvement in the decision-making process. It proposes to replace Habitat Conservation Planning, currently a cumbersome process for deciding how to save a species in its habitat, with Community-Based Recovery Planning, which will give communities a larger say in how the ESA is implemented. In addition, the NWF plan recommends the establishment of multispecies recovery plans and proposes a system that prevents endangerment of plant and animal species on public lands.

**Eight bright ideas that have powered NWF through six decades.** Thomas A. Lewis. *National Wildlife* 34:14-21 Ap/My '96

In 1951, the National Wildlife Federation (NWF) adopted a decree stating that the organization should defend any species that is in any way endangered as to its existence. Since then, saving endangered plants and animals has been a major focus of the organization's actions. Eight ideas that have sustained the NWF over the last 60 years are discussed.

**From war games to wildlife gains.** Mike Lipske. *National Wildlife* 33:46-51 F/Mr '95

Closing military bases may prove to be a boon to conservationists hoping to use vast, undeveloped lands as wildlife refuges. Many military properties are wildlife havens, and nearly 100 federally listed endangered or threatened species inhabit the 25 million acres that the Department of Defense manages. Some locations are a mixed blessing, though, containing much unexploded ordnance, toxic chemicals, and other waste. The article discusses conservation plans for several military bases and lists the most critical habitat/wildlife at 10 bases that are slated to be closed.

**The high cost of saving life on earth.** Bob Holmes. *New Scientist* 149:6 Ja 27 '96

According to 2 recent studies in the U.S., wildlife conservation may be a lot more expensive than people realize. The results from a survey by the Nature Conservancy suggest that many species in the U.S. are in danger of extinction. In addition, a report by the U.S. General Accounting Office estimates that the costs of plans for saving endangered species can range from $145,000 to $153.8 million depending on the species.

**South Africa returns wilderness to the people.** Mary Bakker-Cole. *New Scientist* 150:6 My 11 '96

Some 3.5 million South Africans will be able to reclaim property taken from them under apartheid if the government's controversial land reforms become law in June 1996. Under the reforms, large areas of national park land, and some farms and private game reserves, will be given back to their original owners. According to the minister of land affairs, the government is looking for ways of managing parks with local people, while maintaining their conservation status. Tourism could play a critical role in encouraging rural communities to conserve the wildlife on their land, but only if some of the revenue goes to the communities themselves.

**Are wildlife corridors the right path?** Charles C. Mann & Mark L. Plummer. *Science* 270:1428-30 D 1 '95

Wildlife corridors, which connect patches of otherwise isolated habitat, have quietly become a key battleground in conservation, pitting major development projects against the future of valuable nature preserves. Proponents of wildlife corridors contend that they are critical for maintaining biodiversity. Skeptics maintain that empirical research on connectivity is extraordinarily difficult, that corridors may not be needed to provide connectivity, and that corridors can allow disease, predators, and exotic species to spread through a metapopulation. The current battle between Pardee Construction and local environmental activists over a corridor connecting the Los Penasquitos Canyon to the Torrey Pines nature preserves near La Jolla, California, is discussed.

**Court upholds need to protect habitat.** Richard Stone. *Science* 269:23 Jl 7 '95

By a vote of 6 to 3, the Supreme Court has upheld federal rules that limit land use to protect the habitat of endangered species. Timber interests in Oregon, Washington state, and Georgia have challenged a rule that defines "harm" to an endangered species as including "significant habitat modification or degradation where it actually kills or injures wildlife." Writing for the majority, Justice John Paul Stevens declared that the federal definition of harm should include habitat considerations when the survival or health of an endangered or threatened species is at stake. Conservation advocates were delighted, but a fellow at the Competitive Enterprise Institute cited the ruling as a reason why Congress should replace the Endangered Species Act with a narrower law.

**Fertile results: bringing up baby.** Wade Roush. *Science* 271:594-5 F 2 '96

A technique discovered by developmental biologist John Eppig and research assistant Marilyn O'Brien marks a new era in reproductive biology. The researchers, who recently found a way to make egg precursors called oocytes develop into mature, fertilizable eggs, have announced the birth of a mouse developed from an egg grown in vitro. The researchers have laid the groundwork for some potentially revolutionary wildlife conservation procedures and human medical treatments. With infertile human couples, for example, oocytes could be removed and developed in preparation for test-tube fertilization. This would do away with the need to treat prospective mothers with large doses of gonadotropins, hormones that prompt women to ovulate the multiple eggs needed for the hit-and-miss process of conventional in vitro fertilization.

**Focal species offer management tool.** William James Davis. *Science* 271:1362-3 Mr 8 '96

In Australia, patches of untouched vegetation often provide the only suitable habitat for a significant number of endangered plants and animals. It is not always clear, however, how to go about rebuilding this highly impoverished land and stemming the rates of extinction while still benefiting the landowners. One approach to the problem was recently presented at a conference in Brisbane, Australia, by Robert Lambeck, an ecologist for the Commonwealth Scientific and Industrial Research Organization Division of Wildlife and Ecology in Western Australia. Instead of focusing on what is needed to protect a single species, Lambeck has started to gather data on a variety of "focal" species to help define the attributes of a viable landscape. Public officials and scientists can then work with private landowners to preserve biodiversity and the value of the enterprise.

**In Hawaii, taking inventory of a biological hot spot.** Christine Mlot. *Science* 269:322-3 Jl 21 '95

Hawaii underwent the most detailed biological survey ever conducted in a single biogeographic area. In 1992, the state legislature authorized a comprehensive inventory of all of the state's known species. With $260,000 in start-up funds from the John D. and Catherine T. MacArthur Foundation, researchers at the Bishop Museum in Honolulu and elsewhere have begun combing the scientific literature and museum collections for information on all plants, animals, fungi, algae, and other protists ever observed in Hawaii. Names and descriptions are being standardized, and field studies are being commissioned to fill information gaps. The results of these labors will be entered in a database that will also contain bibliographic and museum specimen information. Researchers have already located a few species that were considered very rare or extinct. The Hawaii survey may help the state devise conservation strategies and provide lessons for similar efforts elsewhere.

**IVF project stirs debate over how to preserve pandas.** Zhou Meiyue. *Science* 272:1580-1 Je 14 '96

A proposal to save giant pandas in the wild through in vitro fertilization has sparked a scientific dispute within China over the use of this technology. Although artificial insemination has been used for almost two decades to breed captive pandas, the procedure is still experimental and has had mixed success. Proponents of IVF assert that the panda population, which now numbers about 1,000 in the wild, has declined to the point where new test-tube and embryo transplanting technologies are required to ward off extinction. Opponents claim that reproductive rates of wild pandas, although low, are sufficient to save the species if more is done to preserve their habitat. Pan Wenshi of Beijing University worries that funding an IVF project could drain money from that effort.

**Slow start for Europe's new habitat protection plan.** Nigel Williams. *Science* 269:320-2 Jl 21 '95

Many of the European Union's member countries are late in complying with the EU's Habitats Directive. That law requires countries to identify and protect habitats that the Union has listed as threatened. Lists of proposed habitat sites were due this past June, but most countries have not yet furnished them. Some, especially in southern Europe, lack data on local habitats and species distribution; others are confused by the directive's definitions of habitat types. Many are reluctant to deal directly with conflicts between conservation and development, another important element in EU policy. European Commission official Olivier Diana believes that countries will comply with the directive if allowed enough time to complete their biological surveys, but other observers are less optimistic. The shrinking habitats of the great bustard and other European birds are discussed.

**Bringing back the birds.** Tina Adler. *Science News* 150:108-9 Ag 17 '96

Researchers are refining their techniques for protecting and improving bird habitats. Restoration of bird habitats involves keeping humans out of the birds' way and learning in detail the location of specific birds and their survival needs. Some birds are having their old homes restored or protected from demolition, thanks to new conservation research, state and federal laws safeguarding wildlife, multimillion-dollar legal settlements, and the patient efforts of bird lovers. Few long-term bird restoration projects exist, however, because they pose many problems for researchers, according to Stephen W. Kress of the National Audubon Society in Ithaca, New York. Scientists have little control over many factors that can determine a bird population, and birds encounter many dangers on their travels that cannot be changed. Information on various conservation projects throughout the United States is provided.

**The Institute for Innovative Plunder.** David Helvarg. *Sierra* 80:34+ Mr/Ap '95

Groups that make up the so-called Wise Use movement flaunt green-sounding names to sell anti-environmental messages. Wise Use groups such as the Alliance for Environment and Resources, the Environmental Conservation Organization, the Abundant Wildlife Society, the Wilderness Impact Research Foundation, and Citizens for the Environment form a backlash movement whose most cynical ploy may be the attempt to portray itself as a financially strapped populist movement going up against a powerful, well-funded "green establishment." In reality, these groups are supported by backers from the corporate sector and the political right. The article discusses several Wise Use groups and their backers.

**A sporting chance.** Carl Pope. *Sierra* 81:14-15 My/Je '96

The old alliance between environmentalists and hunters is being renewed as a result of serious assaults on wilderness areas. Mostly urban environmentalists and mostly rural hunters do not usually disagree about basic conservation principles. They are instead divided by philosophical and cultural differences that are clearly tangential to conservation goals, such as animal rights or gun control. Whatever disagreements the groups have are now overshadowed, however, by the assault from their common enemies—timber and oil companies, big mining conglomerates, and developers. In order to build the widest possible movement for wilderness and wildlife, both sides must agree to disagree on some matters. Their ability to overcome their differences and work together is a matter of survival for the wild places that they treasure.

**Wild things.** E. M. Swift. *Sports Illustrated* 84:60-2 + Ja 29 '96

Part of a special section on the new South Africa. Phinda Resource Reserve, a private game park in the Natal bush, is a good-news story in wildlife conservation. Despite its history of apartheid, South Africa has for the last 30 years or so produced the most successful wildlife conservation and restocking effortson the African continent. Much of this success is attributable to the restocking efforts of the 350 or more private reserves such as Phinda. Phinda was formed after the Johannesburg-based Conservation Corporation reclaimed the land, fenced the property, and reintroduced more than 1,000 wild animals to the area. The process of bringing animals to the land continues, and total investment in the property and its animals exceeds $25 million. Hopes for the future include that the private land of Phinda and the public land of the Mkuzi Game Reserve will become open range and ultimately that the fences in the entire eastern part of Natal will be torn down.

**Lost in the wild: is our obsession with pristine nature hazardous to the environment?** *Utne Reader* 74-85 My/Je '96

A special section on wilderness conservation features an introduction by Joshua Glenn and Martha Coventry that considers whether the obsession with pristine nature is hazardous to the environment; an adaptation of an essay from *Uncommon Ground: Toward Reinventing Nature*, in which the writer argues for a rethinking of the wilderness; an excerpt from the November-December 1995 issue of *National Parks*, in which the writer discusses her opposition to the 1995 Utah Public Lands Management Act; and an article reprinted from the September-October 1995 issue of *Sierra*, in which the writer explains how outdated conservation strategies are killing off wildlife. A list of relevant resources is also provided.

**Benchmarks in breeding.** Deborah A. Behler. *Wildlife Conservation* 99:17 Mr/Ap '96

U.S. zoos have enjoyed recent successes in captive breeding. The first birth of a surviving cheetah through the use of artificial insemination occurred on November 3, 1995, in the Rio Grande Zoo, Albuquerque, New Mexico. Cheetahs have not bred well in captivity, and the Albequerque-based project owes its success to the use of cryopreserved viable sperm collected from wild cheetahs. Elsewhere, the Cincinnati Zoo and Botanical Garden hosted the birth of the first test-tube western lowland gorilla on October 9, 1995.

**Can cats survive?** Maurice Hornocker. *Wildlife Conservation* 99:60 + My/Je '96

Part of a special issue on wild cats. The future of the world's wild cats, despite their natural resilience, is in the hands of humans. There must be commitments to regulate the killing of cats and to maintain their habitats. Both these commitments are dependent on economic, political, and cultural forces. The millions of dollars raised by conservation organizations must be used for more meaningful, realistic action; more long-term commitment at the local level that generates credibility and acceptance; and more field research.

**Denver zoo celebrates its centennial.** Clayton F. Freiheit. *Wildlife Conservation* 99:54-5 Ja/F '96

The Denver Zoological Gardens is entering its centennial year in 1996. The zoo started with a single American black bear, which was followed by a deer and eagle. Today, the mile high zoo has been expanded so that it now occupies 80 acres. It contains a series of naturalistic wildlife habitats such as Northern Shores and Tropical Discovery. The centennial summer of 1996 will be marked by the opening of Primate Panorama, which will include gorillas, orangutans, marmosets, and lorises. Construction of the Wildlife Conservation Center is also expected to begin soon. This center aims to introduce young people from the inner city to the principles of conservation.

**Keeping an eye on the tiger.** Downs Matthews. *Wildlife Conservation* 99:12 Ja/F '96

A new Save the Tiger Fund is going to try to conserve the estimated 8,000 tigers that remain in Asia. Although there are 38 protected areas in Asia for tigers, nearly half the cats live outside these reserves. The new ambitious project will support international tiger-related projects to stabilize the wild populations, to carry out breeding programs, and to educate the public—especially local peoples. The participation of companies, foundations, and the general public is requested.

**Letter from Brazil.** Jose Fragoso. *Wildlife Conservation* 99:6-7 Jl/Ag '96

Jose Fragoso, who works in the forests of Roraima State in northwest Brazil, discusses the danger of extinction that inhabitants of the forest face. Fragoso initially planned to study white-lipped peccaries, which seem to have become completely extinct. However, he has now expanded his work to include beetles, jaguars, palm tress, and the Yanomami Indians, all of which have been adversely affected by the recent gold rush in the area.

**Letter from Patagonia.** Claudio Campagna. *Wildlife Conservation* 99:6-7 Mr/Ap '96

The work of Wildlife Conservation Society field scientist Claudio Campagna as a wildlife biologist for the National Research Council of Argentina is discussed. Campagna lives in Peninsula Valdes, in Patagonia's Chubut Province, where he conducts research on marine mammals. This work has included fixing time-depth recorders and satellite tags to the backs of several animals, which has led to the production of the first maps of ocean use for a number of marine mammals. Campagna has also examined the effects of oil pollution, ecotourism, and fisheries on the Patagonian coastal ecosystem. Much of the field work has involved counting the populations of the various marine mammals. Campagna has written popular articles and has contributed to a book about southern right whales.

**The not-so-enchanted isles.** John L. Behler & Ed Louis. *Wildlife Conservation* 99:16 Ja/F '96

The unique ecosystem of the Galapagos Islands is under threat, partly due to pressures from tourism. The year-round human population is increasing by 8 percent each year, and the fragile island ecology cannot cope with such heavy use. On top of this, last year islanders held national park wardens hostage, harassed scientists, and threatened to kill giant tortoises. This was over a dispute with the government. The Ecuadorian government needs to confront the problems of both people and wildlife, and conservation organizations must offer support.

**The return of the golden fleece.** Joan Downs. *Wildlife Conservation* 99:10 Mr/Ap '96

Vicuna fur is to legally return to the marketplace for the first time since the species became protected under the Convention on International Trade in Endangered Species of Wild Flora and Fauna in 1976. By the mid-1960s, vicuna numbers had dwindled to 5,000. Recognizing the small camel species as a potentially valuable natural resource for the poor campesinos of the Andes Mountains, Peru collaborated with the United Nations Environment Programme to protect and breed the animals. Their efforts were successful, and there are now some 100,000 vicunas in Peru. Loro Piana, the world's largest weaver of cashmere, is to link up with the Peruvian National Society of Vicuna Breeders to manufacture, market, and trade vicuna products worldwide.

**War and wildlife in Georgia.** Cheri Brooks. *Wildlife Conservation* 99:12 Mr/Ap '96

Georgia's declaration of independence from the former Soviet Union in 1989 and the ensuing civil war that tore the country apart in the early 1990s have resulted in a drastic reduction in the country's populations of large mammals. This problem has been mirrored in other republics that declared their independence from the former Soviet Union. A group of Georgian scientists has come together to form the Noah's Ark Center for the Recovery of Endangered Species (NACRES). These concerned scientists believe that captive breeding and release represents the only hope for many of the diminishing species. NACRES has, thus far, released a number of wolves that have been reared in captivity and has also sought and achieved changes on the political front.

# Appendix A

## Organizations

**African Wildlife Foundation**
1717 Massachusetts Ave. NW
Washington, D.C. 20036
phone: (202) 265-8393
fax: (202) 265-2361
http://www.awf.org

**Boone and Crockett Club**
Old Milwaukee Depot
250 Station Dr.
Missoula, MT 59801
phone: (406) 542-1888
fax: (406) 542-0784
http://www2.boone-crockett.org/b&cclub/

**Conservation International**
1015 18th St. NW, Ste. 1000
Washington, D.C. 20036
phone: (202) 429-5660
fax: (202) 887-5188
http://www.conservation.org

**Defenders of Wildlife**
1101 14th St. NW, Ste. 1400
Washington, D.C. 20005
phone: (202) 682-9400
fax: (202) 682-1331
http://www.defenders.org

**Earthtrust**
25 Kaneohe Bay Dr.
Kailua, HI 96734
phone: (808) 254-2866
fax: (808) 254-6409
earthtrust@aloha.net
http://www.earthtrust.org

**Ecotourism Society**
P. O. Box 755
North Bennington, VT 05257-0755
phone: (802) 447-2121
fax: (802) 447-2122
info@ecotourism.org
http://www.ecotourism.org

**Environmental Defense Fund**
257 Park Ave. S.
New York, NY 10010
phone: (212) 505-2100
fax (212) 505-0892
http://www.edf.org

**Friends of the Earth**
1025 Vermont Ave. NW, Ste. 300
Washington, D.C. 20005
phone: (202) 783-7400
fax: (202) 783-0444
http://www.foe.org

**International Wildlife Coalition**
70 E. Falmouth Hwy.
East Falmouth, MA 02536
phone: (508) 548-8328
fax: (508) 548-8542
http://www.webcom/iwcwww

**National Audubon Society**
700 Broadway
New York, NY 10003
phone: (212) 979-3000
fax: (212) 353-0377
http://www.audubon.org

**National Park Service**
P. O. Box 37127
Washington, D.C. 20013
phone: (202) 208-4747
http://www.nps.gov

**National Wildlife Federation**
1400 16th St. NW
Washington, D.C. 20036-2266
phone: (202) 797-6800
legislative hotline: (202) 797-6655
http://www.nwf.org

**Natural Resources Defense Council**
40 W. 20th St.
New York, NY 10011
phone: (212) 727-2700
fax: (212) 727-1773
http://www.nrdc.org

**Nature Conservancy**
1815 N. Lynn St.
Arlington, VA 22209
phone: (703) 841-5300
fax: (703) 841-1283
http://copper.ucs.indiana.edu/ ~ shee-
han/conservancy.html

**North American Wildlife Foundation**
P.O. Box 3128
Bismarck, ND 58502
phone: (701) 222-8857; (888) 987-3695
fax: (701) 223-4645
http://www2.portage.net/ ~ dw4ducks

**Sierra Club**
730 Polk St.
San Francisco, CA 94109
phone: (415) 776-2211
fax: (415) 776-0350
http://www.sierraclub.org

**U.S. Fish & Wildlife Service**
1849 C St. NW
Washington, D.C. 20240
phone: (202) 208-5634
http://www.fws.gov

**The Wilderness Society**
900 17th St. NW
Washington, D.C. 20006-2596
phone: (202) 833-2300
fax: (202) 429-3958
http://www.wilderness.org/wild_alaska

**Wildlife Conservation Society**
Bronx, NY 10460
phone: (718) 220-5100
http://www.wcs.org

**Wildlife Forever**
12301 Whitewater Dr., Ste. 210
Minnetonka, MN 55343
phone: (612) 936-0605
fax: (612) 936-0915
http://www.ool.com/wildlife-forever

**Wildlife Habitat Council**
1010 Wayne Ave., Ste. 920
Silver Spring, MD 20910
phone: (301) 588-8994
fax: (301) 588-4629
http://www.wildlifehc.org/wildlifehc

**Wildlife Preservation Trust International**
3400 W. Girard Ave.
Philadelphia, PA 19104
phone: (215) 222-3636
fax: (215) 222-2191
http://www.columbia.edu/cu/cerc/wpti.ht
ml

**World Wildlife Fund**
1250 24th St. NW
Washington, D.C. 20037
phone: (202) 293-4800
fax: (202) 293-9211
http://www.wwf.org

# Appendix B

## Biographies

The following individuals involved in conservation were profiled in H. W. Wilson's *Current Biography*, a reference work published since 1940 whose hardcover annual cumulations can be found in public and school libraries the world over. (Also available on CD-ROM.) The birth (and, in some cases, death) dates are followed by the year in which the profile appeared.

| | | |
|---|---|---|
| Ansel Adams | (Feb. 20, 1902–Apr. 22, 1984) | 1977 |
| Joy Adamson | (Jan. 20, 1910–Jan. 3, 1980) | 1972 |
| Roy Chapman Andrews | (Jan. 26, 1884–Mar. 11, 1960) | 1941 |
| Lester R. Brown | (Mar. 28, 1934– ) | 1993 |
| Rachel Carson | (May 27, 1907–Apr. 14, 1964) | 1951 |
| Frank M. Chapman | (June 12, 1864–Nov. 15, 1945) | 1946 |
| Gerald Durrell | (Jan. 7, 1925–Jan. 30, 1995) | 1985 |
| Thomas Eisner | (June 25, 1929– ) | 1993 |
| Dian Fossey | (1932–Dec. 1985) | 1985 |
| Kathryn S. Fuller, | (July 8, 1946– ) | 1994 |
| Biruté M. F. Galdikas | (May 10, 1948– ) | 1995 |
| Jane Goodall | (Apr. 3, 1934– ) | 1967, 1991 |
| Bernhard Grzimek | (Apr. 24, 1909–Mar. 13, 1987) | 1973 |
| Roderick Haig-Brown | (Feb. 21, 1908–1976) | 1950 |
| Jay D. Hair | (Nov. 30, 1945– ) | 1993 |
| Richard Leakey | (Dec. 19, 1944– ) | 1976, 1995 |
| Wangari Maathai | (Apr. 1, 1940– ) | 1993 |
| Sharon Matola | (June 3, 1954– ) | 1993 |
| Peter Matthiessen | (May 22, 1927– ) | 1975 |
| Russell A. Mittermeier | (Nov. 8, 1949– ) | 1992 |
| Cynthia Moss | (July 24, 1940– ) | 1993 |
| Norman Myers | (Aug. 24, 1934– ) | 1993 |
| Fairfield Osborn | (Jan 15, 1887–Sep. 16, 1969) | 1949 |
| Nathaniel A. Owings | (Feb. 5, 1903–June 13, 1984) | 1971 |
| Roger S. Payne | (Jan. 29, 1935– ) | 1995 |
| Eliot Porter | (Dec. 6, 1901–Nov. 2, 1990) | 1976 |
| Peter H. Raven | (June 13, 1936– ) | 1994 |
| Laurance S. Rockefeller | (May 26, 1910– ) | 1959 |
| George B. Schaller | (May 26, 1933– ) | 1985 |
| Victor B. Scheffer | (Nov. 27, 1906– ) | 1994 |
| Richard Evans Schultes | (Jan. 12, 1915– ) | 1995 |
| Peter Markham Scott | (Sep. 14, 1909–Aug. 29, 1989) | 1968 |
| Elwyn L. Simons | (July 14, 1930– ) | 1994 |
| Arthur Cecil Stern | (Mar. 14, 1909–Apr. 17, 1992) | 1994 |
| Merlin D. Tuttle | (Aug. 26, 1941– ) | 1992 |
| William Vogt | (May 15, 1902–July 11, 1968) | 1953 |
| Conrad L. Wirth | (Dec. 1, 1899–July 25, 1993) | 1952 |

# Appendix C

## Endangered Species Facts[1]

**Number of Listed Species  (as of April 30, 1995)**

- U.S. species—956
- Foreign species—560
- Total—1,516 (dual status species are counted only once)
- Of the U.S. species, 430 are animals; 526 are plants.
- Of the listed U.S. species, 759 are "endangered," 203 are "threatened." Six U.S. listed animals have dual status.

**Recovery**

- 513 (54 percent of listed U.S. species) are covered by approved recovery plans.
- 232 additional species have draft recovery plans.
- As reported in the 1992 Report to Congress, nearly 40 percent of listed species are stable or improving.
- The status of 27 percent of species is unknown.
- 2 percent of listed species are believed extinct. (The service has been conservative in removing possibly extinct species from the list because of the chance they might be rediscovered.)

**Proposed and Candidate Species**

- 106 candidate species are currently proposed for listing.
- 293 candidate species are listed as "category 1" candidate species. These are taxa for which the service has sufficient information to support a listing proposal.
- 3,698 are listed as "category 2" candidate species. These are taxa for which additional information is needed to support a proposal to list.

*Source*: U.S. Department of the Interior

[1]Chart from *Congresssional Digest*  75: 68-96 Mr '96. Reprinted with permission of the Congressional Digest Corporation, Washington, D.C.

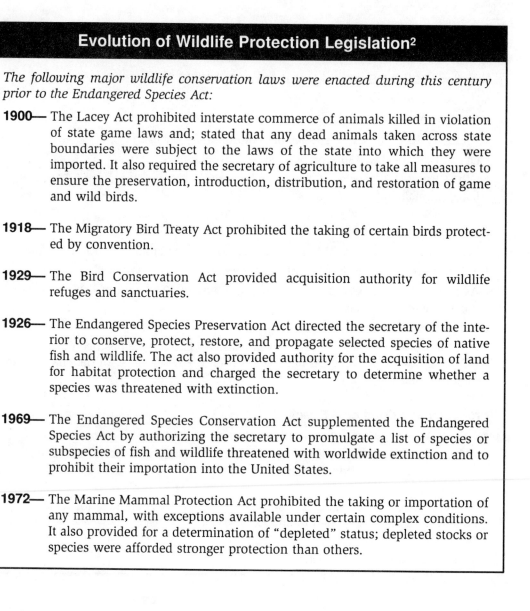

## Evolution of Wildlife Protection Legislation[2]

*The following major wildlife conservation laws were enacted during this century prior to the Endangered Species Act:*

**1900—** The Lacey Act prohibited interstate commerce of animals killed in violation of state game laws and; stated that any dead animals taken across state boundaries were subject to the laws of the state into which they were imported. It also required the secretary of agriculture to take all measures to ensure the preservation, introduction, distribution, and restoration of game and wild birds.

**1918—** The Migratory Bird Treaty Act prohibited the taking of certain birds protected by convention.

**1929—** The Bird Conservation Act provided acquisition authority for wildlife refuges and sanctuaries.

**1926—** The Endangered Species Preservation Act directed the secretary of the interior to conserve, protect, restore, and propagate selected species of native fish and wildlife. The act also provided authority for the acquisition of land for habitat protection and charged the secretary to determine whether a species was threatened with extinction.

**1969—** The Endangered Species Conservation Act supplemented the Endangered Species Act by authorizing the secretary to promulgate a list of species or subspecies of fish and wildlife threatened with worldwide extinction and to prohibit their importation into the United States.

**1972—** The Marine Mammal Protection Act prohibited the taking or importation of any mammal, with exceptions available under certain complex conditions. It also provided for a determination of "depleted" status; depleted stocks or species were afforded stronger protection than others.

[2]Chart from *Congresssional Digest* 75: 68-96 Mr '96. Reprinted with permission of the Congressional Digest Corporation, Washington, D.C.

# Index